Chicken Soup for the Soul®

Think Positive

Chicken Soup for the Soul: Think Positive
101 Inspirational Stories about Counting Your Blessings and Having a Positive Attitude
Jack Canfield, Mark Victor Hansen, Amy Newmark. Foreword by Deborah Norville

Published by Chicken Soup for the Soul Publishing, LLC   www.chickensoup.com
Copyright © 2010 by Chicken Soup for the Soul Publishing, LLC. All Rights Reserved.

The publisher gratefully acknowledges the many publishers and individuals who granted Chicken Soup for the Soul permission to reprint the cited material.

Front cover photo courtesy of iStockphoto.com/Irochka_T (© Irina Tischenko). Deborah Norville photo on back cover courtesy of Timothy White. Interior photo courtesy of iStockphoto.com/ Yuri_Arcurs (© Jacob Wackerhausen)

Cover and Interior Design & Layout by Pneuma Books, LLC
For more info on Pneuma Books, visit www.pneumabooks.com

Distributed to the booktrade by Simon & Schuster. SAN: 200-2442

Publisher's Cataloging-in-Publication Data
(Prepared by The Donohue Group)

Chicken soup for the soul : think positive : 101 inspirational
stories about counting your blessings and having a positive attitude /
[compiled] by Jack Canfield, Mark Victor Hansen, [and] Amy Newmark ; foreword
by Deborah Norville.

   p. ; cm.

   Summary: A collection of 101 true personal stories from regular people about the power of positive thinking in their lives and how they use positive thinking, count their blessings, and are grateful.

   ISBN: 978-1-935096-56-6

1. Optimism--Literary collections. 2. Optimism--Anecdotes. 3. Attitude (Psychology)--Literary collections. 4. Attitude (Psychology)--Anecdotes. 5. Conduct of life--Literary collections. 6. Conduct of life--Anecdotes. I. Canfield, Jack, 1944- II. Hansen, Mark Victor. III. Newmark, Amy. IV. Norville, Deborah. V. Title: Think positive

PN6071.O7 C45 2010
810.8/02/0353   2010930826

PRINTED IN THE UNITED STATES OF AMERICA
on acid∞free paper
18 17 16 15 14 13 12   11 12 13 14 15 16 17

Chicken Soup for the Soul®

Think Positive

101 Inspirational Stories about
Counting Your Blessings and
Having a Positive Attitude

Jack Canfield
Mark Victor Hansen
Amy Newmark
Foreword by Deborah Norville

Chicken Soup for the Soul Publishing, LLC
Cos Cob, CT

www.chickensoup.com

Contents

Foreword, *Deborah Norville* xi

❶
~Words that Changed My Life~

1. The Day I Met Norman Vincent Peale, *James Scott Bell* 1
2. Dancing in the Rain, *Jeannie Lancaster* 5
3. Each Day a Masterpiece, *Dallas Woodburn* 7
4. Words of Wisdom, *Kay Conner Pliszka* 10
5. Two Strangers, *Maggie Koller* 11
6. Listen to Your Mother, *Debbie Acklin* 15
7. Just Show Up, *Saralee Perel* 19
8. Finding the Real Me, *Melanie Adams Hardy* 23
9. License to Smile, *Julie A. Havener* 28
10. Hearing the Worst, *Lois Wilmoth-Bennett* 30

❷
~Health Challenges~

11. I'm Positive... Really, *Shawn Decker* 37
12. Ironman Lemonade, *Ruth Heidrich* 41
13. A Wink from God Himself, *Kathleen M. Muldoon* 45
14. Walking Through My Paralysis, *Saralee Perel* 48
15. Down But Not Out, *Sage de Beixedon Breslin* 53
16. Just One More, *Beth Morrissey* 56
17. Walking Forward, *Joyce E. Sudbeck* 59
18. Faith to Share, *Jean Kinsey* 63
19. I Am Woman, *Sage de Beixedon Breslin* 67
20. My Purpose, *Jean Kinsey* 71

❸
~Every Day Is Special~

21. Every Day a Friday, *Elaine L. Bridge* 79
22. The Gift of Brain Cancer, *Tom Schumm* 81
23. Eleven Minutes, *Heather Gallegos* 85
24. It's in the Little Things, *Diane Stark* 94
25. In Full Bloom, *Annie Mannix* 97
26. A Timely Lesson, *Lindsay A. Nielsen* 100
27. Unwrapping the Present, *Tsgoyna Tanzman* 105
28. The "Who Cares?" Bin, *Saralee Perel* 109
29. Childhood Delights, *Jean Ferratier* 112
30. People First, *Jennifer Oliver* 116

❹
~Role Models~

31. The Queen of Parking Spaces, *Deborah Zigenis-Lowery* 123
32. A True Thanksgiving, *Alyssa Simon* 126
33. Unbreakable Faith, *Jodi L. Severson* 129
34. The Power of Illusion, *Donna Milligan Meadows* 132
35. Cheer Leader, *Lydia A. Calder* 135
36. Throw Away the Key, *Deborah Shouse* 138
37. Breakfast with a Friend, *Erin Fuentes* 140
38. She Altered My Attitude, *Kris Flaa* 142
39. Thank You, Mr. Flagman, *Jennie Ivey* 146
40. A Shining Star in the Midst of Darkness, *Debbie Roloson* 148

❺
~Counting Your Blessings~

41. Counting Our Blessings, *Jane McBride Choate* 155
42. Getting Old Gratefully, *Barbara Blossom Ashmun* 158
43. Cancel the Pity Party, *Patricia Lorenz* 162

44. Shiny Nickels, *Garrett Bauman* 165
45. Power Out, *Shinan Barclay* 168
46. One Hundred Blessings, *Miriam Hill* 172
47. Life Is Not an Emergency, *Debbi Stumpf* 176
48. Death Star, *Paul H. Karrer* 179
49. From Nuisance to Blessing, *Terri Elders* 183
50. Living in Barbie's Dream House, *Annmarie B. Tait* 187
51. Pressed, Stressed and Blessed, *Linda L. Leary* 190

❻
~Overcoming Adversity~

52. From Fear to Joy, *Brenda Dillon Carr* 197
53. We Go On, *Jo Weinert* 201
54. World Travel with Asperger's, *Roy A. Barnes* 204
55. Life View, *Spring Stafford* 208
56. I Can Get Through This, *Theresa Sanders* 211
57. There's Always an Exception… I'm Usually It,
    Grace Gonzalez 215
58. Positively Uncertain, *Jennifer Berger* 219
59. No Complaints, *Donna F. Savage* 223
60. Beyond the Diagnosis, *Deborah Shouse* 225
61. His Badge of Courage, *Jessie Miyeko Santala* 228

❼
~Attitude Adjustments~

62. Word Gifts, *Janet K. Brennan* 235
63. Choice, *Cindy Gore* 238
64. When Health Fails, Paint Nails, *Shawn Marie Mann* 241
65. Weeds, *Kathi Lessner Schafer* 244
66. Magic, *Saralee Perel* 245
67. A Positive Step, *Beth M. Wood* 248
68. Seeing the Good, *Erika Hoffman* 251

69. Survival Steps, *Emily Parke Chase* 255
70. Moving Forward, *Shawnelle Eliasen* 258
71. Half Full, *Linda Newton* 262
72. Drops of Inspiration, *Gerald L. Dlubala* 265

8

~Silver Linings~

73. Sudden Clearing, *Carol A. Grund* 271
74. Walking Wounded, *Lee Hammerschmidt* 275
75. Working Out for the Best, *Mei Emerald Gaffey-Hernandez* .. 278
76. Writing a New Story, *Tulika Singh* 282
77. Downsized Dad, *Matt Chandler* 285
78. Everything Happens for a Reason, *Linda Saslow* 289
79. Unexpected Rewards, *Melinda McDonald* 293
80. Wake-Up Call, *Debbie Dufresne* 297
81. Italian Lessons, *Sheila Sowder* 302
82. Around the Bend, *Karen Majoris-Garrison* 306
83. If Only I Had Time, *Jennifer Flaten* 310

9

~Moving Forward~

84. I Feel Like Crap Today, *Kathleen Shoop* 317
85. Our Family Motto, *Toni L. Martin* 321
86. Savoring the Sweetness of Life, *Janet Perez Eckles* 325
87. Finding My Religion, *Betsy S. Franz* 329
88. The Power of Mark, *Phil Bauer* 331
89. The New Apartment, *Jennifer Quasha* 334
90. The Miracle, *Lynn Sunday* 338
91. Lucky to Be Alive, *Thomas Schonhardt* 342
92. Beauty in Breakdown, *Shannon Kaiser* 345

⑩

~Gratitude~

93. The Gratitude Journal, *Nancy Baker* 353
94. Unexpected Gift, *Susie Bee* 356
95. Catching Ants, *Rachel Spencer* 359
96. Magic Stains, *Nikki Deckon* 362
97. The Color of Gratitude, *Barbara McKinney* 364
98. Simple Joy, *Victoria Koch* 368
99. First Class Attitude, *Mandie Maass* 372
100. Adopting a Positive Outlook, *Sandi Brown* 375
101. Waiting with a Smile, *Leah M. Cano* 378

Meet Our Contributors 382
Meet Our Authors 399
About Deborah Norville 401
Thank You 402
About Chicken Soup for the Soul 403

Foreword

Change your thoughts and you change your world.
~Norman Vincent Peale

can't remember how long it's been since I first heard those words. "Change your thoughts and you change your world." It's a simple enough phrase, but wow—those words are packed with power. They have been something of a lifelong mantra for me. *Change your thoughts and you change your world.* When times are tough, when I feel so frustrated by disappointments and not reaching my goals, I repeat those words in my head and make a conscious, almost physical effort to change course, recalibrate, and steer my little ship of self in a fresh, more *positive* direction.

The other day I was speaking to a group of women in the financial industry and one woman asked to what I credited my long television career. I had to think for a moment. I *have* been blessed in the television business. I started working at the CBS station in Atlanta when I was still in college and interviewed then-President Jimmy Carter on live TV when I was only nineteen years old. (I don't know which was more exciting: Interviewing the President or having ABC's White House Correspondent Sam Donaldson asking me afterward what he said! You could have shot me and my tombstone would have read, "She died happy.")

Even when my career took some unexpected tough turns, I somehow managed to pull myself and my career back together, pick up the pieces and start over. But what was the secret to my long and still successful career? As I pondered the question, I realized there were probably three qualities that have worked in my favor — and the good news is anyone can develop them. I have an extraordinary capacity for **hard work**, an insatiable **curiosity**, and a (sometimes) ridiculous ability to look on the **bright side**. All of us can work hard, put in a few more hours at work, and try a bit harder to master a challenge. Contrary to the old saying, curiosity didn't kill the cat or anyone else. Learning new things, exploring topics about which we know nothing — that's what gives life its zest. But finding the bright side? Well, how does one do that when you've lost a job, gotten a dire diagnosis, or seen your personal life shattered?

For me, finding the silver lining in life's clouds was something of a coping mechanism. As a little girl, my mother battled chronic illness. I remember when school was dismissed, I'd hear other kids see their moms' cars in the pick-up line and complain their playground time was cut short because "Mom is here already." I was thrilled when my family's station wagon was among the cars. It meant Momma was having a "good day." Later when she died (I was twenty at the time), I was able to find gratitude in the knowledge that she was no longer in pain.

When I started my television career before I graduated from the University of Georgia, I had to deal with plenty of naysayers. How would you respond to a woman who said to you, "You have no business being here and are taking away a job from someone who is qualified?" I will never forget that moment in front of the vending machines at Channel 5. I stammered out a reply along the lines of "Well, the boss is giving me this chance and I hope to prove him right." I also resolved to make the most of the opportunity as long as it lasted. Who knows, the boss might be persuaded the female reporter was right!

Later when my career *was* derailed, I discovered that while I couldn't control what happened in my life, I *could* control how I let it impact me. The Greek Epictetus said it quite elegantly, *"Ask not that events should happen as you will, but let your will be that events should happen and you will have peace."* I must confess I only made *that* discovery after wallowing in depression and self-pity for a time.

It is NOT easy to do. How many times have you not gotten the job? Haven't you felt kicked in the teeth when denied opportunities, been frustrated when someone not nearly qualified enough got the green light instead? Maybe health problems have rearranged your family's life. It just isn't fair! I know I've felt that way. It *isn't* fair. But here's the thing. I've given birth to three children and at no point was there ever anyone in the delivery room looking at that newborn and saying, "Kid, from here on out, it's all fair." Life just doesn't work that way.

Some people don't seem to be affected by that. Just as there are those who can walk through a field of poison ivy and never have the slightest discomfort, there are some people who can be hammered by all of life's negatives and still remain unscathed. I am not one of them. Deny me entry to the club, and part of me wants to sob in the corner wondering why I'm not good enough. But the bigger part of me has realized it's no fun going to a pity party. The better I get at resisting the temptation to give in to sorrow, frustration, or stress, the more successful I seem to be both personally and professionally.

Was this real—or was this something I was imagining? I have spent the last several years researching these kinds of values: gratitude, respect, resilience, and faith. What is it that makes some people more resilient? How are some people able to let the difficulties of life roll off them like water off a duck's back? Why do some people just seem *stronger*? The answer is in this book's title—*Think Positive*. Recent scientific studies have proven that a positive attitude actually has measurable benefits. Grateful, positive people report they have better lives and more positive memories. People who can recall positive events have been proven to be more resilient, even in the most difficult of situations. People who keep track of the "good things" in their lives are healthier, more active, more productive—and held in higher regard by those around them. There's peer-reviewed proof of this!

What's more, people who are able to "accentuate the positive" are smarter, better able to make cognitive associations and connections. They solve problems faster and more correctly. Kids who summon up positive memories do better on tests.

But how do you summon up positive memories when you're in a really tough spot? Plenty of people are right now. The collapse of financial markets wiped out jobs and life savings. Retirements have been postponed and homes foreclosed upon. Terror scares have changed the way we travel and the way we look at people from other countries.

Change your thoughts and you change your world.

Let's face it. It isn't always easy. When things aren't going your way, those peppy little sayings—*Count your blessings instead of sheep, When life gives you lemons, make lemonade,* and *If you see it, you can be it*—are just plain annoying. Maybe they make good needlepoint pillows for the family room couch, but somehow when you're in the midst of a really difficult situation in life, trite sayings just don't help much. But this book will.

This wonderful new volume of 101 inspirational stories, *Chicken Soup for the Soul: Think Positive* is filled with the experiences of real people living everyday lives with real problems—yet they've found the inner strength to overcome those challenges or just ways to make their lives more meaningful. Their examples can help you find the keys to think positively, enhance your own life, and provide that little bit of motivation that will help you get over the speed bumps of life.

In fact, the tale of the Chicken Soup for the Soul series is a great example of thinking positively. I fell in love with the series when it debuted years ago—but I love the story of how it came into existence even more. I cite it often in speeches as a great example of perseverance. Jack Canfield and Mark Victor Hansen were convinced their little collection of inspirational stories had the power to make a meaningful difference in the lives of readers. Trouble was—they couldn't find a publisher who agreed with them. They took their book to publishing conferences and literally hundreds of publishers ignored them. Finally they found a small publisher who would print a few thousand books for them and they started selling *Chicken Soup for the Soul* from the backs of their cars as they drove around making speeches and doing book signings. Eventually the book, that wonderful "little engine that could," turned into a worldwide bestseller and Chicken Soup for the Soul became a publishing phenomenon, one of the most successful lines of books in history.

You just gotta believe. Like JB, the foster kid in the movie *Angels in the Outfield*. Every night the little boy went to bed with the hope that tomorrow would be the day he found a family. "It could happen," JB would say as he snuggled under the covers. In true Hollywood form, the movie ends with JB being adopted by the baseball coach George Knox, played by Danny Glover.

JB never gave up hoping that "it could happen." The founders of Chicken Soup for the Soul never gave up on their dream of changing lives through inspiring stories. George Patton said "Courage is fear hanging on one second longer." I like to paraphrase General Patton by saying "Success is failure trying one more time." Most of us don't succeed because we give up too soon. Did you know the average customer has to be pitched five to seven times before he will make a purchase? The average salesman gives up after two or three attempts. Want to read the ultimate tale of persistence? Pull out your kid's copy of *Green Eggs and Ham*. Count up how many times Sam I Am offers up that plate of green eggs and ham. Sixteen tries! As we all know, when he finally gave it a taste, he liked it after all!

It could happen for you too. You just gotta believe. The stories that follow will help you summon up that extra bit of energy and positive attitude that you need to help you reach your potential. They already have for me.

Change your thoughts and you change your world. I didn't know until I did a computer search that those were the words of Dr. Norman Vincent Peale. Did you know he too suffered from self-doubt? After his manuscript for *The Power of Positive Thinking* was rejected for the umpteenth time, he tossed it in a wastebasket, where it was retrieved by his wife Ruth. It went on to publish 20 million copies in 12 languages. Ruth Peale, who died in 2008, was quoted as saying of her husband, "I don't have as much self-doubt as he did."

You'll love James Scott Bell's story of how the now-bestselling author first met the "father" of positive thinking. Bell tells how meeting Norman Vincent Peale influenced his life and helped him get through the anxiety of being a lawyer turned author.

Got a dream you want to pursue but afraid to give it a shot? Just do it. When unemployment hit both her and her husband, Debbie Acklin was terrified to start a new business but circumstance had backed her into a corner. Starting from scratch, she made up flyers advertising computer training, rented out a space, and fielded enough clients to launch a successful new business. Her example has me strategizing how I can extend my own fledgling yarn business into something more.

Health issues are something every family must confront but it's not always easy to see the blessing in such unfair adversity. My cousin Dan has fought a long, painful and incredibly brave battle against multiple sclerosis. His repeated hospitalizations have cheated him of many of the experiences a young man in his twenties should get to enjoy, but it hasn't robbed him of his ability to make a positive difference in the lives of others. His most recent hospital stay was a tough one, prompting friends, many of whom now live far away, to visit and share reminiscences of Danny's impact on their lives. The mom of one friend recalled how even during sleepovers, Danny would always say his prayers before going to bed. What a blessing for his family to know their son's sheer "goodness" was apparent to all. The chapter "Health Challenges" is filled with similar stories in which unforeseen medical misfortunes changed lives but also offered opportunities. People like Shawn Decker, a hemophiliac who contracted HIV from a childhood blood transfusion. Instead of turning bitter, Shawn is upbeat and grateful for life. Now a leader in the HIV community, he's coined the term "positoid" for people in his situation.

Sometimes the magic is in the moment. Surveys show nine out of ten of us say we are "extremely pressed" for time (and the other ten percent were too busy to talk to the pollster, I bet!) The stories in the "Every Day Is Special" chapter remind us that sometimes there's nothing better than an average mundane day. Elaine Bridge used to treat herself to a special coffee on Fridays and always had an upbeat attitude on those days. Then she realized she could have that fancy coffee and that positive attitude any day of the week. Why not make every day a special day?

Heather Gallegos had gone to the local track a bit reluctantly for her morning run when she was confronted with an incident that underscored how an ordinary day can turn out to be anything but. When a man collapsed on the track in front of her, she administered CPR compressions for *eleven minutes* until paramedics arrived. As she put it, it was "Enough time to save his life. Enough time to change mine."

They say God never gives you more than you can handle, but you have to marvel at the strength and resilience of the people who share their stories in the chapters called "Role Models" and "Overcoming Adversity." Are you living the life you were meant to live or does something feel "not quite right?" Shannon Kaiser was a young woman who seemed to have it all — except she didn't feel that way. In the "Moving Forward" chapter she describes how she dissected every aspect of her life and really honed in on what she felt would give her the meaning it lacked. You'll be stunned at just how incredibly fate intervened and helped her reach her goals.

You all know the emphasis I put on gratitude and giving thanks. Jane McBride Choate's story on how a gratitude journal helped when her husband's business hit on hard times will probably encourage many of you to try the technique. As I've written in my own books, weaving gratitude into our daily lives empowers us to lead happier more productive lives. This powerful book ends with a chapter on "Gratitude," with inspiring examples of how the power of "thank you" can make an incredible impact.

As you read along, dog ear the stories that particularly resonate for you. You'll want to refer back to them on those days when you're feeling like "life" is getting the better of you. I also suggest you keep a pencil and paper handy to jot down the questions you might find yourself asking of *you*. Each of these 101 stories has a lesson of unique benefit. What you take from the stories might be different from what

I learn or what a friend might discover from the story. As you go through the book, you'll begin to see a pattern to your scribbles. The questions you write—and the answers you offer to them—can provide a template to help you live your own life more authentically and more fully.

Are you living the way you feel you are meant to?

What are the benefits that come from your own adversities?

What blessings have happened this day, this week?

Who serves as a role model for you? Have you told them?

How can you celebrate the mundane and the ordinary?

What is it your life lacks that would give it greater meaning?

Share this book with family and friends. Give a copy to someone who needs a boost. And when you need a reminder that life is filled with blessings, benefits, opportunities, and joy return to this book. You'll find you're looking ahead with grateful, positive happy eyes that recognize all the good in your life now—and to come. I'm just positive of it!

~Deborah Norville

Think Positive

Words that Changed My Life

Words have the power to both destroy and heal.
When words are both true and kind,
they can change our world.

~Buddha

1

The Day I Met Norman Vincent Peale

Four things for success:
work and pray, think and believe.
~Norman Vincent Peale

"Why are things so bad now?" Cindy, my wife of twenty-eight years said. "Why does it have to be so hard?"

I didn't have an answer because I felt exactly the same way.

We were sitting in our family room that morning, sipping our coffee. Cindy had just suffered a major setback in her real estate work. Another agent had done something unethical, cutting her out of a commission she'd earned. It looked like things were heading toward litigation, with all the attendant stress.

And I, a writer of thrillers, was facing the biggest hurdle of my career—a jump to a new market that was anything but guaranteed.

So we sat there for a moment in silence, and then this popped out of my mouth. "We have to be more Norman Vincent Peale-ish."

I hadn't mentioned his name in awhile, but now it seemed exactly right. Because once, some thirty years before, his words delivered me from a very dark time in my life.

I was acting then, living in Hollywood, working sporadically, auditioning, going through the rounds. If there's any profession that is full of defeats, it's acting. Rejection is your constant companion, doubt your chatty next-door neighbor.

One dismal summer day in 1979 I was standing on the corner of Hollywood and Vine. I'd just come from an audition and was heading back to my apartment. I paused on the most famous crossroads in Hollywood as a bus drove by and spewed a stream of black exhaust my way. A wave of despair washed over me. What was the point of all this? Like in the old Peggy Lee song, I wondered, "Is that all there is?"

Feeling more than a little desperate, I walked down to Pickwick Bookshop on Hollywood Boulevard. I went to the religion section, thinking maybe what I needed was a recovery of my faith.

After high school, I'd gone on to college. It wasn't long before I was into many of the things I'd heard happen at "party schools." Sundays were not for church, but sitting at the beach drinking beer. Now, three years removed from graduation, I was hoping that I could find in a book some relief for the darkness I felt crushing my spirit.

As I scanned the titles I saw the name Norman Vincent Peale featured prominently. I'd seen the movie *One Man's Way*, the biopic about Dr. Peale. Well, I reasoned, they made a movie about the guy; he must have something going on.

So I bought *The Power of Positive Thinking*, went back to my apartment, and started to read. I followed the steps Dr. Peale laid out at the end of each chapter. Some months later I moved to New York to study acting and work in the theatre. I found lodging at a rooming house on West 23rd Street, took a job as a temporary typist, volunteered to move scenery at an Off Broadway theater, and generally fell into the pattern of the city. Which meant a lot of hurrying around and more than a little urban anxiety.

At some point I remembered that Dr. Norman Vincent Peale had been a preacher in New York at Marble Collegiate Church. I wondered if he was still alive. (This was in the days before the Internet and Google!) I looked up the church's address in a phonebook and went by to inquire about Dr. Peale. They told me he was not only still alive, but preaching every Sunday—at nearly eighty-two years of age.

The next Sunday I was there. It was March 9, 1980. I was in the balcony as Dr. Peale delivered his sermon entitled "You Can Win Over All Defeats." I remember being struck by how deep and resonant and expressive his voice was. Especially when he said, "There's an invulnerability that flows out of faith. I love that word. Invulnerability! And undefeatable! That's what you are! You think I'm building you up too much? I do it on the basis of the Bible that says, 'This is the victory that overcometh the world'—that means anything in the world."

I purchased a tape of the sermon. I still have it. On the label is a note I scribbled in ink: "The day I met him."

After the sermon I'd gone to his office, hoping I could shake his hand. A nice secretary said if I'd wait, Dr. Peale would be happy to meet me. I could hear his dynamic voice booming as he spoke to someone on the phone.

Presently, Dr. Peale marched out with a smile as his secretary brought him over to me. I introduced myself and he pumped my hand. "Well I am certainly glad to meet you!" he said.

We conversed for a few minutes. He asked me about my interests and work. It struck me that Dr. Peale was the living proof of the value of his philosophy. He had the energy and enthusiasm of a man half his age. When he spoke, he looked me in the eye and for that moment I felt he was treating me as the most important person in the world.

Life took its twists and turns. I got married, moved back to Los Angeles, went to law school, started raising a family. I also began to write. Through those years I'd occasionally re-read Dr. Peale's books and remember fondly his voice resonating from the pulpit.

Now Cindy and I were in this long period of challenge. During those weeks and months we would constantly remind each other to "stay Peale-ish." It wasn't always easy to be positive, but being Peale-ish got us through many a dark day.

And then our prayers were answered.

After many weeks of uncertainty, Cindy's controversy was settled with a simple conference call. She received just and fair compensation and the prospect of protracted litigation lifted off her shoulders.

My waiting stretched into months. And more months. The publishing industry was going through a challenging time. No one in the business seemed to know how it was all going to shake out.

It took a lot of reminding for me to stay Peale-ish during this time.

The day finally came when my agent called with the good news. The multiple-book contract I'd been waiting for had come through, and it was everything I'd hoped for.

After Cindy and I celebrated with a little jig around the family room, it struck me how crucially important that day was years ago when I walked into Pickwick Bookshop and found Dr. Peale's book. Also the day I met him and heard him speak.

Whenever I need them, his words are right there waiting for me: "Invulnerability! And undefeatable! That's what you are!"

~James Scott Bell

Dancing in the Rain

Anyone who says sunshine brings happiness has never danced in the rain.
~Author Unknown

My husband and I had just finished having dinner at a local restaurant and were enjoying strolling through the stores in an adjacent shopping center. We went into a shop that sold handcrafted items in hopes of finding a few last-minute Christmas gifts. The scent of handmade soaps and potpourri teased our noses as we walked through the door.

There was a lot to see. Every shelf and wall was loaded with different crafters' handiwork. As I walked through the store, I noticed a wooden plaque hanging unceremoniously on a wall. I turned to take a second look and remember shaking my head "yes" at the message printed on the plaque. Moving on, I enjoyed looking at other items in the store, but found myself being drawn back to the plaque.

Standing in front of the plaque, I felt a little like a child who, when digging through the sandbox, finds some unexpected treasure—a shiny quarter or a lost toy. Here among the other handmade items, I found a very simple, yet profound treasure hidden in a message. A message I needed.

"Life isn't about waiting for the storm to pass," the plaque proclaimed. "It's about learning to dance in the rain."

As I pulled my husband over and directed his attention to the plaque, I could see that he too appreciated the simple lesson the plaque shared. How often in our daily lives had we put conditions on our happiness? When we get the house paid off, then we can be happy. When things settle down with the kids, then we'll be able to do more together. There is so little joy for the here and now in the uncertainties of the whens and thens.

Looking at the plaque, I found myself thinking back to a hot and muggy day the summer before, when I unknowingly lived the plaque's message. Dark clouds had rolled in along the foothills of the Rockies, heavy with their burden of moisture. Rain began falling lightly by mid-afternoon, building to a downpour that filled the gutters with rushing water and then moved on as quickly as it had come.

Light rain continued to fall as I walked out to get my mail. Water was still running high through the gutters. I don't know what came over me, but I suddenly felt compelled to do something a little crazy for my fifty-plus years.

I slipped off my shoes and stockings and began walking barefoot through the water. It was deliciously warm, heated by the pavement that had been baked by the summer heat.

I'm sure my neighbors thought that I had lost my last vestige of sanity, but I didn't care. For in that moment, I was alive. I wasn't worried about bills, the future or any other day-to-day cares. I was experiencing a gift—a pure and simple moment of joy!

The plaque now hangs in my living room, a Christmas gift from my husband. I walk past it multiple times each day and frequently pause to ask myself, "So, am I dancing in the rain?"

I think I am. I know I try to. I'm definitely more committed to taking time to pause and recognize and be grateful for the immense blessings that are all around me—the joys that were too often going unnoticed in my rush to future happiness. I celebrate more fully my dear blessings, such as a son with special needs learning to drive alone, the love of good friends and the beauty of spring. Yes, one step at a time, I am learning to dance in the rain!

~Jeannie Lancaster

Each Day a Masterpiece

Very often a change of self is needed more than a change of scene.
~Arthur Christopher Benson

I never thought I would move back in with my parents after I graduated from college. In fact, all through my senior year, I told myself that moving from the exciting cultural metropolis of Los Angeles back into my childhood bedroom in the sleepy, small beach town where I grew up was out of the question.

So, I applied for fellowships to travel abroad. I poured hours into my applications—revising essays, collecting letters of recommendation, researching programs, practicing interviews. I made it to the final rounds for two prestigious fellowships, but ultimately was not chosen for either.

Refusing to dwell on my disappointment, I applied to graduate schools across the country. Four months later, my mailbox was filled with nothing but rejection slips.

It was now April. I had only a month left before college graduation spit me out into the Real World. I went online and searched for jobs in the Bay Area, where my long-distance boyfriend had one more year left as a student at San Francisco State. I figured I could get a job up there, live close to him, and enjoy the creative stimulus of a new city.

Then, weeks after graduation, my boyfriend and I broke up. My college friends scattered to all corners of the globe. I packed my belongings into my parents' minivan and moved back home, feeling like a complete failure.

Don't get me wrong. I adore my parents, and I understood how generous it was of them to let me move back home and take some time to find my post-grad bearings. When I left for college, they probably shared the same belief I did: that I was moving out for good. But instead of being grateful, all I could focus on was how I felt like a loser. I had a fancy college degree, yet here I was, back where I had started four years before. I was sad about the breakup with my boyfriend. I missed my college friends. I felt like everyone but me was out in the world doing exhilarating, impactful things.

After a few days of wallowing, I came across a popular quote: "Make each day your masterpiece." I realized that I didn't have to be living out on my own in an exciting new city to make my days masterpieces. I could start that moment. I taped up the quote on my bathroom mirror. I typed it into my cell phone background. I added it to the signature line of my e-mails. "Make each day your masterpiece" became my own personal motto.

What did a "masterpiece day" look like? I pondered this question. For me, a day that was truly a "masterpiece" would include time with my loved ones, time spent exercising and taking care of myself, time volunteering to help others, and time devoted to my passion of writing.

I used this knowledge to organize my days.

I shifted my mindset and began to see my time at home as a gift in that I was able to spend a lot of time with my parents. My role in the household no longer felt like that of a child; rather, my parents treated me as an adult, and our relationship matured into one of mutual respect and consideration. Nearly every day I visited my grandfather, who also lived in town, and soaked up his stories. I reconnected with a few close high school friends from whom I had drifted away during the past couple of years.

In college I had often been too busy or stressed to cook healthy meals or exercise very much. Now that I was focused on making each day a masterpiece, I carved out time for nurturing my health. I began waking up early and running every morning at the park nearby my house. I visited local farm stands and bought more fruits and vegetables and scoured the Internet for healthy recipes. Within two weeks, I felt stronger and more energized than I had in years. My morning exercise became my treasured time to think and stay in touch with my inner self.

I volunteered in classrooms, teaching writing exercises and tutoring kids in reading. I spent time at the nursing home visiting with senior citizens. I got in touch with my hometown's volunteer center and helped out at beach clean-ups and fundraising events.

And I began to write for two hours every day. I knew I wanted to make a career as a writer, but my writing schedule in college was erratic—twenty minutes some days, none for weeks, then a whole weekend cooped up in my room with my laptop. Establishing a writing routine helped me more easily shift into the "writing groove." Some days, the words flowed easily. Other days, I spent the better part of my two writing hours staring out the window and scribbling down disjointed notes. But my pages of writing began to add up. I wrote articles, essays, short stories. I even started a novel!

Some days weren't as balanced as others. Tasks and problems popped up unexpectedly; not every day unfurled as planned. But as I lay in bed each night, reflecting on the day, I felt a deep sense of contentment and pride in myself. I really think the cliché is true that "things happen for a reason." Looking back, moving home after graduation was the best thing I could have done. Now, as I prepare to leave for graduate school in a few months, I feel focused, rejuvenated, and happy with who I am.

I was not a failure—I never had been. I realize now that my negative mindset is what held me back more than anything. My "success" is not dependent on what other people think or what my peers are doing or what I feel like I "should" be doing. My life is a success when I am living by my motto and making each day a masterpiece.

~Dallas Woodburn

4

Words of Wisdom

I don't like that man. I must get to know him better.
~Abraham Lincoln

t was the first day after I gave up teaching in a classroom to become the high school student assistance coordinator. I asked the woman who was retiring from that job how she tolerated working with a principal who was extremely narrow-minded and negative in his approach to teachers.

Her answer was so amazingly positive and beautiful that I embraced it immediately. It spared me unending hours of frustration and became the solution for conflicts throughout my life.

She said simply: "I pray for him. It's very difficult to dislike someone for whom you are praying."

~Kay Conner Pliszka

5

Two Strangers

Good fortune shies away from gloom. Keep your spirits up.
Good things will come to you and you will come to good things.
~Glorie Abelhas

My charmed life has been full of humorous moments—tidbits for laughable dinner table conversations with friends. I've noticed that often my life stories begin with the words "Guess what happened to me," followed by stories of horrible dates or embarrassing situations. While comical and entertaining, none of these moments have held great significance or importance. I didn't realize that a truly profound moment was heading my way one humid day in July when my car broke down in St. Joseph, Michigan.

A mere seven weeks before this breakdown, I left Michigan after walking out of a meaningless job, heading to Colorado to begin a new life and career at the age of twenty-six. I felt deeply that this was my chance to make my way in the world—living out a dream working with kids at the YMCA in Colorado Springs.

This dreamed "new life" never happened. Instead, I spent four of the seven weeks sick before facing the fact that the altitude did not agree with my asthma. Forced to leave what I thought was my new, exciting life, I faced the unpleasant reality of returning to my ho-hum existence in Michigan where my life status would read: twenty-six-year-old woman, single, unemployed, living at home with parents and no idea what to do with her life.

Driving 1,400 miles alone, sick and down-in-the-dumps was awful, although the word "awful" doesn't fully describe how bad the reality was. The constant wheezing, shortness of breath, and heavy pain in my lungs caused me extreme discomfort and the medication I consumed made me constantly drowsy.

Relief appeared as I reached the Michigan border at about 10:00 PM. Tired and facing a four-hour drive, I pulled off in the town of St. Joseph, rented a room at a motel, and immediately went to bed. I hadn't noticed the exhaust fan in my car was still running as I walked into the hotel. I definitely noticed when my car wouldn't start the next morning.

At that minute, in the parking lot of the motel, I wanted to cry. I wanted to scream. On top of all of the medical and mental stress heaped on me over the past seven weeks, I now had to tackle not only a physical breakdown, but also a car breakdown. I just wanted to be home. Home. But here I was—stuck, sick, tired of driving, mad at having to leave opportunity behind, and mad at the world. I've grown up listening to people tell me that, "God never gives us more than we can handle." It seems in moments like these that He likes to push the envelope.

After a tow to the nearest dealership, I settled in the waiting room for a two-hour repair. That's when I started talking to an older woman who sat a few chairs away from me. She had a friendly face lined softly with wisdom, and an approachable, motherly look.

"So you're having some repairs done?" she asked with concern in her voice. I guessed she could see the frustration on my face.

"Yes," I said with a sigh. "My car wouldn't start. I have no idea what happened." I leaned back in my seat, put my head back against the blank wall behind me and stared up at the dull, fluorescent lights on the ceiling contemplating how many hours I would be sitting there.

That's when unexpectedly, unknown to me, and at the strangest time, my significant moment began to unfold. It began normally as this kind lady and I started to talk. She asked me to tell her about what happened to my car. I did, and then we settled into comfortable, casual conversation — the stuff you talk about with strangers in waiting rooms like vacations, the history of weather in Michigan, and places to eat. Then our conversation shifted from the obscure to more personal things. She talked about her struggle with feelings of guilt as she contemplated putting her eighty-five-year-old mother in a nursing home. I tried to sympathize and told her how my parents, themselves into their sixties, were talking about getting insurance in case one or both wound up needing nursing home care. We talked about life — real life. We talked about my trip to Colorado, my asthma, her home, her husband retiring, my parents retiring.

"Your car is ready ma'am," said the service manager to the woman.

"Oh, thank you," she said.

She stood up and I smiled at her. She wished me luck as she gathered her purse and car keys from the seat next to her. But then as she was about to walk away, she hesitated and then turned back to me.

"You know, I have to tell you something," she said, and I could see a serious expression color her face. The brightness in her blue eyes dimmed a bit as she glanced at the floor and then looked straight into my eyes. "My daughter died a few years ago. It's so hard even now to do just the simple things." She swallowed hard, exhaled deeply and went on, "But every now and then I meet someone who reminds me of my daughter, and today, you reminded me so much of her." She smiled with tears in her eyes and went on. "I believe that sometimes God puts people in my path to remind me of her and to show me that my daughter is still with me and that I can get through this. I've so enjoyed talking to you today." A genuine smile covered her face. "When you get home I want you to hug your parents. They are very lucky to have you."

I gulped down an enormous lump in my throat. I didn't know how to respond. I felt tears of my own welling up in my eyes, and all I managed was to mumble a lame sounding, "Oh gosh, thank you." I was dumbfounded, confused, and most of all sad. I felt so moved by what she said, so touched by this revelation about her daughter and the whole-hearted sentiment she put into telling me this. I'm a person who normally hides my emotions, but that day I stood up and hugged her and said, "I enjoyed talking to you too," and I meant it.

A few hours later, I pulled into the driveway at my parents' house. My mom came outside with her usual broad, inviting smile, and she wrapped me in a huge hug—the kind that generates love and warmth that only a mom can give. I was home. I hugged my mom with all my might. Since that day I've never questioned why bad things, crazy things, funny things, or just plain everything sometimes happen to me. And I'll certainly never ask "why me" when I have car trouble again.

~Maggie Koller

6

Listen to Your Mother

The person who is waiting for something to turn up
might start with their shirt sleeves.
~Garth Henrichs

My grandmother always said, "Can't never could until he tried." My mother took up the mantra and recited it to me many times during my childhood. She normally used it to try and coerce me into doing something I didn't want to do. It was like waving a red flag in front of a bull. Irritating as it was, it took root.

Many years ago, my husband was downsized out of his job, leaving us with a single income — mine. We were a two-income family with two-income bills and two children to support. He had been given a generous severance, but that money would only last so long. Just when it looked like things couldn't get any worse, they did. I lost my job too.

While my husband was out pounding the pavement, knocking on doors, making calls, and scanning the papers for another job, I stayed home and did my best to figure out how to make the most of every cent. It was often difficult to maintain a hopeful, positive attitude, but we did our best.

One day I took some milk from the refrigerator and noticed that it was lukewarm. We could not afford to call a repairman, so we just turned the refrigerator up as high as it would go and prayed for the best.

Anxious about our situation, I tried to think of something that I could do to earn some money. Even a little would help. Maybe we could at least get the refrigerator repaired. But what could I do? I, too, began searching the want ads, applying for anything for which I was even remotely qualified.

One day I had lunch with a former coworker who insisted that I would be great at teaching computer classes. I had used word processing software extensively at my former job and was definitely an expert, but could I sell that skill? Was it possible that people would actually pay me to teach them? The only teaching I had ever done was in Sunday School. I remembered my mother's mantra—"Can't never could until he tried."

I wasn't sure where to start. Finally formulating a plan, the first thing I did was check on the availability and the cost of a meeting room. After securing a room, I went down to the Chamber of Commerce and got a list of local business addresses. I typed the addresses into my home computer and printed them on labels. I then designed a brochure that could be mailed, advertising my class. I sat on the den floor, folded my brochures and stuck address labels and stamps on them. The next day I sat in my car and prayed outside the post office, then went in and mailed the brochures. We could not really afford to spend the money that all this had cost.

I was filled with self-doubt as I waited for responses. I had absolutely no experience in running a business, even a small endeavor like this one. I had no training experience. I just had a need and I remembered my mother's words, "Can't never could until he tried." Well, "Can't" was trying.

Every day, I waited eagerly for the mail. On the third day, I got my first response. I ran inside to show my husband. "Why haven't you opened it?" he asked. I carefully opened the envelope to find a check and two registrations. I couldn't believe it! I needed ten people to break even on my expenses. Over the next two weeks I got more checks and registrations in the mail. On the day of my first class, I had seventeen students.

I had rented computers, but could not afford for them to be

delivered and set up. "Don't worry, honey," my husband said, hugging me. "You've got me. I'll help you out. We can do it." On the day of my class, he and I left early and picked up the computers. It took two trips to get them all to the classroom. We spent the next hour unloading, setting them up and installing the software. Then my husband left and there I stood, alone, waiting for my first student to arrive.

Over the next fifteen minutes, I made two trips to the bathroom, checked my hair and make-up three times, and had a small panic attack. What the heck did I think I was doing? These people were going to want their money back!

The first people walked in. I smiled, introduced myself, and checked them off my attendee list. One by one, my students wandered in and took their seats. I did my best to pretend I was busy getting set up, turning to smile nervously at the class a few times. Once everyone was present, I passed out the course sheets and began. Within minutes I was relaxed, guiding them through, answering all their questions. The hours passed quickly.

When my husband came to help me break down the computers, I ran to him excitedly. "They loved the class! They asked if I was doing others so that their co-workers could attend."

"Great!" he said, a little dazed. I'm not sure that he thought I would succeed, but he had remained supportive.

Over the next months, I did several more classes. I discovered metered mail, set up a business phone line, and got a business license. I made enough money to cover my expenses and have a little left over each time. I wasn't going to get rich, but I was helping keep us afloat, and that felt wonderful!

I will never forget the day that our new refrigerator was delivered. It was much larger than our old one. I paid for it with my training money. I could not have been more proud if I had been paying for a new car. Well, okay, that would have been a pretty big deal. Nevertheless, I had a tremendous satisfaction that I had tried and succeeded!

Eventually both my husband and I found full-time employment.

My new boss told me that the two things that made my résumé stand out were my training experience and the fact that I had run my own business, indicating that I could handle projects and work self-directed. I have been with that company for sixteen years.

Whenever I am handed a seemingly overwhelming project or I have to work with something new, I still hear my mother's voice, "Can't never could until he tried." Thanks Mom!

~Debbie Acklin

7

Just Show Up

Courage is being afraid but going on anyhow.
~Dan Rather

While walking in the woods near our home on Cape Cod, I met a man who taught me a three-word lesson that has altered my life.

His name was Morris and he seemed to be in his seventies or eighties. He told me, "I walk here every day, rain or shine."

Noticing that I was wearing a neck brace and holding onto a tree with one hand and my cane with the other, he said, "So, is it hard for you to get around here?"

"Sometimes."

He nodded in understanding and remarked, "But you still do it." We seemed to form an unusually special bond on that day in the woods as we both spoke from our hearts.

"Frankly," I said. "It's harder for me to get here than it is to walk here. And that has nothing to do with needing a brace or a cane. It has to do with my thinking."

"You get caught in maybe-I-will, maybe-I-won't land. That's the problem."

"Yes!" I laughed at how perfectly he put that. "And that one second of debate is enough of a time gap for me to come up with a perfect excuse to talk myself out of it and press the button on the TV remote instead."

Then he said the three magical words I now say to myself nearly every day: "Just show up."

Later my husband, Bob, asked me what Morris meant.

"Well, here's how I understand it. When the thought enters my brain, 'I should go exercise,' I instantly start thinking about every single step it takes to get around to doing it. First I have to shower. Then I have to find something to wear. Then I have to find everything I need for safety. Then I have to—blah, blah, blah. I think what Morris meant was to scrap all of those thoughts. In other words, I should replace talking-myself-out-of-it thinking with the words: 'Just show up.'"

Bob started practicing Morris's philosophy and it's working for a lot of things. "I get overwhelmed at the computer with all the details I have to do," he told me. "Sometimes I just avoid it, but that's crazy. So instead of thinking about the big picture, I say, 'Just show up,' and I do."

Now, this new way of approaching things was working fine and dandy until a fellow named Kelvin and his wife, Amy, contacted me. They organize and operate the Cape Cod Challenger Club. They've read many of my newspaper columns. My topics often include disabilities. That's why they got in touch.

Kelvin e-mailed, "We provide year-round athletic, recreational and social activities for physically and developmentally disabled youth on the Cape."

He continued, "We pack the park with hundreds of people every Sunday during our baseball season. We would be honored if you would be our opening day speaker and throw out the first pitch."

I held my head in my hands. Public speaking is my number one phobia. But I couldn't say no. So I instantly had the altruistic and benevolent thought, "I hate you, Kelvin."

The next day Bob went with me to meet Kelvin at Dunkin' Donuts. "Please don't make me give a speech," I pleaded with this delightful young man who had the crazy notion that since I write stories, somehow that implied that I could form words—out loud.

"Just a few sentences?" he said.

I was able to buy time by licking the cream cheese off my bagel. Bob kept kicking my leg and touching his mustache, which I found out way too much later meant that I had a huge wad of cream cheese on my upper lip.

I reluctantly agreed.

In the middle of the night before my speech, I shook Bob awake. "What if I can't talk and just hiccup for ten syllables instead of saying words?" (That did happen at our wedding.) "What if I can't walk that day? What if I have a panic attack? What if..." And Bob sweetly silenced me.

He said, "You know there's only one thing that matters."

I knew.

And so, I decided to "just show up" for the opening game.

It went beautifully. And by that I do not mean I did a good job giving my speech. It means that I faltered and stammered and even went blank twice. Should I have been embarrassed? Of course not. All I had to do was look around at the children and their parents, teachers, volunteers—and the beautiful expectant looks on everyone's faces. They were seeing someone disabled, like them, who simply got up there and tried.

I did the weirdest thing for my speech. I told the truth. Here's what I said:

"I am so excited to be here today with you wonderful people of the Cape Cod Challenger Club. I'm honored that Kelvin and Amy invited me.

And... I'm also scared to be talking in front of such a large group. But I'll tell you—I'm scared of a lot of stuff and I try to do it anyway.

So my message to you is this:

Winning doesn't matter.

Being scared doesn't matter.

The only thing that matters... is that we try!!

Now, who's going to help me toss the first pitch?"

Many children, all disabled, raised their hands. "I will! I will!" They excitedly came running over to help me. I was very wobbly. My crew of helpers kept me from falling. I had the children hold onto my arm and the ball so that they also felt they were tossing the first pitch. And when we did, we all yelled, "PLAY BALL!"

Then someone handed me a huge bouquet of flowers.

You know, I found out that it wouldn't have mattered if I lost my balance. It wouldn't have mattered if I suddenly had trouble talking or any of the bad things that sometimes happen to me.

The only thing that mattered was that I just showed up—for the children's sake—for the caregivers' sake—and for mine.

Thank God I had that chance encounter in the woods that day with Morris. Although he told me he walked there every day, I haven't seen him since.

And even though I know over forty people who walk that same path in the woods, not one of them has ever seen Morris. Kind of makes you wonder.

~Saralee Perel

Finding the Real Me

He is a wise man who does not grieve for the things which he has not,
but rejoices for those which he has.
~Epictetus

It started out as one of the best days of my life, and certainly, of my career. My staff and I had been named the number one unit in our company, and I was taking them out for a celebratory lunch. I worked with a wonderful group of people and we were proud of what our hard work and team spirit had accomplished during the prior year.

Lunch was fun, the food excellent, and the camaraderie at the table made me smile. I was proud of this group, who laughed, cried, and loved each other, and I felt blessed to be their leader. The weather was crisp, cool, and sunny, and I thought to myself "it just doesn't get any better than this." It was a perfect day.

After lunch, we returned to work. As I checked my e-mail, an urgent message popped up for a mandatory teleconference later that afternoon. We had these types of teleconferences quite a bit to cut costs versus expensive management meetings, so I thought nothing of it and continued to catch up on work and phone calls I had missed during lunch.

Two o'clock came — time for the teleconference. I put my phone on speaker so I could work and listen at the same time — multi-tasking as usual. I heard our associate director's voice, usually so friendly and upbeat, take on a somber tone. He stuttered and stumbled, which was not like him, and finally gave us the bad news.

"You are all being relocated to Ohio, if you are willing to move," he told us with a tremble in his voice, "and if you cannot move, you will be given a severance package, and sixty days notice."

I felt numb. How could this be happening? Most of us had been at the company for years and had been told our jobs were some of the most secure in the organization. None of us, for various reasons, would be able to relocate, and there were no other jobs available within the company in our area, so it appeared my team and I would soon be out of work.

I had the heartbreaking task of sharing the news with my staff. As their leader, I had to be strong, upbeat, and courageous, but inside I was scared to death. While I gave them words of encouragement, I felt my world was slowly coming to an end.

My husband and family consoled me, but I was scared. Really scared. Financially, I knew we would be okay—my husband had a good job, and the severance and other savings I had would keep us going for quite a while, but I had worked full-time my whole life and did not know if I could deal with losing my job. It had become my identity—who I was and how I defined myself. I was a leader, and I felt, a good one. What would I be with that taken from me?

The first few days after my job ended, I didn't want to get out of bed. I kept up a brave front for my children and husband, but moped around the house, not really knowing what to do. After working non-stop for twenty-five years I was lost. I sent out résumés, but due to the economic conditions, job postings in my field were few and far between. It looked like I would be out of work for quite awhile, and I didn't know what to do with all my newfound extra time.

One day, after sitting around feeling sorry for myself, I turned on the television and watched a program about a missions group that helped children and hungry people all over the world. I felt guilty knowing that even though I had lost my job, we had plenty of good, healthy food on the table every night. The words spoken by the missionary seemed directed specifically at me—she told viewers that the "best way to be blessed and to forget about your own problems is to help someone else."

Ashamed, I realized that I had been wallowing in self-pity when I had so much to be thankful for—a loving husband, beautiful children, and family and friends who needed me. I could either continue to focus on what I had lost and be miserable, or I could count my blessings and bless others.

I decided to get up, get dressed, and cook a great meal for my family that night. I had always loved to cook, learning at the side of my mom and grandmothers, all wonderful Southern cooks who taught me their secrets. I also thought I could make some extra food to take to our neighbors who were retired, and brighten their day as well.

I began to assemble the ingredients for my dinner, humming to myself a little as I prepared our meal. I was starting to feel like my old self again. Just then one of my daughters walked into the kitchen and asked if she could help me cook dinner. As we stirred and sifted, basted and baked, our dinner came together. We laughed, talked, and shared stories. I told her how my mom and grandmothers had let me help them cook when I was a little girl, and I still used many of their recipes. I forgot about how depressed I had been, and when we put the meal on the table for the rest of the family, we were both proud of the delicious dinner we had made and basked in the compliments we received.

After dinner, as I cleaned up the dishes, it occurred to me that I had never taught my children to cook. I had been so busy being a "career woman" that I had not taken the time to show them how to make the wonderful dishes I had learned to make as a child and young woman. I had always cooked for my family, but had not given them the gift that I had been given—the gift of learning how to prepare a meal for my loved ones. I was saddened by this, and decided that I was going to use my unexpected free time to change all that.

The next morning I announced to my family that I was going to start a cooking school for them. This was met with groans from my kids, who all had busy lives and plans of their own. But I convinced them to give it a try and we decided we would prepare supper the next night. I let each child pick a dish to prepare for the meal, with my guidance. We decided to do this weekly and make extra food to share with friends or neighbors in need in our community.

The next morning, we shopped for our dinner at our grocery store and local farmers market. We unloaded our ingredients, put on our aprons, and started cooking. I shared cooking techniques, short cuts, and the background behind many of the recipes we had decided to prepare. While making my grandmother's famous lemon meringue pie, I remembered the many times I had stood in her kitchen, licking the beaters thick with white, fluffy meringue, sweet and cloudlike, and how much fun those times had been. Now I was sharing them with my own children. I could almost see Grandmother smiling down from heaven, watching my children and I carrying on her traditions. Nothing had made her happier than cooking something wonderful for her family, and now I knew how she felt. Instead of rushing to put something quick on the table between business meetings and reports, I got to take the time to enjoy cooking and eating the beautiful meal we were creating. Plus, I got to share the company of my children—listen to them joke, find out what was going on with each of them, and appreciate the personalities of each one. All four of them were so different, yet so special, and brought so much joy into my life—I had just been too busy to notice that before. I had been so busy providing for my family financially, and basing my worth on my career, that I had forgotten what was really worthwhile, and who I really was—a wife and a mother to these amazing people who deserved my time, my guidance, and affection.

Cooking school continued each week. It became a time we all looked forward to—a time of laughter, love and learning. And, of course, some really great meals. Cooking with my kids was just the start—I began doing things with them and for them that they enjoyed—going to the library, movies, playing tennis, or lounging by the pool. For the first time, I was able to really focus on and enjoy my family, without deadlines looming in the background, working on my laptop, or checking my e-mail at the same time. Instead of multi-tasking, I focused on the one task that mattered most—making sure my family knew that they were loved and were number one in my life.

I did eventually go back to work, but I found a job that was more flexible and allowed me to spend much more time with my husband and children. It turned out to be an even better job than my previous one—it paid better, was much less stressful, and gave me the flexibility I needed to be there when my family needed me. My priorities had changed, and I never again wanted to put my loved ones in second place to my career.

I had thought losing my job was the worst thing that had ever happened to me. But, it turned out to be a blessing in disguise. While I had thought that losing my job was the end of who I was, it was really only the beginning of discovering the real me.

~Melanie Adams Hardy

License to Smile

A cloudy day is no match for a sunny disposition.
~William Arthur Ward

Anyone who knows me well would almost certainly label me an optimist. I believe in embracing hope and finding something positive even in the most difficult circumstances. My own optimism stems from a strong, personal faith in a loving God who I believe is very interested in the personal details of our lives, not just the "big stuff." I also believe that things happen for a reason and that if we keep our minds and spirits open, our invisible God often becomes visible, sometimes in ways that are quite humorous!

With that being said, even optimists can temporarily lose hope. This was the case for me on a particularly cold and gloomy January day. I felt overwhelmed by the painful challenges I was dealing with in my personal life. Marital, health, and financial struggles had joined forces to create a tornado of emotion that threatened to crush my spirit. I felt angry, frustrated, burdened, and distanced from the presence of God. The weather seemed to reflect my mood—the gray sky blocked even a single ray of sunlight. As I drudged through my workday, I just couldn't shake a sense of hopelessness and despair.

About midway through the day, I left work to get some lunch. Still feeling pessimistic and negative, I noticed that the sun had come out for a brief moment. I began to think about my negative attitude and reminded myself that I was responsible for choosing my state of mind. While I could not ignore the pain I was going through, I could choose to dwell on the negative or I could choose to shift my thinking to a more positive focus. Even as I consciously reminded myself of this truth, I felt incapable of making the shift. So I gripped the steering wheel and prayed an honest, heartfelt prayer. "God," I cried, my tears ready to spill out, "where are you? I don't want to feel this way but I am miserable and hopeless today. Please lift me out of this dark, gloomy place!"

As I stopped at a red light, I looked at the car directly in front of mine. The personalized license plate caught my eye—it read "SUNZOUT." This brought an immediate smile to my face. It felt like a reminder from God that the sun was shining after all, and in the midst of the longest, darkest, coldest winter in years, this in itself was a blessing. But then my eyes moved to the car that was perfectly parallel to the SUNZOUT vehicle. The license plate on that car read "GROUCH." So as I read these two license plates side by side, I said out loud "SUNZOUT, GROUCH." This brought more than a smile to my face as I laughed out loud! Seeing the two very opposite license plates right next to each other at that exact moment in time also strengthened my previous recognition of my ability to choose my outlook despite my circumstances. I felt my spirits and mood lift as I made the conscious decision to choose a positive attitude.

I returned to work and shared my story with several co-workers who responded with warm laughter at what I referred to as my "message from beyond." I learned that day that when we are feeling too discouraged to bring ourselves out of a state of negativity, relief is only a prayer away!

~Julie A. Havener

Hearing the Worst

If you don't like something change it;
if you can't change it, change the way you think about it.
~Mary Engelbreit

S
ue and I sped along the highway at seventy-five miles per hour as we began our climb up the curving mountainous roadway where North Carolina intersects with the southern border of Virginia. Sue, my youngest daughter, also a mother and grandmother, is a young-at-heart fifty-year-old widow. I suppose she could be identified as a "tweener"—between me and her younger family—since I've often asked her to drive me long distances or to do other things I can't or don't want to do for myself.

The more politically correct term, I suppose, is that Sue is now a member of "The Sandwich Generation." These young to middle-age men and women are still raising their families, even if they are mostly grown, and suddenly they find themselves also responsible for their aging parents and must add additional responsibilities to an already busy lifestyle.

I leaned back in my seat and enjoyed the luxury of the comfortable ride, while taking in the sunshine and scenery so different from that in Florida. I had to admit there were times when I longed to see the mountains and rolling hills, and missed the colors of the changing seasons. Still, Florida had been a good place for me to live after retirement and while caring for my aging mother—except in situations such as this when my son developed a potentially serious medical problem. I was happy that my daughter had been willing and able to transport me to see him through surgery. It was a free trip for her, too, a chance to visit with old friends and other family members.

As we entered Virginia, the trees and valleys glistened ever more brightly with deepening shades of green reflecting the sunlight of late spring. One of the most beautiful spots along the ascending highway featured a vertical drop to picturesque valleys on the right, looking over many miles of neatly manicured farmland dotted with white buildings of civilization. On our left were even steeper cliffs rising skyward with trickles of running water, jutting rocks with mossy patches and scattered growth of new plant life highlighting the incline of the mountain. Occasionally, small piles of rock and dirt had broken loose from their moorings and lay as evidence of man's failed attempt to conquer the hilly terrain.

I twisted my body to the right in my seat, trying to find the mountain with the "bite" taken out of the top. I assumed it was a "man-made" bite to make way for utilities and other signs of civilization, but it had become a game for my family, looking for the sign that we were approaching the area where Uncle Charlie used to live.

It was April 28, 2009, a day I should not forget—but for how long would I truly be able to remember it?

My cell phone rang, breaking the tranquility of the pleasant scene. I glanced at the caller ID and answered with a degree of trepidation. I had been waiting for this particular call.

"Hello, Ms. Bennett," the cheery voice said. "This is Annette in Dr. Jay's office. He wants you to know that your PET scan results are in. They're consistent with Alzheimer's disease."

I gasped! No friendly word foreplay to break the ice or soften the blow—just the dreaded diagnosis—one which I expected but dreaded nonetheless. I had even asked to have the PET scan (an imaging technique—positron emission tomography—producing three-dimensional images of a body process) done.

"He wants you to start taking Aricept right away," the caller added. "I'll call in a prescription for you. You have a good day now, you hear." And just as quickly, she was gone.

I closed the cell phone, put it back in my purse, and said nothing, just stared at the scenery, which had lost some of its magical luster.

"Who was that?" Sue questioned.

"Just someone at the doctor's office," I replied, trying to show at least a half-smile. "She's calling the pharmacy with a prescription for some of my memory problems."

Sue turned her head toward me and started to speak.

I placed my hand on my daughter's arm, stopping her before she could question me further.

"Better keep your eyes on the road, sweetie. This road is really curvy—and steep. Looks like those clouds are dropping right on top of us."

I was not ready to share my diagnosis with family or anyone else at this time even though nothing had really changed—it had just become formal—no longer a suspicion, but now a reality.

Had I been driving, my thoughts could easily have led me down a dangerous path. The callousness and lack of empathy with which the news was delivered sent chills racing up and down my spine as my eyes strayed to the steep descent to the valley below. For a split second I wondered if I'd be better off just to leave the highway and sail through the air and trees and brush to my ultimate fate, rather than spending years dependent on others and living in the foggy mental state that surely lay before me.

But reason prevailed and in that instant, I made a major decision.

I will not become a victim. I will take each day as it comes and deal with it. Beyond that, it's out of my hands. But, I will never consider myself just a number or a victim—I'll do what I can to try to slow the process down, but never, ever will I be a victim.

~Lois Wilmoth-Bennett

Think Positive

Health Challenges

*Being in a good frame of mind
helps keep one in the picture of health.*

~Author Unknown

11

I'm Positive... Really

Positive anything is better than negative thinking.
~Elbert Hubbard

The second son of a middle-class family, I presented more challenges for my parents than did my big brother, two years my elder. I was born with the bleeding disorder, hemophilia, meaning that each move I made, from crawling to learning how to walk, was closely monitored for fear that the most insignificant fall could result in a serious bleeding issue. In those early years one physician told my parents that I might not survive childhood.

Being born in the mid-1970s meant that I got to sport the latest in red bell-bottoms made specifically for toddlers. More importantly than that, I was the beneficiary of advances in the treatment of hemophilia. If I got a bump, bruise or nosebleed, I could get an injection of concentrated blood plasma that would help control the bleeding. Often times, I was back on the playground with friends within hours of taking a health-related delay of game.

A more normal life for those with hemophilia had started to set in, and I enjoyed all the perks of growing up in small-town America, from neighborhood reenactments of my favorite movies with friends to farm league baseball, playing right alongside my brother.

Over time, the trips to the hospital stopped being stressful and traumatic. Instead of resenting the unexpected bleeds that took me away from the neighborhood games, I grew to enjoy the opportunities to hang out with my "grown-up" friends, the nurses and doctors who patched me up. In the hospital, I'd see people who were really having health problems. My mother made a special point of teaching me about spirituality, that nobody knows for sure what happens after we pass, but that she felt our spirit lives on. Based on the love I received at home and in the care of my grown-up friends at the hospital, I couldn't find a reason to doubt that belief.

That conviction came in handy when, just before I hit puberty, another medical drama rocked my family. At age eleven I tested positive for HIV—infected by tainted blood products used to treat my hemophilia.

Unlike hemophilia, there weren't any treatments for HIV at the time of my diagnosis. Worse still, HIV was viewed much differently than hemophilia. Many of the parents of my best friends wouldn't let their children spend the night with me. I was expelled from my sixth grade class two months before the end of the school year. There was so much fear and misinformation.

Once the initial shock wore off, I went about life as usual by making new friends, dating and worrying about my complexion. In other words, I became a "normal" teenager. Admittedly, I used my HIV status on more than one occasion to stay home from school to sleep in and play video games. (I'm sorry, Mom and Dad. I wasn't sick most of those times!)

Though I enjoyed that particular perk, one thing I didn't like anymore were the trips to the hospital to see my new doctor, an HIV specialist. Though the appointments were only four times a year, I'd argue against them so hard that my mom had to pretend that she was taking me to school—then hop on the interstate for the hour-long drive to the big city. Instead of leaving the hospital with a medical problem fixed, I left with the cruel reminder that I was HIV positive and might have one Chuck Taylor in the grave.

Still, with each year that passed I gained more confidence that I might just survive this thing, and though I slacked on my responsibilities in school, I managed to graduate with my classmates right on schedule. Not only that, my peers gave me the greatest honor of my life up to that point when they anointed me as their Homecoming

King. Even though I never openly admitted that I had HIV, most of my peers had heard the rumors. The moment was surreal for my family, who weren't sure I'd live to see graduation, much less a quite literal crowning moment.

Often times when people hear my story, I am the object of sympathy because of how I contracted HIV, or that it happened when I was a child. In actuality, I'm quite fortunate in how the timing played out. Hemophilia taught me that life is to be enjoyed on a daily basis, and that friends could be peers as well as mentors. And with HIV, I learned about discrimination based on fear of someone who is perceived to be different. When I came to terms with the fact that everyone has challenges, and mine happen to be medical, I felt lucky that mine were so painfully obvious to identify.

By the age of twenty I'd lived half my life with HIV, and I was finally comfortable with the idea of not only talking about my status, but doing what I could to help others cope with the virus or stay safe from contracting it to begin with. When I put up a website and started a blog, I was surprised to discover that I had a knack for writing. A word that I made up for those living with HIV—"positoid"—started to get used by people in the HIV/AIDS community. I was totally comfortable with HIV's role in my life, and figured that if others weren't, then that was their problem and not mine.

One of the questions I've been asked over and over is: "Would you trade your life for someone's who didn't have HIV?" For me, the answer is no. Why spend all these years learning the lessons I've been taught to trade in my adversity for a whole new, unknown batch of problems? Plus, if I wasn't born with hemophilia and didn't have HIV, I wouldn't have met Gwenn, an HIV educator who was looking for someone with HIV for an educational project, and ended up finding me.

That was ten years ago, and we've been together ever since.

I strongly believe that the toughest parts of our lives provide us with the best opportunities to grow, and as a result of my medical conditions I have been the recipient of a tremendous amount of love, support and compassion, all of which has outweighed the negativity

I've encountered. As a happily married man in my mid-thirties, I take my health very seriously because I know there are a lot of people who have not been as fortunate. Those who didn't live to see the advent of HIV medications, or who currently live where there is no access to such treatment.

To live my life without a deep appreciation for that would be an insult to their memories, and an insult to everyone who provided their help in making my happiness a reality. I love my positoid life.

~Shawn Decker

12

Ironman Lemonade

Cancer is a word, not a sentence.
~John Diamond

I was forty-seven years old and believed I was as healthy as I could possibly be! Talk about being positive, I thought I had it all! My career was taking off, my kids were successfully launched, and I loved all the travel that my job provided. I'd studied nutrition in college and ate what I was told was a very healthy diet, with lots of chicken, fish, and low-fat dairy. I was in the best physical shape of my life except for a little arthritis, which I was told everybody gets by the time they're thirty. I'd started running daily at the age of thirty-three and found I loved it! So, at this time, I'd been a runner for fourteen years and had even run a bunch of marathons.

What I didn't know was that my life was about to be turned upside down. While in the shower that morning, I found a lump in my breast. I got right in to see a doctor, but he just remarked, "Oh, you're too young for breast cancer." He did, however, order a mammogram, "just to be sure." The results were "negative," a false negative as it turned out—because of my dense breasts, it didn't pick up any abnormality. I was told to come back for yearly checks. The next year, the same result. The third year, however, the lump was golf-ball-sized and very visible! The doctor looked shocked and ordered an immediate biopsy. The diagnosis: Infiltrating Ductal Cancer, an invasive cancer that had already spread, indicated by "hot spots" in my bones, a lung tumor, and elevated liver enzymes!

I was so stunned and disbelieving that I got second, third and even fourth opinions. Each doctor confirmed the findings, and as for my prognosis, none could tell me whether I had three months, three years or what, just that it was "not good." They all recommended the standard chemo, radiation and tamoxifen. I could not believe my body betrayed me in such a manner! I was doing all the right things to be healthy.

I was slated for chemotherapy but dreaded going down that path. I started searching for alternatives, any kind of help, anything—I did not want to die! That was when I found a tiny three-line newspaper item, "Wanted, women with breast cancer to participate in cancer/diet research study." I ran to the phone and was put right through to the doctor. He said, "Get your medical records and come down to my office right away."

"Hmmm," said the doctor as he looked at my lab results. "You know, with cholesterol of 236, you have as high a risk of dying from a heart attack as from the cancer."

I was stunned by what was happening—cancer, arthritis, and, now, heart disease? I was a marathoner, for goodness sake! These things didn't happen to people like me! The doctor said, "Don't worry, all of this can be reversed and avoided. Change your diet and you'll lower your cholesterol, lower your risk of heart disease, and reverse the cancer. And, in order to show that it's the diet that's responsible for these changes, you must not have any chemo or radiation. It's very simple—eliminate all animal foods and oils from your diet. Your diet will consist of plant foods: fruits, vegetables, whole grains and legumes."

No "transitioning" for me—in less than two hours, I was vegan!

I found the diet amazingly easy to follow. I already loved brown rice, whole grain breads and oatmeal; I just had to replace the chicken, fish and dairy with vegetables and fruit, and throw out all the oils.

My body responded immediately. The next morning I discovered I'd been constipated all my life but never knew it. I now know what "normal" is.

When I returned to the oncologist, I told him what I was doing. He responded by saying that diet had nothing to do with my getting breast cancer and I couldn't possibly get enough protein, calcium, and essential fatty acids on my new vegan diet. I made a mental note to check that out with my new doctor. In addition to the hot spots in my bones, I was having serious bone pain that medication could not relieve. A month later, those hot spots had significantly receded, and within three months, they were gone, as was the bone pain. The chest X-rays, however, to this day, still show an encapsulated tumor in my left lung. It hasn't grown in twenty-eight years, and my liver enzymes are now normal.

It was during all this turmoil that I happened to see the Ironman Triathlon on TV. I was awestruck and thought, "I've GOT to do that!" I saw the 2.4-mile swim, the 112-mile bike ride, and the 26-mile marathon. I knew I could handle the marathon and thought just adding swimming and biking would be a piece of cake. Then it hit me, I've got CANCER and, besides, looking at all the young bodies, at forty-seven I'm way too old to do this. I then realized what an opportunity I was being given: diet DOES affect cancer and I can show people that you can do one of the toughest races in the world on a vegan diet and at a relatively advanced age to boot! I got excited at the possibilities and joined two running clubs, got a swim coach, took a bicycle repair course, and was obsessed with training in all three sports. Training daily, I could see amazing progress in my speed and endurance. What's more, I was enjoying my workouts, gaining confidence that I could attain one of the most ambitious goals I'd ever set for myself—to be an Ironman.

I did have to dig deep, however, as I was challenged like I'd never been before. Crossing that finish line of my first Ironman, I experienced indescribable feelings—a mix of joy, empowerment, exhilaration, and total fatigue. I could not have gone another step.

Since my diagnosis in 1982, I have completed the Ironman six times, run sixty-seven marathons, have won nearly 1,000 gold medals including eight gold medals in the Senior Olympics, won the title of "One of the Ten Fittest Women in North America," and have a fitness age of thirty-two, although chronologically I am seventy-five.

Because of the history of osteoporosis on both sides of my family, I track my bone density and have found significant increases with each test. I am obviously getting enough calcium on this diet. I was also very pleasantly surprised to discover that my arthritis disappeared. Now I actually do my own little daily triathlon as part of my regular training! How about that? A seventy-five-year-old triathlete! I never thought my life could take such a positive turn and am thankful that I found out, in time, the positive impact diet has on our health.

How's that for turning cancerous lemons into Ironman lemonade.

~Ruth Heidrich, Ph.D.

13

A Wink from God Himself

Oh, my friend, it's not what they take away from you that counts —
it's what you do with what you have left.
~Hubert Humphrey

My Irish grandmother, who raised me, could find a blessing in the direst of circumstances. She proclaimed our poverty a gift from God, because the Lord had a special place in His heart for the poor. Whenever I bemoaned the fact that my clothes came from church rummage sales, Gran directed my eyes to one of her favorite Irish blessings which she'd painstakingly stitched and hung over the kitchen table in our tiny apartment:

"May you enjoy the four greatest blessings:
 Honest work for your hands to do.
 A hearty appetite to nourish you.
 A good man or woman to give you love,
 And a wink from God himself above."

Shortly after my twenty-third birthday, however, I encountered a situation that I believed even Gran would have found impossible to consider a blessing. The sudden onset of an autoimmune disease caused a systemic inflammation in my blood vessels and gangrene in my lower legs. Neither surgery nor chemotherapy halted its spread, leading to the eventual amputation of my right leg and leaving my left leg with nerve damage and encased in a brace.

Gran had died two years earlier, but even her legacy of faith couldn't pull me out of the self-induced isolation in which I put myself when I was discharged from the hospital. The chemotherapy had left me bald, and the enormous steroid dosing bloated my body so that I went from a size eight to a size twenty. I no longer recognized myself and did not want to be seen in public. I hung pillowcases over both mirrors in my apartment so I wouldn't see myself, and my new prosthesis gathered dust in the closet. I think my friends were glad that I no longer communicated with them; their visits to me in the hospital had been painfully awkward. What could they say?

I allowed myself to wallow in self-pity for a few weeks before I got sick of my own company. I had turned down the opportunity for outpatient physical therapy when I left the hospital, but now I began a self-designed program, wearing the prosthesis and hobbling around the apartment for longer periods each day. Amazingly, the pain in my stump began to lessen. I took the pillowcase off the closet mirror and watched myself walk, keeping my eyes on my legs and off my bloated torso.

Then one day I did study my body. Could I do without the cortisone pills that had assailed it? I called my doctor, and he agreed to wean me off the pills. It would take the better part of a year, cutting me down a half tablet every two weeks. I felt a surge of hope as the pounds slowly melted off with my decreasing medication and increased exercise.

I began to believe that I could work, but not at the nursing aide work I'd done previously. I remembered that at some point in the hospital a social worker had told me of a job-training program for which I qualified. I called her, and soon I was taking a special van back and forth each day, learning office skills that would qualify me for work as a secretary.

During my van rides, I made friends with some of the riders. One told me about a social group for adults with disabilities. I attended one of their get-togethers, and within six months I was an officer in their group. I'd also begun dating a handsome fellow amputee I met there.

A week after I graduated from the business school, their administrator called me. Their secretary was moving out of state. He offered me the job and I accepted. When the school closed two years later, I got an administrative job at a local university, where I went to school at night and majored in journalism, a career I'd never considered but discovered I was good at.

Not too long ago, I was packing to move from Pennsylvania to Texas when I came across the sampler Gran had stitched. It was yellowed and frayed, but its words still spoke volumes. I closed my eyes and pictured Gran, her eyes full of faith, pointing at the blessing. I knew just what she'd say about that awful day I lost my leg. Had that not happened, I would not have met the man I love, nor have a career as a writer — honest work indeed, which brought me food for nourishment and, most decidedly, "a wink from God himself above."

~Kathleen M. Muldoon

Walking Through My Paralysis

Some see a hopeless end, while others see an endless hope.
~Author Unknown

I t has taken me seven years to consciously relive the events of January 22nd, 2003. It's not that I've developed courage to face what happened. I relive it in my dreams. Many nights my husband, Bob, wakes me because I'm screaming. I should have stopped repressing the memories years ago. It is time to tell my story.

Many concerned people have asked me the specifics of what happened, yet apologize for prying. Nobody's prying. It has been my fear of facing as well as telling the truth. As Christopher Reeve said, "Living in fear is not living at all."

Cape Cod, where I live, is a kayaker's dream. For years, Bob and I were four-season kayakers. We planned our work schedules around the tides. Two days before my breakdown, Bob and I had taken a beautiful winter excursion in Cape Cod Bay, where curious harbor seals escorted our boat.

That night, weird symptoms began. In bed, I couldn't keep my legs still. Until dawn, I sat watching TV while continuously needing to swing my legs back and forth.

The next night it became hellish. I needed to stand up and sit down constantly. Then it felt like electrical impulses gone haywire.

My legs, seemingly on their own, were flinging up as far as legs could go. I couldn't stop them.

Bob called our friend, Judy, who's a chief doctor at a Boston hospital about two hours from our home. I could tell Bob was trying to control his panic.

"What did she say?" I said.

"It's not good."

"Just tell me!"

"She said, 'Take Saralee to my hospital's emergency room right now. I'll meet you there.'"

"What does she think is wrong?"

"She thinks it's your spinal cord."

I was shocked. "I didn't have an accident! And I don't have pain!"

"I told her that. But she said, 'Something's happening very fast.'"

When I was wheeled into the hospital, I couldn't walk and had no feeling in my hands. I was petrified.

Three neurologists tested me. I looked away as they touched sharp instruments to my body. I felt nothing. Bob saw the startling abnormalities. For my sake, he never showed his terror on his face.

A CAT scan ruled out a brain tumor. Nearly everything was ruled out: multiple sclerosis, bone disease, rheumatoid arthritis.

I needed an MRI but their machine was down. Now I had no feeling in my legs and arms. Since I was losing precious function so fast, we decided to go to another hospital.

A neurologist rushed to stop us. "If you leave here," he said, "you could become a quadriplegic and permanently on a vent." So of course we stayed.

By the time of my MRI, I had no feeling in my torso.

The chief neurologist of several Boston hospitals had been called in. My medical team observed as we looked at my MRI images.

Two vertebrae in my neck had completely disengaged and were rapidly crossing over each other choking off my spinal cord. Without immediate surgery, the cord would be severed entirely and I'd be completely paralyzed.

Why did this happen? Nobody knew.

It happened spontaneously.

"Can you fix it?"

"No." He was a straight shooter. "What's done is done. We can hopefully stop the progression surgically."

"Hopefully?"

"There's no guarantee of improvement. There's a fifty percent chance that even with surgery you will never walk again."

I slung my arms over the ledge of the nurses' station. I was in an advanced state of spasticity. Everything was moving on its own. My arms and legs were uncontrollably swinging widely through the air. "Are you telling me that even if surgery stopped the progression, I could spend the rest of my life like this?"

"Yes."

The surgery did stop the progression.

My neurologist said, "If there's any improvement, ninety percent will occur in the first three days. The only other variable that could help is time. Whatever state your body is in two years from now, you will always be."

Bob asked if occupational therapy, physical therapy, or medication would help. He shook his head no. My doctor's words felt as authoritative as an edict from God.

I'd rather not name my doctors. They did terrific surgery. I love them all and we get along beautifully. However I'm disappointed in myself that I initially took their words as gospel. Christopher Reeve didn't listen to his doctors. He said, "It's pretty irrefutable that you can help yourself. I just don't believe in ultimatums."

I wish I had been prepared for the psychological and physiological aftereffects. Bob was angry. "They sent you into a whole new world without telling you one thing to expect."

There was no improvement in those three days.

I kept falling. My brain was sending incorrect signals, such as how high to lift my foot over a two-inch obstacle. Had the medical professionals told me two words—"look down"—many dangerous falls would never have happened.

Christopher Reeve said, "Gratitude, like love, needs to be active." When I regained use of my typing fingers, I started using them with gusto.

I'm privileged to help others by writing for the Christopher and Dana Reeve Foundation, though I'm still surprised every time I see myself described on their website as a "woman living with paralysis." Paralysis is defined by the foundation as a central nervous system disorder resulting in difficulty or inability to move the upper or lower extremities. As Christopher said, "Living a life with meaning means spreading the word. Even if you can't move, you can have a powerful effect with what you say." Using my writing to help other people with disabilities has become a mission for me. After all, Christopher also said, "Even if your body doesn't work the way it used to, the heart and the mind and the spirit are not diminished."

In these seven years, I haven't been able to change some malfunctions… yet. Walking feels like I'm on a tightrope while moving through molasses. Though I can walk, I can't climb one step. With no balance, I can't stand still. But I've become determined to help myself. Again I take inspiration from Christopher Reeve, who said, "I gradually stopped wondering, 'What life do I have?' and began to consider, 'What life can I build?'"

I learned that there's no greater antidepressant than helping others. It is dramatically gratifying to make a difference in others' lives through my writing. The countless readers' responses I receive have without a doubt brought meaning to what happened in 2003. I am eternally grateful for all who have helped me by telling me my words are important to them.

My wish is that those who read this story might re-think the words "try" and "hope."

Before my spinal cord collapse, I spent nearly every day kayaking in the magical world of Cape Cod Bay. I assumed those days were gone for good, but now I know they are not. Bob and I have taken five small excursions back to the bay. The curious seals are still there, probably wondering where we've been all these years. I tell them, from my strongest heart and resounding voice, what Christopher

Reeve said: "I refuse to allow a disability to determine how I live my life. There is only one way to go in life and that is forward."

At that two-year mark, which is when my neurologist said that whatever I was, I would always be, I could walk no further than twenty feet. This year, which is seven years later, I made it ten miles.

~Saralee Perel

15

Down But Not Out

The human spirit is stronger than anything that can happen to it.
~C.C. Scott

I t was nearing spring in my second year of graduate school that I discovered what I was really made of. I had been writing my Comprehensive Exams for two weeks, primarily seated in front of the computer and taking very few breaks. As I neared completion of my first draft, I realized that I needed to do further research. Tired and hungry but wanting to finish, I trudged off to the library. Once there, I flung my knapsack on a comfortable chair and headed to the stacks with a large leather bag. I filled the bag with books, then leaned to the side to pick it up. As I straightened with the load, I felt a strange sensation that ran from the base of my spine to the top of my scalp. I shrugged it off, hefted the sack to my chair downstairs, and set out to read what I'd found.

Hours later, I stood to go home, only to feel the sensation again. Once again, I shook it off and headed home. By evening, I'd become so nauseous that I headed to bed.

I woke the next morning feeling even more uncomfortable than I had the previous day. I made it to work, but by lunch I was driving to the University Health Services. I was assessed by a young med student who was quite impressed that I could touch my toes (I was an aerobics instructor after all), but thought little of my achy back and flu-like symptoms. He sent me on my way with a bottle of 800 mg Motrin and wished me well.

That evening, I hosted a work party that had been scheduled for weeks. After the guests left, I fell apart. I called the After Hours Healthcare line and expressed my concern about my growing back pain and general malaise. They told me to lie down on a hard surface and hope that my back would sort itself out. Unfortunately, once on the ground, not only did the pain increase, but I couldn't get up. My husband lifted me to the bed, gave me my Motrin and turned out the light.

I awoke the next morning to sun streaming in the window and the birds chirping. I tried to roll onto my side to get up, but nothing happened. It took a few moments for me to realize that I no longer felt any pain in my back, then only a few more seconds to comprehend that while I no longer felt pain, I no longer felt anything. I began to panic when I realized that I couldn't move at all and woke my husband. He telephoned for an ambulance and the paramedics arrived shortly thereafter, backboard in tow so that they could transport me to hospital. They gingerly wedged the board beneath me, then cinched the first strap down. I heard a high-pitched scream, but confused, didn't realize that it was coming from my own mouth. As the paramedics cinched the second strap, everything went dark.

I came to a few times during the ambulance ride to the hospital, but each time only long enough to know that consciousness was not a good plan. When I was finally alert, I found myself in a hospital bed. Confused, I rang for the nurse and was told that I had herniated three of the discs in my lower back and that the spinal column was impinged. The rupturing had caused the paralysis, and the doctors were evaluating the options for me.

I lay in the hospital bed, waiting for the doctors to decide what to do with me. After three days, the Chief of Orthopedics informed me that in his professional opinion I would never walk again without surgery. I lay there, twenty-two years old, graduate student and athlete, trying to contemplate what that meant. I had always been active and learned most things by doing. I couldn't grasp what it would mean to be unable to do so. I was also deathly afraid of having surgery on my back, and really unable to even consider the option. My husband had gone to work, my family lived 2,500 miles away, and my dear friend Jen could offer little to soothe me. When the doctor left and I started sobbing, Jen stroked my face and spoke softly to me until I drifted off to sleep, then, unbeknownst to me, made the most amazing set of phone calls.

Jen contacted our Department Director, who promptly called his wife, who just happened to be the Director of Sports Medicine. She then called her team, who committed to providing round-the-clock integrative medical care for me until I was walking again. Jen then contacted my husband, who contacted my family (three of them physicians), who then called the hospital and demanded that the new team be allowed to treat me.

A day later, I was being hoisted into a Hubbard tank to begin my hydrotherapy (three times per day). I was fitted for a whalebone and steel corset that was designed to keep my spine straight, whether or not I could stand. The massage therapist came next, and after her, a physical therapist. Even the hospital dietician played a part as she designed a diet that would enhance healing and enable my body to function better. Jen just sat at the side of my bed smiling as each new cast member popped into the room.

I fell the first time they lifted me to my feet. I fell the second and third times, too, but eventually, as the compression eased, I began to regain feeling in my feet, and I was able to stand with a walker. When I was discharged from the hospital, my gait was so bizarre that most people thought I had cerebral palsy. But with a lot of assistance from dear, committed friends, I forced myself to swim two miles per day in the campus pool, went to physical therapy five times per week, and engaged my body to do the unthinkable. Armed with a mind set on full recuperation, after six months I walked into an aerobics class with my physical therapist at my side. The students clapped and my teacher wept.

Twenty years later, as a mother of five, I ran the La Jolla Half Marathon. Those who raced with me will never forget my primal yodeling as we ascended each hill—urging on those at my side to celebrate every step as we made them.

You never know what you've got till you think it's gone.

~Sage de Beixedon Breslin, Ph.D.

16

Just One More

Toughness is in the soul and spirit, not in muscles.
~Alex Karras

"Okay Beth, one more, that's it, just one more."

I huffed and puffed my way through another sit-up, red-faced and exhausted, then collapsed back onto the mat and stared up at the ceiling. My physical therapist leaned over me, a smile on her face and her hand outstretched, waiting for me to lift my arm and slap her five.

"I can't," I said. "Give me a minute."

As I gazed up at the peeling paint of the physical therapy room's ceiling I wondered again how I'd gotten to this point. Five sit-ups? I could barely make it through five sit-ups without having to stop and rest? What had happened to the girl who could swim five kilometers at a time? What happened to the woman who did yoga several times a week? What had even happened to the peppy lady who would walk an hour to work just because the sun was out?

"She's gone," the physical therapist said gently, sympathy radiating from her kind face. "Whoever you were, she's gone. You have to concentrate on being who are you now."

Squeezing my eyes shut against sudden tears, I inhaled deeply and the smell of stale sweat and antiseptic filled my nostrils. I exhaled slowly, shakily, my diaphragm protesting under even that much use.

I didn't want to be who I am now. I didn't want to have myasthenia gravis (MG), a rare form of muscular dystrophy that causes great muscle weakness. In my case it started with a droopy eyelid, then affected my arms until I could no longer wash my hair without weakness and eventually attacked my legs until walking up stairs became a problem. Physical activity just for the fun of it became a thing of the past and "fitness" became a measure of what tiny fraction of my past routine I could get through in any given day.

With a sigh, I rolled over to my side, pushed up with one arm and eventually drew myself into a seated position. I reached out and gave the PT a high five. She smiled at the evidence that at least I was still trying.

"It sounds so pathetic, but I don't want to be who I am now," I said, admitting it for the first time since my diagnosis.

"I know," she said simply. "If it helps, remember that fitness isn't a competition. From here on out you have to measure yourself against yourself and that's it. If you could do five sit-ups today you have try to do six tomorrow. If you could walk for ten minutes today you have to try for eleven tomorrow."

I nodded, knowing that what she said was important. But deep inside there was a small child who wanted to clap her hands over her ears and sing, "I can't hear you! I can't hear you!"

We got on with the session that day and I took her advice to heart in the coming months, particularly after I had to have a full sternotomy in order to take out my enlarged thymus gland in an attempt to alleviate the MG. After the surgery I chanted "just one more, just one more" as I fought to put one foot in front of the other, feed myself, cut my own food and finally climb stairs. When the surgery didn't bring about the results for which we'd hoped, I chanted "just one more, just one more" as I learned to walk with a cane, then a crutch. These weren't things I wanted to do, in fact I downright resented that simply walking could make my legs weak and on hot days a short stroll to the corner could make me sweat as if I'd gone for a long jog. Yet every time I wanted to stop I promised myself I'd do just one more and, most of the time, I'd do a lot more than that before I finally finished.

Now that I've adjusted to life at this slower pace there are few days I still get caught up with how much I can't do. But every now and then I'll watch someone dance or run or swim or even carry a baby and I can't help but compare myself to her. Then I'll hear the PT's voice in my head telling me that fitness isn't a competition and I only need to think about myself. I can still walk and even dance a little, I can swim in my own way and I can carry a baby for short amounts of time. I may not be as healthy or physically fit as others, but I'm still committed to being as healthy as I can be, to doing just one more of whatever I need to do.

Just one more. It's not so much, but there's little more important.

~Beth Morrissey

17

Walking Forward

The only disability in life is a bad attitude.
~Scott Hamilton

As I sat facing the doctor, I posed the usual question, "What is the prognosis, Doctor?" He said, "It is going to be necessary to amputate your leg just below the knee."

A sudden wave of nausea swept over me. I felt like I was going to faint. Looking back, I can never remember having anything shock me quite as much as those words from the doctor.

Gaining my composure, I asked more questions. It became apparent that it had to be done. Although the amputation was considered elective surgery, the choice wasn't if, it was when. I was twenty-eight years old and out of options.

The doctor explained. If I waited, I would risk gangrene setting in. Then, the amputation site would be dictated by the line of demarcation (a puffy, red line that forms between the healthy and gangrenous tissue). I was familiar with gangrene, as I had already lost two of my toes. My chances of having a well-fitting limb, afterwards, would be more favorable if the doctor determined the site.

On the drive home, between bouts of tears, I thought of all the ways an amputation would affect my life. The picture seemed pretty grim. I was terrified.

I had already suffered for four years. My bone grafting surgery had developed complications, followed by residual infections that literally destroyed my whole foot. It had been a tough four years, but

I had never expected it to end this way. Wearing an artificial limb wasn't what I anticipated. However, there was nothing more anyone could do to restore my foot and leg. The damage had been far too extensive.

The doctor had made it clear I needed the surgery, and soon. I dreaded telling my husband. We had suffered financial devastation during those four years of numerous surgeries, hospital stays, and treatment. In those days, we had no medical insurance and still had old bills we were paying on monthly. My husband worked so hard. Now, there would be even more expenses. I felt like such a burden.

Things moved quickly after that fateful day. The doctor amputated my right leg about six inches below the knee. My stump healed beautifully since the infections were gone. He was able to work with healthy tissue.

Back then, the usual waiting period for the first fitting was eight weeks. I was ready in six. Being young and fairly healthy helped a whole lot. After a five-day hospital stay I came home on crutches. I was glad it was over. I wasn't suffering any more pain than I had been before, on a day-to-day basis. Knowing this pain would eventually go away filled me with new hope.

My husband worked as a body man for a salvage yard. He managed to purchase a burned automobile and completely restore it over the six weeks I was waiting for my first fitting. The price he received for that automobile covered the exact amount needed for the hospital bill plus the new limb. It was remarkable.

To this day, I believe receiving that precise dollar amount came directly from "divine intervention." Otherwise, how did the dollars work out to the penny? Coincidence? I don't think so.

The rest is history. In retrospect, after being an amputee for forty-six years, I can tell you that it is not the worst thing that could ever have happened to me. I walk very well for age seventy-four. I have no more complaints than most folks my age have about their discomforts. In fact, I probably have a lot fewer because I am quite active.

Breaking it down into a percentage, my missing part is only

about ten or fifteen percent of the "entire me." That's not a whole lot. Before, it was painful, disfigured, and threatened to undermine the health of my entire body. It was a miracle that it could be removed and my health restored. What more could anyone ask?

I'll admit there have been times when I have been disgruntled over fitting problems. At those times, I have been frustrated and cranky, but on the whole, those times have been few and far between. The technology of today's prosthetics is absolutely amazing. Most people never notice I am wearing an artificial limb (nor do I).

The secret—adjusting to the change and having a willing attitude about your new way of getting around.

If you are satisfied with watching life pass you by while you sit, then you will never get where you are going. If you really want to be a part of life, you certainly can be. The best part about being busy is that you forget about the prosthesis. At least, that's how it has worked for me.

People have always complimented me about "my wonderful attitude." I guess the thought of losing part of your body has a deeper emotional impact upon people than internal ailments. Probably because it is so visual.

So, why would I have anything but a good attitude? After all, I have two legs, two arms, and a healthy body to live with every day.

I have a strong belief that God has been carrying me forward since the day the doctor "pronounced my doom," or what I thought was the end of world for me. It was only fear of the unknown that caused such anguish.

I couldn't have been more wrong. There are so many things I can do, and have done.

Obedience training three large dogs, seventy-five pounds plus, presented a challenge, but the wonder was, I "trophied" with all three.

I am no longer as fast a swimmer as I was before the amputation (missing one of my flippers) but I can swim like a fish.

Can I dance? You bet. Not particularly the slow dances like a waltz or tango that require long strides and perfect balance. I can dance them, but not gracefully. I can certainly jitterbug, polka, cha-cha, or do any of the dances that have quick, short, steps.

I played recreational volleyball two different periods, in past years, and was a terrific "spiker" at the net.

My home has always been clean and organized as we raised our family. Even now, I cook healthy, tasty meals every day, and feasts for the holidays. My life has been filled with activity. I am humbled and grateful for any, and all, of my accomplishments.

I cannot relate to "handicapped," "crippled," or even "physically challenged." To me, better words would be "slightly limited," but aren't we all in some way?

Bragging was not my intent. I only spelled out some of my "can do's" as an example of what is possible.

I acknowledge all the rich blessings that have been bestowed upon me over my lifetime. I have been able to keep walking forward to reach whatever destination I chose. Only through my faith in God, in myself, and with prosthetic technology could I have kept walking this long course.

Life is good.

~Joyce E. Sudbeck

18

Faith to Share

Every evening I turn my worries over to God.
He's going to be up all night anyway.
~Mary C. Crowley

"I hate the way chemotherapy makes me so sick. I wish I could go the rest of the summer without these treatments." My husband Glen picked up my hand as we sat in our side-by-side recliners in front of the television screen, neither of us caring what was on it. Having made a living by operating heavy equipment for thirty years, even the palms of his hands had always been rough. I noticed how soft they were becoming. "I don't even know why I bought that boat. It won't do anybody any good tied up at dock all summer. I wish the kids would go ahead and use it, but you know they won't."

"The kids will use the boat all right—with us." I squeezed his hand. "I believe you'll get an extension on your break from chemo. We'll be camping and fishing soon. And we'll take our family vacation again this year, too. You just wait and see."

"Oh, I'll be back on chemo for the rest of the summer. I've been off it since April. I hate this stuff, but I guess if it prolongs my life, I'll have to take it. Being with you and the kids means a heck of a lot more to me than putting up with a little nausea and needle sticks, so I'll take the chemo again." He spoke in a low but determined tone. "But you do know, don't you, that there will come a time when I will have to say 'no more'?"

I swallowed to keep the lump in my throat from choking me. "I know, and it is your decision. We have agreed not to influence you. When that time comes, you will know, and we'll understand." I tried to lighten my voice. "But for now, we will enjoy your vacation from chemo and nausea. We'll enjoy the next three months."

"I don't have a clue what you're talking about. The doctor said I can't be off that rubbish more than a few months, or the mass will double in size. Don't you remember he said that?"

"I know what the doctor said, and I know how much being able to spend these summer months relaxing with the family means to you. But, you see, I have it on a higher authority that you won't be taking treatments for three more months. We'll have this summer together, so plan the vacation. Rachel wants to go to Myrtle Beach, I think."

My husband of forty-two years looked at me as if I were mad. He had been suffering from lung cancer for two and a half years. It had spread into his lymph nodes and the adrenal gland, but chemotherapy was keeping the lungs stabilized and preventing the mass from spreading to other vital organs. When Glen wasn't suffering from the side effects of the chemo, such as violent nausea and extreme exhaustion, he appeared quite healthy. His breathing had become almost normal. The doctors who did his study were amazed.

Although the chemotherapy did a good job fighting the cancer, after so many treatments, his body demanded a rest period. His blood vessels and his nervous system couldn't handle any more poison being pumped into his body. The damaged nerves in his feet caused so much pain he could hardly walk, and his veins wouldn't hold the needles. So, the doctors decided to give his body a break from the torture of chemotherapy. He had been resting and gaining strength all spring, but the threat that stopping the treatment would allow the masses to grow in leaps and bounds hung over us. Now it was time to see the doctors and get the results of the latest scans.

"What in the world are you talking about, woman? How could you know something like that? Why would I be off for another three months?"

"Because that's what I asked for—three months," I answered.

"Oh, I know. You're talking about religion again." He let go of my hand and fumbled with the remote control. Deciding there was nothing on TV to hold his attention, he switched off the set. "Hon, I wish I had your faith, but the truth is, I don't, and you better be prepared to accept what the doctor has to tell us."

I wasn't ready to accept such a summation. "I asked God to give us just three months to enjoy this summer. He said 'yes.' That's all there is to it."

My husband turned toward me, giving me his full attention, his eyes probing my face. "You know I'm not much of a churchgoer, but you are so confident you almost make me believe." He touched my fingers to his lips.

I searched my heart, asking God to give me the right answer, before I replied. "Okay, Glen. Please, just try it this way. If you don't have enough faith of your own, try leaning on mine for a little while. I promise you there will be no more chemotherapy for three months." I'm not sure if my faith or my stubbornness kept my voice from trembling as I made that promise.

Our daughters, Rachel and Beth, met us at the Kentuckiana Cancer Institute the next morning. They never missed any new scan reports. You wouldn't believe a twenty-nine-year-old and a twenty-seven-year-old could be such Daddy's girls. Beth sat on his knee, while Rachel stood, arms around his neck, waiting for the doctor to come into the room.

"Don't you girls go worrying, now." Glen's jovial mood turned sober. "We're gonna get a three-month reprieve." My eyes widened in surprise. Had I heard him correctly? Then he added, "Mama says so." I thought he was joking until I perceived the somberness in his voice. He did believe.

The door opened and the doctor, smiling as always, bounced in. "Well, Glen, we got good news. I don't know how, and I sure can't explain it, but the cancer cells haven't doubled in size; actually, they've shrunk. I don't think we'll need any treatments just now." And then he said the magic words: "Come back in three months."

As he shook the doctor's hand, Glen said, "My family's been praying."

"Well, you tell them to keep it up," the doctor said before he exited the room. "You know you really shouldn't be here. You should have left us two years ago. Yeah, you tell the family to keep on praying."

Sunday morning, Glen was dressed and waiting for me to get out of bed. "Well, come on, woman, get up and get ready. We don't want to be late for church today."

With a smile in my heart and a lilt in my voice, I hummed "Amazing Grace" all the way to church.

~Jean Kinsey

19

I Am Woman

When you treat a disease, first treat the mind.
~Chen Jen

n 1997, I learned what it meant to be a woman. Not how other people define womanhood, mind you—I was well past puberty, had already been married and experienced childbirth twice. I learned how to define myself in other ways, as I faced the loss of what I thought made me female.

Six months after the birth of my daughter, I went for my annual exam. I'd been exercising and feeling great and had no worries. The doctor completed her exams and I returned home. A week later, the doctor called and told me that she needed to perform a cervical biopsy, based on my test results. Scared and a bit squeamish, I appeared dutifully for the colposcopy. A week later, I was told that the cells were not cancerous, and that lowering my stress would likely improve my cervical health. I was informed that I would be returning to her office twice per year to have exams instead of annually due to the increased risk.

Two months later I met with the doctor again, this time because I was pregnant with my second child. Despite a few hiccups with the pregnancy, things went relatively well, and I gave birth to a healthy son eight months later.

Six weeks after the birth, I headed to the doctor's office for a postpartum exam. While I thought that all was well, the doctor was concerned about some "suspicious" skin discoloration near the suture sites. While it seemed reasonable to me that the area might be freaking out given what I'd been through, the doctor was not so pleased. I was told that I would be returning to her office for a biopsy the following week. After the last biopsy, I wasn't looking forward to any other procedure being performed in the area, but agreed to do so anyway.

A long week later, the doctor did a punch biopsy. I left the office sore, and began the long wait for the results. A few days later, we learned that there was no cancerous explanation for the radical change in coloration—it was, as I'd suspected, just a part of my reaction to childbirth.

I felt like I had a new lease on life! Two close calls, but all clear now! I enjoyed my children, my family and my work, and settled into the working mother routine. I tried to focus on what was positive and to distract myself from the stressors that seemed to be creeping in day by day. I made marketing calls, attended networking events, and when my son was six months old, I entered training as a Medical Intuitive. I was going to be all that I could be, no matter what else was happening in my life.

As much as I loved the training and felt like I'd finally discovered myself, I watched the distance grow daily in my marriage. I had entered a new world, filled with Light and healers—a place where he didn't fit. He travelled more often, and the silence between us grew. When we interacted, it was about the house or the children, but little else. I distracted myself from the reality I lived in, until one morning I found a lump in my left breast.

I contacted my doctor, who gave the lump a cursory exam and ushered me into Radiology. The tech performed an ultrasound, and I watched as the amorphous beast appeared on the screen. While I was used to the tiny fibrocysts I'd had all my life, this mass was much larger than anything I'd ever felt, and its presence on the screen shocked me. Appearing a little pale, the technician left the room and returned with the radiologist, something I'd never experienced despite the fact that I'd had numerous ultrasounds during my pregnancies. The radiologist turned to face the screen and grimaced. She then turned her gaze to me and told me that the mass had to be biopsied and likely removed, and that I would need to meet with a breast surgeon immediately. She left the office and returned with a sheet of paper as I pulled my clothing back in place. I was to head over to the surgeon's office while she called to schedule an emergency appointment.

I drove across town, finding it difficult to breathe. A half hour later, I was sitting in yet another doctor's exam room, being told that no biopsy would be performed due to the inherent risk of a potentially-cancer-filled mass leaking its mutant cells into my chest cavity. And, as the surgeon scheduled a radical lumpectomy for my left breast, the tears came like a torrent. I was thirty-one years old and in the previous twenty-four months, I'd had two children, and had faced cancer scares in all of the organs that I thought made me inherently female. Somewhere, here, there was a message for me.

I spent the weekend not with my husband, or even my children, but with a group of healers of all kinds. I had my palm read, got a massage, had some acupuncture, then spent hours in past life regression. In all of the lives in which I died as a result of bodily injury or illness, the healers diligently worked to resolve and release the energy trapped there. Then, on Sunday, anxious but more at peace, my tribe and I went to see G.I. Jane. After two hours, I came out physically and emotionally exhausted. Over dinner, I told my women friends that if Demi Moore could shave her head and be a badass, then I could certainly surrender my breasts in order to survive.

Monday morning found me on a gurney, staring up at the man who was about to remove most of my left breast. We made an agreement that if the path slide were positive for cancer, he'd remove both of my breasts and schedule reconstruction as soon as possible. I slipped into the nothingness of anesthesia, chanting my prayers, as I was wheeled into the operating room.

I awoke to the most incredible blue eyes staring at me, smiling.

"Ah, good, you're awake!" greeted the doctor.

I still felt so fuzzy, but wanted to know what they had found. I tried to reach up to my chest, but I couldn't seem to move my arms.

"That'll wear off soon," the surgeon soothed. "But, you don't need to check—they're both still there," he said, smiling again.

Then, as my tears of joy consumed me, he reached out to touch my arm. He leaned in close to me, with his lips just to my ear and whispered, "I don't know what you did, but I've never seen cancer vanish! You think someday you can teach me that trick?" He stood up, gave me a wink, and strode away.

My whole life, I thought that being a woman was about having a uterus, a vagina, breasts, and long hair. But, in 1997, I learned that being a woman was about acknowledging the awesome Light within, filling every crevice with peace, joy and love, and knowing that no body part would ever again define me.

~Sage de Beixedon Breslin, Ph.D.

20

My Purpose

He who has a why to live can bear almost any how.
~Friedrich Nietzsche

"Syringo-my-what?" My eyes widened and my heart skipped two beats as my neurosurgeon gave me the diagnosis.

"Syringomyelia—a very rare disease. You have a syrinx, or a cyst, inside your spinal cord. It's growing toward your brain. Should do surgery soon as possible."

What was going on? I hadn't been sick—just some numbness, tingling and a few sensations resembling electrical shocks. Scary but not painful.

"I don't understand. What are you saying?" I wasn't sure I wanted to hear the answer.

The doctor patted my shoulder and spoke softly. "If that thing continues to travel upward, you have only a few weeks to live."

"What's the prognosis if I have the surgery?"

He sat on a stool and swiveled it to face me. Gentle concern filled his eyes. "I am a Christian and I pray before every surgery, but sometimes God has his own plans for my patients. This is a dangerous operation; I will not lie to you." He waited a moment for me to absorb what he said. "You may never walk again or you may die. You could be quadriplegic, or you could be well. I have to puncture the spinal cord, insert drainage tubes, and decompress the hindbrain. I promise to do all I can."

"But, Doctor, I can't die. I have two small children. They need me."

"Then we better get started. Do you want me to set a date?"

"Have — have you done this surgery before?" Again, I feared his answer.

I was more frightened when he answered, "Yes, one, and the results were good."

Telling my husband was almost as hard as hearing the words coming from my doctor's mouth. "Honey, we need to get a second opinion," he said. But this doctor told me he never went into surgery without praying first. I wanted him!

Several weeks later, I walked out of the hospital. I wore a neck brace and dragged my foot, but with the help of a walker and God, I walked!

Until this time, I had considered myself a good Christian person, who went to church — when it was convenient, who loved my church family — when I thought about them, who taught my children to say their nightly prayers — when we weren't too busy or too sleepy. Sometimes skipping them until the next night, or the next. The word "miracle" seldom crossed my mind.

Thank God, my church wasn't as lax as I. My pastor, who couldn't sit upright because he'd recently undergone a spinal fusion, rolled himself into the backseat of his automobile while his wife drove him to see me every day for the many weeks I was hospitalized. After returning home, several weeks later I was able to attend church. My loving church family had prepared a special seat so I could sit without hurting my neck. I no longer had my top seven vertebrae.

My life, as I knew it, came to a halt. I learned to expect the unexpected and to accept the unacceptable. My condition forced me to learn new skills and gracefully put the old ones behind me. I learned to appreciate the few true friends who stuck around through it all. I learned what a financial drain a prolonged illness can have on a working-class family.

But most important, I learned what love can overcome. My husband and I had planned to travel as school schedules allowed. He surprised me earlier than I'd anticipated. One day he came home driving a big brown, used motor home.

Shocked, I looked at those big steps leading from the ground to the entrance. "Did you forget I can't do steps? Can you take it back? I think our plans may have to be put on hold or maybe canceled."

"Yes, I can take it back. I haven't closed the deal yet. But did you forget I have arms? I can carry you up the steps." He pointed to a vacant spot in front of the window. "A comfortable recliner or even a lift chair will fit just fine there." We kept the motor home.

I had been an avid bowler for years, bowling in two leagues a week. By the time the winter season began, I had improved somewhat, yet I was still weak, wore my neck brace and used a cane. My teammates asked me if I would come and watch just to cheer them on. But when I got there, they said, "Of course, if you think you can do it, we still need a bowler. We decided not to replace you just yet."

"I can't. Besides, I'd kill all chances of you having a winning team." We'd won the league two years in a row.

"We want you, if you'll try."

"Well, maybe," I answered. Since I couldn't hold onto my heavier ball, I chose one of the children's balls, put on my bowling shoes, held onto the ball return and laid the ball on the lane. It stayed on and I picked off three or four pins. The building full of people began to applaud. I returned to my spot on the team, hobbling on a cane, neck brace and all. It didn't take long for my 165 average to drop into the low eighties, but I was bowling! I even won a trophy. My team ordered me a special one, engraved "Most Courageous Bowler." It's still my most cherished trophy. We received a team trophy also—we earned last place!

Perhaps I would have never stopped to evaluate my friends, my family and my Christianity if I had not been stricken with syringomyelia. I even learned that I had a hidden talent. I began to write articles for the American Syringomyelia Alliance Project newsletter. "FACES" profiled SM sufferers from around the country, helping individuals to feel less alone. I started a local support group and joined a group of peer supporters, answering calls from frightened SM sufferers from all over the world. I feel blessed that God has taken a misfortune and turned it into a blessing, making me a better person.

But, alas, time has taken its toll. The cyst has elongated the length of my spine. There are no more surgeries for me. Someday, unless God intervenes, and I believe He can and might, I may lose the remaining use of my arms, legs or both. But the beautiful truth of this is that I know as long as the Lord has work for me to do, He will make a way.

My cloud has a silver lining that refuses to dissipate as long as I know I have a reason to exist. Some say it is a miracle that I still have even limited mobility in all my limbs after twenty-five years of living with this malady. But I say, God has worked His miracle on me, not by miraculously giving me a new body, but by giving me peace within myself.

~Jean Kinsey

Think Positive

Every Day Is Special

Each day comes bearing its own gifts.
Untie the ribbons.

~Ruth Ann Schabacker

21

Every Day a Friday

Monday is a lame way to spend 1/7 of your life.
~Author Unknown

I love Fridays, and I'm not alone. Most people associate the last day of the workweek with feelings of relief, relaxation, and anticipation of good times to come in the weekend ahead. You know there has to be something special about a day when the feeling of celebration that accompanies its arrival is even commemorated in the name of a restaurant chain!

And so I, too, celebrate Fridays. After dropping my son off at school I head to Starbucks, to pick up a coffee treat of one type or another. Then instead of driving straight home I generally take a long route through the most scenic roads I can find, which usually includes my favorite corner of the local state park. On and on throughout the day I find myself smiling and happy for no other reason than that the day's name starts with an "F" rather than a "M," "T," or "W."

When I pick my son up again hours into the afternoon we high-five physically and vocally, our chorus of "FRIDAY!" resonating at least as loudly as our hand slap. Then we point out to each other the signs of beginning celebration in the college town we drive through. We see footballs being passed on fraternity lawns, hamburgers being thrown on grills, people parked on front porch swings, and parties everywhere swinging into action. Sometimes it seems as if the whole world is celebrating Friday!

The other day I emerged from a doctor's office happy over a

positive prognosis in a health situation I was concerned about. My good mood was amplified by the signs of spring that were bursting all around me—flowers blossoming, birds singing, bright sunshine warm upon my back. I was suddenly ready to celebrate, and java-scented thoughts wafted through my brain. I whispered the word "Cappuccino!" and headed for the specialty coffee bar that was conveniently located just around the corner.

My mind rebelled. "What are you doing? It's Tuesday! Coffee treats are reserved for Fridays!" And suddenly I realized how ridiculous that line of thinking was! Why should Fridays be any more special than any other day of the week? Why waste six days while waiting to rejoice on the seventh? Minutes later I was walking back to my car with a big grin on my face and a raspberry mocha in my hand.

A small victory, to be sure, but it's also an accurate example of how many of us live our lives. We're waiting for conditions to be right before we allow ourselves to enjoy our time here on earth. Maybe when we finally graduate from college and get a job it will be time to celebrate, or perhaps when our toddlers are old enough to be in school all day. We'll rejoice when the car is paid off, or enjoy life when we're finally able to retire. And in that waiting we waste so much of the life that God has given us and the happiness that can be found in our todays. What if we moved a little of that "Friday feeling" into our rainy-day Mondays, our gloomy Tuesdays and our mid-week Wednesdays? Surely our lives would be much happier as a result.

It's interesting to note that T.G.I. Friday's isn't open for business on just the last day of the workweek! No, they celebrate all week long and into the weekend.

So should we.

~Elaine L. Bridge

22

The Gift of Brain Cancer

The excursion is the same when you go looking for your sorrow
as when you go looking for your joy.
~Eudora Welty

In August 2002, I received the greatest gift of my life when I was told that I had terminal brain cancer and would be dead in four to six months. I had been married exactly five months when this happened. My career was going well, my family and friends loved me. I was as happy as I had ever been. So why was this such a great gift? Why?

Because I had to face my death.

It was the middle of the night in January 2003. I was wandering outside in the cold, alone and bitter. The clinical trial I had entered was fraught with uncertainty and danger. I could only participate because I was terminal, my survival quite unlikely. I was confused, constantly nauseous, and hardly able to walk, even with a cane.

I was infuriated by my circumstances: I hated the cancer, myself, the doctors, and God. I found myself shouting, screaming, crying, raging against the injustice. For the first time in fifty-four years I had finally found happiness in my life, and now this horrific disease was ripping from me not only the joy of life, but also any semblance of stability, comfort or peace. Was I destined for continuous detestable rotting away every day in my pathetic limp to a cold grave?

Then suddenly, amidst all the virulence, came the inspirational voice of a very dear old friend, employer, and mentor, W. Clement

Stone, one of the first people to write about Positive Mental Attitude, or PMA. In my mind I could hear him say, as he had thousands of times, "Every Adversity carries within it the seed of equivalent or greater benefit to those who have a Positive Mental Attitude!"

What?

Are you serious?

Greater Benefit?

What on earth was the greater benefit of dying of brain cancer, old man? (I was unaware that Mr. Stone had passed away just five months earlier at the age of 100.)

His words kept running through the part of my brain that was still functioning. Not some adversity, he had said, but every adversity, EVERY adversity, carries within it that seed of equivalent or greater benefit! You have to be kidding!

Fortunately, the many years of his being my mentor, teacher and hero had left its mark—the words "I reasoned" were ablaze like sun above my head. He used "I reasoned" frequently—very often in describing critical situations he faced in life. Once, a loaded gun was held to his head by a desperate, depressed, and hopeless person who told him that he had lost everything—he was going to kill Mr. Stone, and then turn the gun on himself. While most of us would panic in such a spot, Mr. Stone said calmly, "I reasoned," and then proceeded to think of a logical plan to save not only himself but the other person as well. He later set the person up in business, where the man was successful and prosperous the rest of his life.

"So," I said to myself, giving in to his message, "Let's reason." Immediately, I was at peace and felt rational—for the first time in months.

So… what were the possibilities for me? After all, life at that point had not provided me with very good options.

I certainly didn't have the option of "live happily ever after"—or did I?

The fact is one of two things was going to happen: I was either going to die very shortly, or, much less likely, live a long time.

So what if I died soon?

Well, "I reasoned," if I were bitter and angry, then I would have spent the last few months of my life in sorrow and isolation, making a living hell for my loved ones, and would be remembered, if at all, as a bitter old man who let brain cancer defeat him. I would receive their temporary show of sympathy, but in the end they would only have contempt for me and how I left them.

On the other hand, what if I were positive and hopeful? It wouldn't change the date of my death one bit!

But, it would mean that I would spend the last months of my life breathing deeply and clearly, contented, blissful, and in love with my family and everyone I met. I would die a happy man, and be remembered as that brave soul who faced a terrible death with courage, fortitude and aplomb. I would be cherished by those who knew me.

On the other hand, what if I made it? What if I lived?

Then I had no reason to be bitter and tormented! Why waste months of my life wailing about an end that wasn't even near?

So there it was—I had every reason to be positive about my condition, and absolutely no reason to be negative.

It was at that point, that very moment in time, for the first time in my life, that I stopped dying and started living.

I started telling everyone I met and knew that having brain cancer was the greatest thing that had ever happened to me, and today I believe that with all my heart.

A little over a year ago, I learned that the brain cancer had returned. Treatment today is more researched and predictable, prognosis is better; however, the outcome is never certain. After a year of radiation and chemotherapy the tumor board doctors have decided to continue my chemotherapy indefinitely and have scheduled me for monthly MRIs, with absolutely no promises.

How has this disturbing news affected me? It has made me even more positive!

From that special moment—that cold, dark night in January 2003, I have not wasted one second of my life fretting about dying. All the moments of all of my days are spent living.

Brain cancer the first time made me a better man. The second time is making me a good man. Brain cancer is the greatest thing that has ever happened to me.

So what about you? You will have good things and bad in life. Sometimes life will give you great fortune, other times it will rip you like a brick across the face.

What happens to you will happen, and you only have two ways to respond—you can be positive and happy, or negative and miserable. That's it. The good news is that the choice is always up to you! You choose how happy you will be every day of your life, every way that life happens, no matter when, no matter what, no matter who.

Make the decision today to live, not die. To be positive, not negative. Don't endure a tragedy such as mine to figure it out. Live every day, live every minute, live every second of your life.

~Tom Schumm

23

Eleven Minutes

Act as if what you do makes a difference. It does.
~William James

Wednesday starts ordinarily enough. I turn off my alarm and drift back into the warm softness of my bed, listening to the soft breathing of my husband and my daughter's rhythmic sucking on her fingers as they sleep.

As I start to go back to sleep, I force my eyes to open and sit up. There is a reason I want to wake up at the ridiculous hour of 5:30 AM! I quickly put on my running gear and head out to the car.

It is still dark as I drive to the track and I wonder if I'll ever get used to getting up before the crack of dawn. Orion is still very bright in the sky, even as the horizon lightens.

I don't recognize the people running or walking together around the unlit track. I see a woman walking by herself. Is that Marisa? She said yesterday she might not be up to coming today. I stretch my hamstrings waiting to get a closer look.

Nope, not her. Just a stranger wearing a navy windbreaker.

Walking onto the track, my leg feels pretty good today. I am up for some good running spurts today as soon as I warm up. I walk past the bleachers and off to my right on Cherry Avenue, I see Leanne and her running friends jog swiftly past. One day I'll be able to keep up with them.

A runner passes me on the left. He looks like Leanne's husband Todd. Does he come to the track while she runs, too? No, that wouldn't make sense. I bet Todd is home with…

WHAM!

The runner collapses. Hard. His head hits the track with a sickening thud, like a bowling ball dropped on concrete.

"Oh!" exclaims the woman in the navy windbreaker, jumping back. She is a few feet away from him.

"Is he all right?" I call out. I'm about thirty yards away, and walk quickly to get to them.

The man on the track makes no sound. No screams of pain.

"Does anyone have a phone? Call 911!" says Navy Windbreaker.

I pull out my phone and dial 911. He's breathing harshly. Ring. His eyes are open, but staring, his tongue sticking out. Ring. His legs are bent at an odd angle. Ring. I walk around him looking for a leg injury.

"Hello, what is your emergency?"

"A man just collapsed at the Willow Glen High School track on Cherry Avenue. Please send an ambulance."

"Okay, one moment."

The rest of the folks at the track are starting to gather, murmuring quietly. No one touches him.

"Can you tell me what hurts? Are you okay?" I ask loudly. I don't understand why he isn't talking. It still hasn't hit me that his injuries aren't visible. He looks fairly healthy and is probably in his mid-forties.

The dispatcher on the phone says, "Hello, what is your emergency?" I realize that the long pause was the call being transferred to the local San Jose 911 dispatcher.

"A man just collapsed at the Willow Glen High School track on Cherry Avenue. Please send an ambulance," I repeat.

"Okay, one moment."

We are all quiet, watching. Waiting for something. His breathing is slowly getting quieter and quieter. Less air now. Even less air. Now just a soft wheezing.

Oh… My… God!! He is dying right in front me! We all are frozen for a moment as we realize this.

"He's not breathing!" I yell into the phone. "Does anyone know CPR?" I shout. It has been years since I was trained. I'm squeamish about giving mouth-to-mouth, but I remember how to do chest compressions so I move in to get started.

I straighten his legs first and then kneel down next to his chest. I don't adjust his head or check his pulse or listen for a heartbeat. I hold the phone against my face with my left shoulder and immediately start chest compressions.

"One and two and three and four and," I count off and then pause.

"He's not breathing. Can someone give him mouth-to-mouth?" I call out to no one in particular.

"One and two and three and four and," I press down at each count on his chest, pumping his heart.

I touch his face, cup his cheek and look in his eyes. His skin is smooth and clammy. His eyes are open and unseeing. It looks like his tongue might be blocking his airway.

Barbara, a fit and active grandma with thick, bobbed gray hair, kneels down to adjust his head. Her hands are shaking.

"Squeeze his nose," someone suggests behind me.

"Put his head back," another person calls out.

"One and two and three and four and…" I count and compress.

Barbara tries to move his tongue with her finger. He bites her in an unconscious response. "Ow!" she exclaims.

"One and two and three and four and…"

Barbara valiantly pinches his nose before giving him a breath. His chest rises and the air rushes out again.

The 911 dispatcher starts giving instructions for CPR.

Another big breath from Barbara. "Stay with us!" she yells at the man. "It is not your time yet!" Movie scenes flash in my head where a disembodied spirit is floating above us, watching us working on him. I wonder if that is happening now.

The dispatcher is telling me how to hold and place my hands, etc. I am frustrated hearing detailed instructions about things I'm already doing while trying to coordinate the compressions and check for his breathing.

"But I've been trained," I interrupt the dispatcher irritably.

"Ma'am I just want to make sure you don't do it wrong!" I get it. I shut up and let her talk.

"Now, you need to do six hundred compressions."

"Six hundred?" I'm confused.

"Yes, six hundred. Don't stop. Count as you go. I want to hear you count."

"One... two... three..." I'm counting out loud.

Barbara gives him another big breath, and it looks like he is starting to breathe on his own.

"We're not ready to have you go yet!" she continues to yell at him.

"Nine... TEN... one... two... three..."

I get into a rhythm and almost drop the phone. My neck is starting to hurt holding it against my shoulder. I ask someone to hold the phone for me and put it on speakerphone.

"Nine... THIRTY... one ...two ..."

Barbara has stopped giving mouth-to-mouth as he is taking big shuddering breaths on his own. His tongue is still slack in his mouth and the exhale is a loud and welcome sound.

"He is breathing on his own now," I tell the dispatcher.

"Eight... nine... ONE HUNDRED... one... two..."

"Wow," a man says behind me. "He has had a massive heart attack. Just massive."

It finally occurs to me that his injuries must all be internal. I cannot stop what I am doing. I am pumping his heart for him! For the first time I think to check his pulse in his neck. I don't feel anything. Maybe I'm feeling in the wrong spot? I keep my counting and compressions.

"TWO HUNDRED... one... two..."

It seems like forever since I first called 911. Where are the paramedics? There is only so much we can do.

"Eight... nine... TWO EIGHTY... one... two..."

"Do you need a break?" someone asks behind me. "Are you doing okay there?"

I don't look up. "No thanks, I'm okay."

My lower back is starting to feel a little tight, but I am afraid to stop long enough to let someone take over. I don't want to stop. I cannot stop. I am in the zone of counting and compressions. Counting and compressions. Counting and compressions.

"Eight... nine... THREE FIFTY... one... two..."

My anxiety settles a bit while I concentrate on counting, but then suddenly realize too much time has passed already! The sun has come up and it is no longer dark.

"Where is the ambulance?" I snap at the dispatcher, irritated.

"They are on their way," she assures us. "Keep going. You are doing a good job."

"Nine... FOUR TWENTY... one... two..."

I can feel the growing anxiety of the crowd.

"They should be here by now!" someone says in frustration.

"Eight... nine..." I lose track counting and guess "... FOUR EIGHTY."

We hear the sirens. They are on the high school's main street behind us.

"They are on the wrong road!" someone exclaims, panicking.

"No, they know where they are going," the dispatcher calmly explains. "Keep going. You are doing a good job."

The sirens come closer and we see a fire truck stop on the street. Firemen in blue uniforms get out calmly and get their gear. They start walking to the track.

"Why aren't they running? They need to go faster!" Someone to my left is upset.

"Eight... nine... FIVE HUNDRED AND TEN... one... two..."

The crowd backs up a bit for the firemen and one puts his bag down and starts putting on his latex gloves, unpacking his gear. Very calm. He assesses the two of us.

"Okay, you can stop now," he tells me. His eyes look sad. "I'll take over."

I stand up and back away as he starts up the chest compressions again. Someone hands me my phone back.

"They are here now," I tell the dispatcher.

"Okay, I see they are on site. You did a good job." And with that, the dispatcher hangs up.

An ambulance arrives and more EMTs join the firemen. They put an air bag on him, and then have to clear the airway and put in an oxygen tube. CPR continues, and they each take turns. The chest compressions the EMT does are really hard... his limp legs move on each push and I am worried that my compressions didn't do the job. Were mine too soft? Maybe they didn't work.

The EMTs don't find a pulse. They work efficiently and quietly together, cutting open his shirt to apply the pads of the AED. The entire team stands up and backs away as someone says, "CLEAR!" and they defibrillate him. His arms and legs jerk as his torso tenses with the jolt.

Still no pulse. More chest compressions. No pulse.

They defibrillate him again. "CLEAR!" His body contorts stiffly and then relaxes.

There is a solemn silence as we all wait to hear the heart monitor.

"Beep... beep... beep."

Everyone lets out a collective sigh of relief as we hear the soft sound of his heart beating on its own.

"They got his pulse back!" someone shouts.

Others around me clap and cheer. They all seem relieved and surprised. Somehow, I don't feel that surprise. It had never even occurred to me that he wasn't going to be okay. Am I in shock?

A fireman finds a house key in the runner's shorts. There is no other ID. No wallet. No cell phone. No way to notify his family about where he is. He must live close by. I'm horrified at the thought of someone waiting for him to return home from his run and not knowing what has happened.

The ambulance is driving off and a few firemen remain to clean up the trash on the track from the emergency supplies. One is the fireman with the sad eyes.

Sad Eyes walks over to me and says, "Wow. We usually don't see that."

"Yeah," adds another fireman. "Usually we don't get them back."

I'm stunned.

"What? Why? People just stand around and watch?"

"No, it's not usually witnessed. They were in another room and find someone on the floor. Maybe it has been too long since it happened or they don't know how long it has been or they don't know CPR."

"How long was it after he fell that you started CPR?" asks Sad Eyes.

I have to think. "Umm. Less than a minute?"

"Well that was it then. One minute is really good. The sooner CPR starts, the better the chances are for recovery." He continues to fill out his report on his clipboard.

Now I understand the sadness I first saw in his eyes. Arriving at the scene, I don't think he expected a good outcome. His rescue experience and knowledge had taught him that, in cases like this, the story was not going to have a happy ending.

Navy Windbreaker is standing next to me and has started to react to what happened. I reach out to give her a hug; she is still really shaken up.

"What's your name?" she asks me, wiping her tears.

"I'm Heather. What's yours?"

"Suzanne. Oh, I could have never done that. Heather, I will never forget you. You did a great job. I just keep thinking that could have been my husband...." she trials off, still emotional.

Navy Windbreaker is now Suzanne.

I check the time on my phone. 6:15 AM. I'm surprised it all happened in less than thirty minutes! It felt so much longer. I don't need to be home until 6:30 AM. Should I run now? I haven't even walked once around the track. I look around and see others starting to run around the track and think it looks odd. To just go on with life… I'm not ready for that yet. I want to go home. I say goodbye to the group and start to walk to my car.

"Ma'am!" someone calls out behind me. I turn around and it is Sad Eyes the fireman again.

"Hey, I just want to say again that you did a great job. I'm going to go to the hospital to pick up my guys who rode with him in the ambulance. If I find out more information about his status, do you want me to call you?"

"Well sure. That would be great. I am really interested to find out how he does. And whether his family finds him." I give him my name and cell phone number and he writes them on his clipboard.

"What's your name?" I ask him.

"Dave." Sad Eyes is now Dave.

"You guys did a great job too, Dave. It is an honor to meet you," I say with a smile.

I get in the car with this feeling that maybe I shouldn't go home. That I should help more, but I don't know what else to do. I wave absently to the policemen on the street and drive home on autopilot. I pass the first intersection and my eyes start to tear up when I realize the gravity of it all. That man could have died this morning! I hope he will make it through okay. I wish I could go tell his family, to not let them worry when he doesn't come home this morning. I think of all the things I could have done sooner. I worry I didn't do enough to help.

The house is quiet when I get home but for the water running in the shower. I am definitely shaken now and consider having a glass of wine to settle my nerves. Since it is 6:20 AM and I need to drive the kids to school, I figure wine is not really a good option right now. Tempting, though.

There is a voicemail from Marisa letting me know that she isn't coming today. I realize how close I came to not being there to help! If I had checked my voicemail or if I had gone back to sleep… I would have stayed home. If I hadn't been there today, then someone else surely would have stepped up, but I can't be sure they would have been there in time or had a cell phone with them.

I am again reminded that everything happens for a reason. I was there today for a reason. To help save a life. To learn my own inner strength and grace under pressure. To be reminded again that there is a higher source I can trust to give me opportunities to live my purpose. I walk back to my bedroom, in a bit of a daze.

"There is a reason I woke up today," I tell my husband.

"Hold on, Babe. I can't hear you. I'm almost out," he calls out from the shower.

I wait in the doorway of the steamy bathroom, absorbing the warmth of the room. I take off my sweatshirt and start to put my phone on the dresser. I pause to check my last call, curious how long I was on the phone with 911.

Eleven minutes.

Eleven minutes for my life to briefly intersect with his. Enough time for me to be his heartbeat until help arrived. Enough time to save his life. Enough time to change mine.

~Heather Gallegos

24

It's in the Little Things

Enjoy the little things,
for one day you may look back
and realize they were the big things.
~Robert Brault, www.robertbrault.com

I t was one of those days when there was way too much to do. I had fallen behind in most of my household chores. I hadn't been to the grocery store in nearly forever and we were out of pretty much everything. The laundry was piled up well above the tops of the hampers and the house was stretching even my reasonably loose standards of cleanliness. And besides all that, I had two article deadlines and needed to spend some serious time at my computer.

All of that, and my four children were on a break from school. They were thrilled to be home and asked me repeatedly how we would spend their day off.

They were going to be disappointed with my plans for the day. There was absolutely nothing fun about them. Nothing special, nothing school break-worthy at all.

The kids woke up that morning, expecting their usual bowls of cold cereal. But we were out of milk, and my kids hate dry cereal. There were no eggs and no bread, which left few breakfast options. I searched through the freezer, hoping for a box of frozen waffles. No such luck. I rooted around in the fridge, finally finding a tube of buttermilk biscuits. I sprinkled them with cinnamon and sugar, baked them, and gave them to the kids.

"I'm sorry that I can't offer you anything better this morning, but I haven't had time to go shopping," I said. The kids didn't bother responding. They were too busy shoving my makeshift cinnamon rolls into their mouths.

After breakfast, I started a load of laundry and sat down at the computer. My youngest daughter, Julia, walked toward me, wearing her I'm-about-to-whine face. "But, Mommy, I thought we were going to do something fun today," she said. "Since it's our day off from school."

"I know it's your day off, but it's not Mommy's day off," I explained. "I have work to do."

"Can you play a game with me?" she begged. "Like *Candy Land*? Or beauty shop?"

I sighed. I really didn't have time to play. I desperately needed to get some work done. But then I had an idea. "Can we play beauty shop while I work?"

So I got my article done, and my toenails painted at the same time.

My oldest, Austin, volunteered to fix lunch so I could keep working. The younger kids were thrilled with his selections. Not exactly the choices the food pyramid people advise, but the kids had fun and I met my writing deadlines.

Shortly after lunch, we made the trek to the grocery store. Austin pushed the cart, while the younger kids collected coupons from the little dispensers scattered throughout the store. I got what I needed—with a few additions from my entourage, of course.

Back at home, the kids decided to play "grocery store" with the coupons they had collected during our trip. They lined up the canned goods on the kitchen counters and the snacks on the island and pretended to re-buy our groceries.

For the remainder of the afternoon, I cleaned house, folded laundry, and started dinner. The kids continued with their game until my husband, Eric, walked through the door.

He spotted me and grinned. "So how was the kids' big day off today?"

I began to explain that we hadn't done anything special because I'd been too busy with chores. But the kids interrupted me.

"Daddy, did you see Mommy's toenails? She let me sit under her computer desk and paint them while she typed!" Julia said. "It was so much fun!"

"And, Dad, we had the best breakfast today," said Austin. "Have you ever made those special biscuits for Dad? They were awesome!"

Eric gave me a questioning look and all I could do was shrug. My two middle kids, Jordan and Lea, piped up to tell their dad about the coupon game and Austin's special lunch. "We had such a great day today, Dad! It was a blast!"

I looked at my children's faces. They were lit up with excitement. Excitement about makeshift cinnamon rolls, a most unhealthy lunch, coupons from the grocery store, and painted toenails.

"You guys really had a good day? You're not disappointed that we didn't do something fun?" I asked.

Austin shrugged and said, "Life is only as fun as you make it, Mom."

I nodded, realizing how right he was. Happiness is far more about our attitude than our circumstances.

I hugged my kids and thanked them for reminding me to look for happiness in the little things.

Julia smiled and said, "And the little things that make you the happiest are us, right, Mommy?"

Wow, my kids sure are smart.

~Diane Stark

25

In Full Bloom

Some people are always grumbling because roses have thorns;
I am thankful that thorns have roses.
~Alphonse Karr

She was outside, looking at the flowers. "I don't think I mentioned this earlier, but one of my hobbies is taking photos of flowers," she said, contemplating the few blooms left in my yard. "Let me get my camera."

"Knock yourself out," I shrugged, wondering why anyone would bother. I had not planted much this year, cutting back on nearly everything since losing my job. But if she wanted to take pictures...

It had been a difficult year. Just when I thought I was done with the bitterness, it would all come rushing back. The last thing on my mind was flowers.

She aimed her lens at a rose. I hadn't seen her in nearly twenty years, since college in New York. The world had changed, yet we seemed the same. We could still party like old times, as long as we were home by eleven, wore comfortable shoes, and took a couple of aspirin and an antacid. And since we couldn't see our crows' feet without our reading glasses, essentially we were the same. Close enough, I reasoned.

I fiddled with the television remote. My laptop was on the coffee table next to a magazine I was reading. That was me, doing a dozen things at once, packing everything I could into a moment. I was busy with graduate school, an arduous job search, and being the stereotypical valiant, strong, single mother of two boys.

She steadied herself near the last rose of the season, quiet and still, taking photo after photo. Eventually even the dog got bored with her endeavor and walked away.

Suddenly a song from *Mary Poppins* filled the air. I was pretty sure it was coming from outside my head. This day was getting progressively stranger.

"That's my cell phone," she remarked. "I set the alarm on it to remind me to take my medicine. 'Spoonful of Sugar'—get it?"

"An alarm for meds?" I laughed. "Are we that old?" I still refused to write grocery lists, insisting on carrying the list around in my head. I'd forgotten many things that way, but so what? It was the principle of the thing. I would get old when I was good and ready.

Anger kept me young, I figured. Those days were bittersweet, my fury harsh but healthy.

"Strange looking pills," I remarked as she pulled them from her purse.

"They're for my liver," she took a drink of water. "Actually, it's not MY liver. I'm just borrowing it." One corner of her mouth curled upward.

Every few hours, Anne took anti-rejection medication to keep her body from attacking her donated organ. Eight years earlier, she had been diagnosed with a rare liver disorder, one so rare that her doctor missed it completely. Somehow, though, she knew something was wrong. But she didn't know exactly what.

"It was a fluke, really," she said. "What are the chances of meeting a liver specialist at a party? And he was cute!"

She had a slew of flukes in her life. After her liver transplant, she came down with thyroid cancer, discovered by chance during a checkup by a doctor touching the base of her throat. "I told him he was examining the wrong end of me," she giggled. She could giggle at the damndest things.

One day she felt dizzy. With her track record, her doctor sent her for an MRI, which revealed a small tumor in her brain. "It's no bigger than your fingernail, and it hasn't grown at all, so that's a good sign. After all, size is everything!" That was Anne—ever hopeful, giggling and fluky. Even a brain tumor was not beyond joking about. I envied her attitude, but certainly not her situation.

She'd be leaving soon. I was just fine alone. It was great to have her here, share old times, but I was comfortable on my own. I didn't need anybody.

With a hug, she was off. I grabbed a beer from the fridge.

Later that day, an e-mail popped up from her, taking forever and a day to load, especially to an impatient, moody grump like me. Sheesh, I huffed, I have things to do.

It was filled with her flower photos—still, clear, and beautiful. She had taken a few blooms and made them glow, made them perfect, made them timeless. Just a few raggedy flowers.

Damn, I thought. She had gotten past the anger, past the pity. She was on the other side, capturing giggles and picking flowers, making an incredible, everlasting bouquet while I grumbled and whined. That, too, wasn't fair.

I wanted to be able to do that. Here I was trying to cram all sorts of events into my life so it would count for something, as she blithely took one moment at a time, polished it until it shined, and shared it with everyone. She made it look easy. Compared to many things in her life, I guess it was.

Quietly she was able to stop the world from turning, keep it still for a moment, insisting that it take the time to look at a single, lowly daisy. Even more extraordinary, the world would do it.

"Wow," I wrote back. "These are incredible." Lame, I know, but for once I was beyond words.

"Annie," she replied, knowing what I was thinking. "We don't know what tomorrow will be. We don't know if we'll even have a tomorrow. So I choose to focus on today. That's why I take pictures. That's why I came to visit you. That's why I'm here."

I shifted my gaze to outside. I got it now. I was stubborn and thick-headed but finally I got it. And I had thought I was the strong one.

She'll be back to visit again—I'm sure of it. Until then, I have her flowers, in full bloom. Actually, I always had them, but it was Anne who got me to really see them.

~Annie Mannix

26

A Timely Lesson

We can only be said to be alive in those moments
when our hearts are conscious of our treasures.
~Thornton Wilder

"The kid was only eighteen. He dropped on the basketball court. SADS. It's what a lot of those young athletes die of."

"Yeah, what's SADS?"

"Sudden Arrhythmia Death Syndrome."

As I listened to the actor's words on *NCIS*, I popped up on the couch, dumping *The New York Times* crossword onto the floor. Extricating myself from the heavy paws of our Lab-mix, Yoshi, I moved to the computer and typed in "SADS."

I wove through research about this syndrome, which is characterized by a cardiac electrical glitch. It was probably what had snuffed out our teenaged son's life seventeen years earlier. Maybe if Josh had been born later, he could have been saved. SADS no longer had to result in sudden death, but it was genetic, so close relatives should be examined.

Jeff and I have always been grateful that our third child, Maliq, born eighteen years after our first, has had solid ground under his feet. Life has tossed this kid very few lemons.

Young life was different for our middle child, Miles. Losing his big brother when he was only eight cast a shadow across his childhood. Miles had held hands with mortality too early. Now at twenty-seven, he was a father himself.

I called him to talk about getting checked for SADS.

"Mom, I had an EKG a few months ago because I had those bruised ribs. They didn't find a problem. Are you worried? Should I be? For Mikah?"

Miles hadn't planned on children. He brought his dad and me the ultrasound picture as a way to tell us that he was going to be a father. He was happy. And terrified.

"Mom, all that can go wrong..."

"Yeah, but all that can go right. Look at you; look at Maliq."

There's a lot Jeff and I, as parents, don't get worked up about since Josh died; fender-benders, money problems, adolescent piercings, and pretty much anything that isn't a death threat stays in perspective.

• • •

Now we were having Maliq checked for SADS. The doctor and nurse swept into the small exam room that was packed full of our family. The doc took one look at Maliq, who even when seated, dwarfed him, and began firing questions: History of eye problems, scoliosis, heart murmurs? I knew where he was going because I had already been there during one of my many Internet searches. Marfan's Syndrome.

"Listen Doctor, I understand I'm not a cardiologist, but I've researched Marfan's thoroughly. Maliq doesn't fit the criteria." I knew even as the sentences flew anxiously out of my mouth that this doctor wasn't taking me seriously.

"How tall are you, anyway?" Just fifteen, Maliq already measured in at 6'3". The cardiologist put stethoscope to chest. His face changed. He listened for a long time, then had his nurse listen.

Damn, I knew that expression. I had seen it enough times with Josh. I looked over at Jeff. His face seemed to lose muscle, sagged as he too recognized the shift.

The doc listened again. "There's definitely a murmur."

Maliq's face, lean and sculpted, was open and mostly unconcerned.

"I think this young man has Marfan's Syndrome."

Maliq looked at us, then at the doc. "What's that?"

"It's a syndrome that includes serious heart problems. Young man, as of right now, you are on complete athletic restriction."

Maliq's eyes registered shock as tears rolled down his face. Maliq's world was spinning. The door was slamming shut on the life he had constructed, on the future he had assumed. Maliq had been a soccer goalkeeper since he was four.

Miles moved to his brother's side, put his arm around Maliq, moved his head in close and whispered in his ear. Time paused as I watched my sons together. Their relationship deepened in that moment, narrowing the span of years between them.

I jumped in to compensate for the doc's obviously underdeveloped bedside manner, my voice stern enough to cause my husband to grimace, and Miles to smile.

"What other tests are needed to confirm or rule out the diagnosis, and when can we get them done?"

The cardiologist looked startled by my tone and set of my jaw. Years of navigating the medical system had helped me be just a little scary, when need be.

"We can do the EKG here. He needs to go over to the hospital for the echo cardiogram."

Maliq had rearranged his face, stopped his tears.

They squeezed the machine into the room. Jeff and I sighed in relief when no long QT, which is a marker related to SADS, and no other abnormality showed in the EKG's squiggly lines.

My schedule was such that I would take Maliq over to the U for the echo. As we walked to the car, I reached up to hug Maliq. He was a good hugger — never gave passive squeezes — but this time he held on a lot harder and longer than usual.

"How're you doing, Darling? Do you have questions?"

Tears showed again. "Is he saying I might have the same thing that killed Josh?

"Yes, but Josh died a long time ago. Things have changed. What Josh had can now be treated."

"Mom, I have never loved soccer as much as I do this very minute. If I have this heart thing, is there surgery so I can play again?"

"Yeah, I think there is."

"Okay, then if I have it, I want the surgery soon, so it won't mess up my season."

And for the first time that day, I started to cry, because here it was, that thing you can always count on embedded in adversity. Within minutes, Maliq's priorities had crystallized. He knew, without a doubt, what he was willing to do to keep the life he had previously taken for granted.

"Mom, is this going to be okay?"

I answered from the logical part of my brain. "It's going to be fine, and here's the good news; this morning, soccer got taken away, and when you get it back you'll appreciate it like you never have before."

"Mom, do you really believe that, or are you just being positive?"

This child knew me well. "I do believe it, and I'm also being positive."

Finally at 9:45 that night, the cardiologist called. "The echo came back clean."

I let out the breath that I hadn't realized I'd been holding. "Great. That means Maliq doesn't have Marfan's or SADS?"

"You still need to meet with the geneticist, put all the pieces together."

The appointment with the geneticist ended up being scientifically interesting but thankfully, clinically insignificant. She found no Marfan's, and ruled out SADS.

Maliq started running sub-six-minute-miles. His soccer team made it to the state tournament and in a shoot-out where Maliq was up against arguably the best goalkeeper in the state, he blocked the most kicks and his team won.

Later, fork paused over the last of about ten meals he had eaten that day, he said, "Mom, I took it for granted before. I figured there was always time to get serious about soccer. Now, I know, I can't take anything for granted; we don't really ever know what kind of time we have."

I was so grateful that a lesson I learned through tragedy, this son was able to learn through a near miss.

~Lindsay A. Nielsen

27

Unwrapping the Present

A happy person is not a person in a certain set of circumstances,
but rather a person with a certain set of attitudes.
~Hugh Downs

I lay snugly in bed trying, yet again, to figure out what to do with my life. "God, what would you have me do? Where would you have me go?"

Too impatient to wait for His response, my mind catalogued everything I expected to hear: "Fight World Hunger." "Save the Children." "Stop Global Warming."

Yet I distinctly heard, "Go to Costco."

"Excuse me? Costco? Really?"

Not that I underestimate the spiritual value of seventy-five rolls of toilet paper, but maybe my to-do list got tangled up in my spiritual call. So I tried again.

"God, what would you have me do today? Where would you have me go?"

No doubt about it— "Costco" was His answer.

Frankly, I was relieved. Costco seemed infinitely more manageable than fighting world hunger, especially since I had to be home before 3:00 PM.

"If you have the nagging suspicion that you're wasting your life," Marianne Williamson, the spiritual teacher, once said, "it's because you are." Our house renovation, which had been my "job" for over a year, was finally finished and I now volunteered only minimally since my daughter had entered middle school. In short, I found myself suddenly out of work with that nagging suspicion Marianne talked about. Admittedly my ego yearned to own a cocktail-party sound bite that would impress when someone inevitably asked, "So what are you up to?"

"Uh… nothing."

In great need of an identity makeover, I'd begun reading spiritual books. What struck me was how often someone found her calling or purpose in life by waking each morning and asking God, "What would you have me do today? Where would you have me go?"

Truthfully it all seemed a little hooey. Could I really dial God 911 and get an answer?

But okay, I'd go with the flow. Maybe this Costco gig was my audition. If God saw that I could handle family hunger, he might give me a go at the world one day.

So I got out of bed and dressed for Costco.

Being Day One of my God-given duty, I approached my calling in, let's just say, a more godly way. Instead of weaving my shopping cart NASCAR-style through the aisles, running intersections, and whizzing through the less busy thoroughfares, I yielded. I turned off my cell phone and gave up being smug about multi-tasking, which I discovered enabled me to remember all of the items I came in for. But as I waited in the checkout line my foot tapped anxiously. I still had to go to the cleaners, the post office and the library and be home in thirty-five minutes. My heart raced faster. Breathe. Be here. Be present.

I redirected my thoughts to my feet and felt them ground me to the earth. As I breathed, tension evaporated. I became less stressed. I felt an opening of grace. I felt lighter.

I arrived home and unloaded my packed SUV. Normally, I'd moan about having to make multiple trips up two flights of stairs, including lugging a three-gallon jug of laundry detergent, but today I found gratitude. First, I was grateful I had the money to buy everything I did. Second, I was thankful my arms and legs were strong enough to haul my goods, and third, I was mindful we now had food for dinner and lunches and I could tackle the piles of laundry that had accumulated.

Gratitude was beginning to run rampant. The more present I became, the more I grasped how blessed I was. I was grateful I had appliances and that they worked. I was grateful every time I turned on the faucet and clean water came out. I was grateful I had a family to cook and clean for. Had my newly found gratitude not caused so much serenity, it could've been downright annoying.

"What's up with you?" my daughter asked, eyeing me suspiciously, as she dropped her book bag and kicked off her shoes. "You look weirdly happy."

I was happy. Not weirdly, just simply.

Being grateful—can that be a calling? My life's purpose?

My husband arrived home earlier than expected.

"Hi," I chirped.

His face was slack and drained of color, his eyes glazed with that "I have something to tell you but I don't want to" expression.

"My job's been 'downsized.' I haven't been fired, but I don't have a job."

I felt the panic of the unknown future surging through my body. What's going to happen? What now? What if? My body tightened. I felt ill.

Okay, gratitude's pretty easy when your pocket's full and the sun is shining, but I wasn't ready for this so soon. Now what, God? This was only my first day on the job.

Then it hit me. God didn't send me to Costco to find toilet paper, and the gratitude thing was really just a warm-up. What he sent me to find was presence.

I'd gotten it wrong. It wasn't God, what would you have me do? It was God, what would you have me be?

Be present. Be in this moment. Be.

I took a grounding breath and hugged my husband, absorbing the warmth of his body. As I stood in that present moment unwrapped, uncontested and accepted for simply what is, I understood that all we ever truly have is the present. Maintaining gratitude, faith and presence were actions I could choose now. Faith is knowing the moon is always full even if I see only a sliver or none at all. And from this deep place of awareness I knew we were, and would be, all right.

~Tsgoyna Tanzman

28

The "Who Cares?" Bin

Only a few things are really important.
~Marie Dressler

don't pray as much as I should. But two weeks ago I prayed as my husband, Bob, was taken by ambulance to Cape Cod Hospital with intensifying pain spreading through his chest.

There's exquisite simplicity and purity in the words "I love you" that two people share when it may be for the last time. And in that instant, everything else, every thought, every action, every other part of your life falls into the "who cares?" bin.

I want to tell you something very important. It is not a big deal to call 911. You call. They come. There'll be sirens, but you'll welcome their sound. The EMTs don't want you to wait until you're positive something's wrong.

Bob, on the couch, saw me struggling to quickly answer their questions through my crackly voice. And I wasn't breathing well. He mouthed the words, "I'm sorry," which, of course, broke my heart even more. Then he was taken away.

Ten minutes later, I hurried through the hospital parking lot with just one prayer. "Please let him be alive."

And my prayer was answered.

Joyously, I flopped down on the chair next to his gurney. Apparently, it wasn't his heart. We were bubbly with happiness.

The nurse connected leads from an EKG machine to different points on Bob's chest. As she unbuttoned his shirt, he looked at me and started to laugh. It was then I remembered his recent mid-life decision to try Grecian Formula to get rid of the gray in his beard. But afraid to try it outright, he had experimented with his chest hair and was therefore sporting brown polka dots. The nurse was quiet. She also didn't say anything while Bob and I tried in vain to squelch a giggling fit.

"What have you eaten today?" she asked before taking blood.

"Jellybeans." By now, he had lost all credibility as a grown-up. After the EKG, he had X-rays. Then he was given a little plastic jar for a urinalysis. It took a heck of a long time for him to come out of the bathroom.

"What was the matter?" I asked when he came out. "Don't they have dirty magazines or something?"

"It wasn't that kind of test," he said, looking around in hopes I couldn't be heard.

So all continued well, until our drive home. Bob, feeling good, wanted to drive, but halfway down Main Street, I saw him reaching for his chest again.

"What is it?" I said, panicking.

He was feeling around. "They left these things on."

"What things?"

"They put BBs on my nipples so they wouldn't be mistaken for spots on my X-rays. But they're embedded in some sort of adhesive and I can't get them off."

I went ballistic. "You've got to get them off! What if we have an accident? What are people going to think if you're wearing nipple buttons?" I grabbed his nipples and started yanking. He swerved to park the car.

So, there I was, leaning over Bob's chest with my face in his nipples trying to wrench the BBs off. And a couple with three kids walked by, looked in the window, said something to each other, then ran away.

I'm learning to pray more. And one thing I've learned lately is to choose my prayers carefully. "Is this really important?" I'll ask myself, because if it's trivial or too selfish, I'll scrap it. And maybe prayer is really a process of evaluation that teaches me what matters and what doesn't.

And I'll tell you something else. Most of those things that fell into the "who cares?" bin during those terrible life and death moments… are going to stay right there.

Which is where, when it comes down to it, they should have been all along.

~Saralee Perel

29

Childhood Delights

So our human life but dies down to its root,
and still puts forth its green blade to eternity.
~Henry David Thoreau

My mother was diagnosed with Alzheimer's long after I accepted the gradual changes I saw in her. I had grown used to partially listening to her repetitious stories and filling in the missing words of her sentences.

I imagine I might have continued to deny my inklings had she not been admitted to the hospital for a short hospital stay. During the night, apparently she had become disoriented and the nurses found her roaming the hallways. A neurology consultation had taken place and the doctor told me that my mother was approaching the middle stages of Alzheimer's.

The doctor was kind and compassionate as we sat in a hospital conference room. He explained that for people with dementia, once a memory was lost it could not be relearned as in the case of a stroke. I thought I understood that concept, but over the coming months, I often had to fight the urge to say, "I already told you that."

My mother lived with our family since her retirement. We enjoyed a deep friendship and she led a very independent life filled with activities. Almost overnight our family life dramatically changed with the pronouncement of that one word: Alzheimer's.

Those happy, active days dropped away from my consciousness as I suddenly felt trapped by the challenges that I imagined lay ahead for all of us. Somewhere in the process of hearing and accepting this diagnosis, my focus shifted from being with Mom to taking care of Mom.

Each day led to a new discovery as I learned what Mom knew and what she could no longer remember. For example, my heart sank the day I realized she could no longer read written directions. She stood in front of the microwave holding her frozen dinner, not knowing what do. That was also the day that I knew she would need someone to stay with her while I was at work. It was the only way I could ensure that she would eat during the day.

I thought about the best way to take care of Mom all the time. I was vigilant in my discreet observations of her. Looking back, I wonder if despite my well-meaning intentions, I arrogantly took it upon myself to decide what I thought was best. Possibly in the process I curbed some of her independence and neglected to consider her capability to express her feelings and opinions in the moment.

Driving the car was a major decision and dilemma as I wondered whether she could drive to the grocery store and find her way home. When was it time to remove her car keys from her purse? Fortunately it turned out to be a mutual agreement when she called me crying from the mall, "I can't find where I parked the car. Help me!" Thankfully she remembered the phone number, probably because she had dialed it hundreds of times over the years.

That one decision struck a major blow for each of us. It signaled a huge loss of independence for Mom and huge dependence on me. I also began wondering how I could convince her to wear a medical alert bracelet with her name and address without destroying her dignity.

Each day more memories were lost but slowly I discovered that every cloud does have a silver lining. Because my mother did not have memories of the past, I grew to know her in new and different ways that were free from the baggage that most of us carry throughout our lifetimes. Resentments with a sister-in-law no longer mattered and she would talk to her on the phone again. She could go to the hair salon on a Tuesday instead of a Saturday because each of her days really did begin with a clean slate.

Slowly I let go of the firm notion of taking care of Mom and being with Mom. We began to share a companionship. Often we would engage in an activity and it was as if she was experiencing it for the very first time. I would see delight on her face blowing out candles on her birthday cake, coloring with crayons, or picking flowers in the park.

It was surprising to see some amazing changes of imprinted patterns that evolved. She forgot that her back bothered her and I no longer had to drive around a parking lot to find the closest parking space to the store. She even began taking walks up and down our street.

One day we went to a buffet and I will admit I was a bit shocked and embarrassed when she stuck her hands in the salad bin and stacked her plate with a wide variety of foods. She didn't remember what she liked or disliked and I watched with fascination as she tried and enjoyed some of those foods.

As time passed, I noticed Mom was able to take care of herself in some new ways. She dressed herself but she didn't care if her clothes matched. This was the same person who bought me matching box-pleated skirts, cardigan sweaters, and knee socks as a child. I noticed with amusement and sadness that she took over the control of the television remote. Her taste in movies changed from her cherished classics to the Western channel.

She was unaware of the growing to-do list added to my schedule. She was free from paying bills, making dinner, driving herself to doctor appointments, laundry and numerous other details that make up a person's day.

Mostly she was happy just to be with me. She would follow me from room to room and was always ready to jump into the car for errands or an outing. Slowly I began to recognize her individuality as she displayed her likes and dislikes and a full range of unpredictable emotions. She was Mom, not just a human being with a disease.

One of my most treasured memories occurred when I took her

to an outdoor band concert. They were playing music from the Big Band Era. By that time she was barely able to carry on a conversation, yet once the music started she sang the words to almost every song! For more than forty-five minutes, I was filled with awe and gratitude that somewhere deep inside her there was still a bridge to the outside world. I can still recall the joy and contentment on her face.

Alzheimer's helped me to learn to appreciate Mom and not just take care of her. As her memory fell away, I discovered in her an almost childlike innocence. She taught me to view the world from a different perspective and to notice how precious each moment can be. It is with a sense of irony that the less she remembered, the more present we both became in our lives.

~Jean Ferratier

30

People First

I always prefer to believe the best of everybody, it saves so much trouble.
~Rudyard Kipling

When I attended Open House at my son's school, I scanned the bulletin board outside his first-grade classroom. I spied Cody's handiwork in a colorful sea of papers tacked to the board. My expectant smile froze.

In one circle he was supposed to write or draw what he didn't like.

"MEN," he scrawled in capital letters.

Uh-oh, I thought as fear iced me. How could Cody not like men? He loved his daddy! Did some man do unspeakable things to my child?!

"Cody," I said casually. "Can you tell me about your work here?"

"Yeah," he replied, then carefully recited each word slowly. "I... don't... like... mean."

Such is the world of phonics, writing words the way they sound.

That exercise served to reinforce how our kids perceived the world, divided into two classes: good and bad.

It didn't matter to them what the person looked like. You were either good or you were bad. Take our neighbor next door, for instance. She was a good person, giving the kids treats when they deserved it. Now the bully on the bus who hit Cody in the stomach...

"He's mean, Mom!" cried Cody. "He's a bad boy!"

"He's not a bad boy," I replied, drying his tears. "What he DID was bad. There's a difference."

That's what the parenting magazines tell us to say. And it makes sense, this mass campaign of programming us to think in terms of "people coming first."

People with or without disabilities.

People with or without a steady income.

With or without a home.

With or without goodness.

People first.

But I doubted Cody understood my logic.

Until one warm Saturday morning.

Cody and I arrived at a pizza parlor where a birthday party was being held for his classmate, Kristi.

"Cody!" Kristi shouted, walking toward him in a cloud of pink ruffles, her thick, blond hair combed into one long braid down her back. She was radiant as she hugged him.

"Why, Kristi," I said, "you look beautiful!"

"Thank you," she responded, twirling around. "Let's go play some games, Cody!"

Cody, unfazed by being the only boy in the handful of attendees, bounced gleefully from one game to another, feeding tokens to hungry machines.

When several pizzas were delivered to the balloon-bedecked tables, Kristi made a point of asking Cody to sit next to her. When Cody asked for pink lemonade, she informed the waitress, with a trace of authority in her voice, "I'll have what he's having."

When it came time for opening presents, she announced, "I want to open Cody's present first!"

He handed her a small package, a pink Ooglie toy that made funny and irreverent noises when one pulled its tail.

"It's for your book bag," Cody said shyly.

"Oh, I love it!" she gushed, hugging Cody. "Thank you!"

While everyone was eating cake, Kristi leaned over to me and said, "Mrs. Oliver, Cody is always so nice to me every single day at school. He's the only one who's never, ever mean to me."

I blinked back tears. Not just because a little girl was sweet enough to acknowledge Cody's sensitivity to his mother. But for knowing how cruel kids could be, especially to skinny-challenged girls like Kristi.

My heart ached from the sudden surge of pride that coursed through it.

All I could think of was, by golly, he got it.

Cody got it.

People first.

~Jennifer Oliver

Think Positive

Role Models

A good example has twice the value of good advice.

~Author Unknown

31

The Queen of Parking Spaces

Could we change our attitude,
we should not only see life differently, but life itself would come to be different.
~Katherine Mansfield

"How do you do that?" I exclaimed, as Aunt Judy pulled into a parking space directly in front of the doors of her busy, neighborhood Round Table Pizza. But, that's my Aunt Judy—the Queen of Parking Spaces. She never parks out in the boondocks. Wherever I go with her, be it to the mall, the grocery store, or her favorite restaurant, Aunt Judy parks up front, always has, always will.

One day we headed for The Jewelry Mart in San Francisco. Traffic stopped before we even got out of Contra Costa County. We crawled with double lines of cars through the tunnel that connected Orinda and Oakland, and of course there was a backup at the toll-booths for the Bay Bridge, even for vehicles using FasTrack passes on their windshields. Once on the bridge it was stop and go, there in the sunshine above the shifting blue water, all the way into the city.

Fortunately, The Jewelry Mart lies in the warehouse district and in a port city like San Francisco, it's only logical the warehouse district should be located near the bay. Thankfully, our exit was one of the first upon reaching the city and off the freeway we crept, Aunt Judy's Mercedes just one in a long line of cars and trucks. We waited through the signal at the bottom of the exit three times before we were able to turn left onto the one-way street passing under the freeway.

At last, the utilitarian structures of the warehouse district loomed before us. Now I knew parking spaces would be scarce here — either on the street or in the rare, distant parking lots. Even street parking is limited by delivery zones. This is, after all, a place where raw merchandise and commodities are delivered to be shipped and sold elsewhere. It is not designed for the suburban shopper. I had come prepared to walk.

Just as we emerged from under the freeway, a parking lot appeared to our right. Aunt Judy did not even glance in that direction. One block, two... she drove confidently. "There it is," she said as the building that housed The Jewelry Mart came into sight ahead and to our left.

Aunt Judy flipped on her blinker and merged into the left lane, slowed as we approached the building, and pulled into a vacant spot right in front of the main entrance. Unbelievable!

"How do you do this?" I cried, gesturing toward the shiny glass doors.

She laughed. "If you don't look for a parking place up front, how will you ever get one?"

It was as simple and as obvious as that.

We passed a thoroughly enjoyable day of shopping and browsing, headed back to her house and stopped at Safeway for a few things, parking two spots from the door, then wended our way home.

Now I am a Parking Princess. I went to Costco this morning and crawled along with a line of cars into the parking lot. Cruising to the back of the lot to avoid the commotion near the front of the store, I turned down the row that opened before the entrance. I parked three cars from the doors.

But Aunt Judy's attitude doesn't just apply to finding primo parking spots. There is so much to appreciate and enjoy in life if one will only look for an opportunity.

The year my husband and I divorced, I found myself flat broke as the kids' summer week with their dad approached. I dreaded the thought of rattling around in our four-bedroom house all by myself. Then it dawned on me. I had airline miles! I started thinking. Where could I go where I wouldn't have to spend a lot of money when I got there? I figured the cost of meals wouldn't matter because I'd have eaten anyway if I stayed home, so all I needed was lodging and entertainment. Where could I go?

Then it dawned on me—Washington, D.C. Almost everything of interest is free in D.C. It could take weeks just to explore all the Smithsonians, and I only had five full days.

I booked my plane tickets and, because it was August, was able to reserve a bargain-basement-priced lodging that included breakfast every morning then set out on one of the greatest trips of my life.

On the day I arrived, I walked The Mall in the late afternoon sunlight, stopping to pay my respects to President Lincoln at his memorial. I could hardly believe I was standing there before him, seeing how huge the sculpture is, how compassionately rendered was that well-known face, and how inspiring were the words he'd crafted so long ago, displayed on the walls around him.

That week I reveled in the art and museums, marveled at the gothic beauty of the National Cathedral, and was awed by the Capitol and Library of Congress. I intend to go back some day.

My Washington trip was the first time I had travelled alone. That week I discovered I could not only do it, but enjoy it. It is not such a long journey from Parking Princess to Travel Queen. However, I might not have found my way there were it not for Aunt Judy and her parking space philosophy.

~Deborah Zigenis-Lowery

32

A True Thanksgiving

I would maintain that thanks are the highest form of thought;
and that gratitude is happiness doubled by wonder.
~G.K. Chesterton

A few years ago, right before Thanksgiving, I was dumped without warning by the man I thought I would marry. The next day, I was laid off from my administrative assistant job. The day after that I turned forty.

I'd lived in New York City for ten years trying to make it as an actress. While I'd had some luck on stage, nothing had paid enough for me to make a living at it. I was single, broke and approaching middle age in a profession that worships youth and beauty.

The last thing I wanted was to go home to Florida for Thanksgiving and catch up with my younger, married and successful cousins. At least we would all meet at Brooks, my favorite restaurant back home and a family holiday tradition for twenty years.

The day before I flew to Florida, I got a terrible cold. I was lying in bed feeling very sorry for myself when the phone rang. It was my mother.

"Darling," she said. "I have wonderful news!"

This made me cringe. Her last report of wonderful news was she had married a man she met online two weeks before. Now, recently divorced for the fourth time and living in a new apartment complex for "active elders," I feared the worst.

"What is it?" I sniffled.

"Well…" she replied, pausing for dramatic effect, "you know how every year we have dinner at Brooks. This year, I've decided to make dinner for the family myself. Well, with your help, of course. Let's see, we should have... twenty-five people, not including us. Won't that be so much fun?"

Could I have pretended she had the wrong number? Yes, if I hadn't been so stoned on cold medicine and thinking clearly. Instead I mumbled "Yeah... great... can't wait" and hung up, pulling the covers over my head before passing out.

The next day, I arrived at the Ft. Lauderdale airport looking and feeling absolutely miserable.

I picked up my luggage from baggage claim and walked outside to look for my mother. A platinum blonde pulled up to the curb beside me and honked the horn. "Do you like it?" my mother exclaimed. She leaned out of the car window to toss her formerly salt-and-pepper curls, now flat-ironed and reaching her shoulders.

"Who are you and why did you steal my mother's car?" I replied.

She laughed like a girl of sixteen. "Silly! This is to celebrate my wonderful new life!"

"Oh. Wonderful," I said.

I should have been happy for her, but at that point my mom looked and sounded ten years younger than me.

The next day was madness. I shopped and cooked more by noon than I had in years. At midnight, I was bent over the sink, elbow-deep in a still-frozen turkey, trying to pull out the gizzards with both hands.

Even though the activity helped take my mind off my troubles, I still felt sad about my life and worried about what I would do when I got back to New York.

Thanksgiving Day, we woke up at 6:00 AM to finish cooking. I never thought we would pull it off, but somehow, we managed to prepare everything, clean the house, fit four card tables next to the dining room table in a one-bedroom apartment, polish the silverware, find matching plates and even create four miniature pumpkin centerpieces.

We put out our casseroles and hot dishes on the buffet, checked the turkey, and just had time to change clothes before the first guests arrived.

Soon the house was overrun with family. No one asked about my boyfriend or if I had gotten any acting work lately. They all just oohed and ahhed over the table. They couldn't believe we did it all ourselves.

Before we ate, we said grace and went around the table to say what we were thankful for. I've always loved doing this each year but now, even though I was proud of helping my mom and glad to see everyone, I didn't really feel like contributing.

Mother's turn came before mine. She said, "I am thankful for my health, my family and my friends. I am especially thankful to my daughter Alyssa who taught me the meaning of gratitude on a Thanksgiving thirty-nine years ago."

I looked up from my plate. What did she mean by that?

She continued. "Alyssa's father Ed had just gotten out of the Army. I was a new wife and mother of a one-year-old. We left Ft. Polk in Louisiana for Pittsburgh because that's where Ed found work. Well, the Army lost all our furniture in the move and we had no money to buy more. We also couldn't afford to go home for Thanksgiving.

"I went out and bought one baby food jar of strained turkey and one of strained carrots for Alyssa and two turkey sandwiches for us. We sat on the floor in our empty apartment and cried over our misfortune. Then we heard Alyssa laughing."

My mother looked over at me with tears in her eyes. "You were so happy. You were singing and having such a good time playing with your food in that cold empty apartment. I pray that you will always find happiness in every living moment, my darling daughter."

I was stunned. I had asked myself how a woman of sixty-five who lived alone on a fixed income decided to become a hot blonde and make Thanksgiving dinner for almost thirty people.

Now I had my answer. She was just following the example I had set so long ago and had forgotten.

When I returned to New York, I had a new sense of purpose and thankfulness for life.

I also went blond.

~Alyssa Simon

33

Unbreakable Faith

Every tomorrow has two handles.
We can take hold of it by the handle of anxiety, or by the handle of faith.
~Author Unknown

L ike most moms of her generation, our Italian mother has mantras for every life event. For medical ailments—whether a broken bone or toothache, her advice is to "take two aspirin and grease it with Vicks." When something she predicted didn't exactly happen the way she believed it would, Mom's reply is, "I may not always be right, but I'm never wrong."

One of the most inspiring attributes of our mom is her ability to face adversity and not come out defeated. She always emerges with a renewed spirit and infectious sense of hope. Her outlook on tragic events is typically met with: "Hey, nobody died, nobody has cancer; we'll get through this, too!" But by far, our mother's most widely used mantra is, "For the love of God, count your blessings! It could be worse!" And she should know. Four of my parents' five children, myself included, are afflicted with a rare genetic bone disease called Osteogenesis Imperfecta, known as "brittle bones," as are three of their grandchildren. Having children who have collectively broken more than 300 bones would lead some parents to question their faith, but our mom refused to let others pity her or let us feel sorry for ourselves. "Hey, it's just a broken bone   it'll heal. There are worse things children could have. If this is the worst thing I ever have to deal with in my lifetime, I'll take it."

I, on the other hand, needed a little more convincing. Let me illustrate a typical day in my O.I. history. I woke up one morning, slipped on something innocuous, fell and broke my wrist. After Dad splinted my arm, we went to the ER, and I was sporting a heavy white plaster cast before 10:00 AM. Most parents would allow their injured child to stay home from school for the rest of the day, but not my mother. She scrubbed floors to pay for all five of us to get a Catholic education and by God's grace, she was going to see to it that we didn't miss a day. Whining was out—and so was reason when it came to dealing with my mom.

"But Mom, I have a broken arm. Can't I stay home?"

"It's just an arm, Jodi. You still have two good legs—now get out of the car and use those good legs to walk into that school."

"But Mom, it's my right arm... I'm right-handed. How am I supposed to write?" Protesting was fruitless because Mom had an answer for everything.

"Hey, that's why God blessed you with two hands—use your other one."

Did I mention I'm now ambidextrous? Not by birth, but by counting the blessing of my two hands. Years later, when I learned that I was carrying twin girls, my joy became short-lived when they were born sixteen weeks early. Weighing in at one pound, three ounces each and just under twelve inches in length, my daughters had a large medical mountain to climb. My mother, by my bedside, holding her rosary in one hand and my own hand in her other, told me with great conviction, "They may be tiny, but they're mighty. Count your blessings." Even after Hayley succumbed to pneumonia and died three weeks after she burst into our lives, my Rock-of-a-Mother was there helping me find a way to go on in spite of my incredible grief.

"I know you want your baby here with you," she said in a gentle, loving voice, "but God must have another plan. Maybe he needs Hayley in heaven to be her sister's guardian angel here on earth. Hayley will watch out for Hanna so Hanna can survive." Mom was right; Hanna did survive. Each day for the past seventeen years, I've looked into my daughter's blue eyes and I've known firsthand that I am indeed blessed.

When Hanna was diagnosed with O.I. and people around me started to feel sorry for us, I replied, "Hey, she's not dying and she doesn't have cancer—she'll survive this. Broken bones heal." Then I started to laugh... I had finally turned into my mother.

In 2003, our mother took ill and had to have surgery. When the doctor relayed the unthinkable diagnosis to my siblings while Mom was in recovery—post-menopausal ovarian cancer—my sister called me and said, "Now what do we tell her? We can't say, 'No one's dead, no one's got cancer!'"

As it turned out, we didn't have to say a word. Mom knew even before she was told, and she soothed us when we should have been comforting her. "Hey, let's count our blessings; the doctor got it all and I'm not dead yet. Let's have some faith." As usual, our wise mother was right. She survived not only this bout with cancer, but five years later, she rebounded from another round of cancer—colorectal. She never needed chemo or radiation because miraculously both cancers were contained and surgically removed; and she has been cancer-free for nearly two years and counting.

"Faith; that's all you need," my mom says firmly as she taps the table. "Feeling sorry for yourself doesn't help anything or solve the problem... pity just adds to your problems. Spend your time counting your blessings instead. You'll see just how well off you really are. That's my motto."

And now we have the good sense to reply, "Yes, Mom... we know, we know!"

Counting blessings is not just a mantra drilled into our heads by our mom. It's become a way of life for all of us. So much so that when I count my blessings, my wise mother is always near the top of the list.

~Jodi L. Severson

34

The Power of Illusion

There is no truth. There is only perception.
~Gustave Flaubert

M any years ago, I was sitting in my dear friend Sara's beautifully wallpapered living room. We were discussing my painstaking effort to successfully hang wallpaper in several rooms at my house.

"I can't get the seams to match," I lamented. "It's not straight at the ceiling and it just isn't nearly as pretty as yours. What am I doing wrong? How did you get yours to look so much better than mine?"

Sara sat quietly listening to all my woes. I noticed a small smile on her lips and wondered if she was, perhaps, laughing a bit at me. She had seen the first room I had finished. Maybe she was chuckling to herself about what a poor job I had done. Finally, I wound down my complaining and gave her a chance to respond.

"Donna," she soothed. "It's all an illusion. The details don't matter. Look at my seams; they aren't perfect either. There is a tear over in the corner, did you notice that?"

I slowly shook my head as I looked more closely at the previously unnoticed imperfections of her living room walls. She continued, "You walk into my house and see the illusion of a beautiful room. You don't notice all the flaws. You did your wallpaper yourself so you know every spot that isn't exactly right. You want your room to be perfect, so you search for anything that may be wrong. No one else will see the mistakes, just like you didn't see mine." As I left her house that day, I knew that she was right and looked less critically at my rooms upon arriving home.

Life went on and I eventually forgot the discussion that I had with Sara that day. Time passed and one of my daughters decided to have her wedding in my backyard. I had worked for many years to make my yard into a beautiful garden—cultivating, transplanting, pruning, trying new varieties of plants. With the help of my husband and sons, we had dug a pond, planted new shrubs and trees and made the area a refuge from the daily world. It was a haven where birds nested, squirrels scampered, and frogs rested on lily pads. I had dreamed that one day one of my children would choose it for a wedding. That day had come and I enthusiastically began planting pale yellow and lavender flowers to match my daughter's chosen colors.

Things were going wonderfully, and then the rains came. Here we were in drought-ridden Colorado and suddenly we were being deluged with day after day of rain. My grass developed a fungus; the weeds thrived with the extra moisture, but it wouldn't stop raining long enough for me to pull them; mushrooms spread from the front to the backyard. The prediction was for clear, dry weather the day of the wedding, but how was I ever to get the yard ready in time?

A few days before the wedding, I was feeling rather desperate. The sun was supposed to be out for a few hours before another thunderstorm was expected. As I was kneeling in mud trying to pull a few obvious weeds, a tree branch brushed caressingly across my shoulder like the soft touch of a tender hand and in the quiet breeze I heard the hushed whisper of Sara's gentle voice from the past saying: "Donna, it's all an illusion. The details don't matter."

And, again, I knew she was right. I looked around and saw that not only had the weeds flourished in the constant downpours, so had the flowers; they were luxurious. The plants and what grass remained green looked emerald and sparkled in the sunlight. The illusion of my yard was a place of peace and tranquility. Once my daughter walked into view in her elegant snow-white dress, with the glow of love in her eyes, no one would notice the weeds or the brown spots in the grass. This outdoor setting was just a fragrant backdrop for an unforgettable event. That's all people would remember, not the details of unfinished gardening.

The wedding was perfect. Well, not perfect, but a perfect illusion of a fairy tale wedding in a magical place. Sara's words of advice to me from many years ago will never again be forgotten. I will always remember as I move through the remaining events of my life: "It's all an illusion. The details don't matter."

~Donna Milligan Meadows

35

Cheer Leader

If I had to sum up Friendship in one word,
it would be Comfort.
~Terri Guillemets

The skies were overcast and the sun wasn't even trying to break through. I stood on the steps of Vancouver General Hospital staring at the cold gray exterior, daunted by the size of the building and all the sadness contained in it. Clutching a bouquet of flowers in one hand and a novel in the other, I tried to get past my dislike for hospitals and focus on the task at hand.

My friend Terri and I were both visiting Vancouver, but for vastly different reasons. I was reconnecting with family and friends, and she was in the hospital for tests.

I slowly walked in, feeling helpless and anxious. I got Terri's room number at the information desk and headed for the elevators. As the doors closed I was conscious, not only of our different purposes in the big city, but of the different paths our lives had taken. I'd been blessed with a pretty normal life. Terri, on the other hand, had a particularly tough life. Sometimes I'd look at her and wonder how she had the stamina to survive. In her early 40s, she had already raised two sons when she took on the care of her two preteen nieces when their mother was murdered. Both girls came with a lot of baggage and the younger seemed to be suffering from fetal alcohol syndrome. Caring for them was a stress-filled full-time job.

Terri also has epilepsy and was having increasing problems with seizures. Everyday activities that most of us take for granted carried the threat of a blackout or a seizure. Naturally she could no longer drive a car and had to take the bus everywhere. During meetings at our church we left the fluorescent lights turned off because their flickering could bring on a seizure. Terri signed up for a computer course at the local college but had to quit because she collapsed twice and had to be rushed to the hospital.

Her doctor decided enough was enough and sent her to Vancouver for extensive tests. She was given a private room and was to be bedridden for an indefinite period of time, electrodes implanted in her skull watching for even the slightest change in brain activity. The doctors wanted to know exactly what stimuli would bring on her seizures. I was hoping my surprise visit might cheer her up a bit.

It was with great trepidation that I followed the nurse into Terri's room. I don't like hospitals, even when I'm a mere visitor, and I always get nervous wondering what I will talk about. Besides, this was a person who was having several seizures a day. Maybe my sudden presence would bring on something catastrophic. Maybe a surprise visit was really stupid.

Terri was laying in bed, in the semi-darkness, eyes closed. "Terri, you have a visitor," the nurse whispered.

As her eyes focused, a big smile greeted me. "Lydia! Wow. I can't believe it. Come and sit down. You don't have to worry about touching me," she said laughing. "You won't get electrocuted or anything!"

As I took a chair she quipped about the dozen wires protruding from her head. "What do you think of my new hairdo? It's pretty wild, ay? I thought it was about time I had a change of hairstyle, but this wasn't really what I had in mind."

I laughed with her but it looked kind of painful to me. "Do they hurt?" I asked.

"No. There's a bit of discomfort now and then, but nothing that bothers me. See that TV screen up there? That's most of the TV I get to watch each day. It shows you my brain activity."

I looked at the TV suspended from the ceiling and watched lines and waves and blips floating along the screen.

"Pretty boring stuff, isn't it? Not what most people would want to watch hour after hour. Let me tell you, I had no idea my brain was so inactive. But it does get exciting when I have a seizure. Then bells ring and the nurse comes running in. If that happens, don't panic and don't leave unless they tell you to. Things will calm down in a minute or two."

I was still staring at the screen. "Are they finding what they're looking for?" I asked.

"Nah. We're all hoping I'm going to have a big one, but it hasn't happened yet. Life is too quiet in here. I keep telling them it's related to stress, and what kind of stress do I have here? No responsibilities, no kids, no husband, no telephone, no noise, no dog driving me nuts. I need action to bring on a big one!"

I spent the next half hour with her. We talked about kids and husbands, church and schools, small town drivers and big city traffic. We talked about the challenges of her life and her hopes for the future.

She was looking pretty happy when I left.

And she'd sure cheered me up.

~Lydia A. Calder

36

Throw Away the Key

Locks keep out only the honest.
~Jewish Proverb

My godparents Bel and Max met in England during World War II. They became mess hall friends for nutrition's sake: Max liked only meat and Bel liked only vegetables. They began their relationship by swapping foods from their mess trays. Soon they were sharing other parts of their lives.

When they moved into a rickety old house in Berkeley, California, Max carried Bel across the threshold. Then he said, "Hand me your house key."

She did, and he took both their keys and threw them out into the yard.

"I want to live in a home that's open to whoever needs it," he declared.

And so they did. Their home was never locked. Friends wandered in and out, stopping for dinner, taking a cold chicken leg from the refrigerator or curling up in an easy chair for a quiet read. Supper time was always a mish mash of opinions and people: the Kurdish student and the Israeli dissident, the Dallas lawyer and the manufacturer's rep from Denver, the rabbi without a congregation from Brooklyn and the priest with the small church in Santa Fe.

Still, Bel had grown up in Chicago and knew well the value of locked doors.

The unlocked house both exhilarated and terrified her. Sometimes she would lie awake in bed, expecting what her mother would have called "the worst." Robbery, rape and death raced through her mind. And all because her *meshuggeneh* husband refused to lock the doors.

One Friday night, well past midnight, Bel heard a door open. She heard footsteps and then stumbling. Her hands turned icy and she clutched the covers. She wanted to scream, but her voice dried up in her throat. Then she wanted to be quiet, so the robber would take what he wanted and leave. Downstairs, the furniture scraped and a drawer opened. She nudged Max, but he didn't wake up. She pushed the covers into her mouth so she wouldn't cry out. Then she heard the squeak of the screen door and the closing of the outer door. She shook Max's shoulder. "Max, someone was just downstairs. I think we've been robbed."

"Are we all right?" Max asked sleepily.

"Yes," Bel said.

"Then let's go back to sleep. We'll assess the damage in the morning."

The next morning, Bel could hardly bear to go downstairs. She took one cautious glance at the living room and saw only its familiar rumpled sofas and stack of papers beside the easy chair. The kitchen drawers were all intact; the refrigerator still stocked with leftovers. The Friday night candlesticks were still on the dining room table, her grandmother's sterling was still in the sideboard. Only one thing was out of place: a fresh loaf of challah bread rested on a doily in the center of the dining room table.

"Max, did you buy that challah?"

Max shook his head.

As they settled at the table and drank their morning coffee, Bel said, "Max, we have to lock the house. Something bad could happen to us."

"Or, something good," Max said, as he bit into a piece of fresh buttered bread.

~Deborah Shouse

37

Breakfast with a Friend

No life is so hard that you can't make it easier by the way you take it.
~Ellen Glasgow

"Good morning." I answered my business line at work.

"Good morning!" came the male voice on the other end. "What do you want to eat this morning?"

The caring voice on the other end was a pleasant surprise. We shared a common interest and problem that neither of us could share with anyone else we knew. There was peace and safety in the early morning question.

Thinking of foods I loved but could no longer enjoy, I responded, "I wish I could have pancakes with lots of butter and syrup."

Feeling tearful over the loss of the sweet pleasure of eating, my mind settled into my new pattern of sadness. The eighty-two-year-old man on the other end of the line interrupted my pity party. "Go get your carrot juice and we'll have breakfast together on the phone."

Running to the refrigerator, I grabbed the all too familiar light blue plastic cup, now permanently stained orange. "Okay, Bill, I've got it."

"Alright," he said from another state, two hours away. "Let's enjoy those pancakes."

Drinking my carrots and celery, I pictured him drinking his juice on the other end of the phone. It was the brightest moment in my dismal mealtime ritual and I was so grateful he'd called to encourage me.

The conversation only lasted a couple of minutes, ending with his signature, "I've gotta go take care of business." His thoughtfulness made me feel like I had my own angel helping me.

A prostate cancer survivor, Bill was remarkable. In his eighties, he still worked from 6:30 in the morning until after 5:00 PM on his lumberyard six days a week, while managing to single-handedly keep up with the other businesses he owned.

The first time I met him I knew he was special. Within moments of meeting me, he asked not about how I could help him and his business, but about my goals and purpose in life. Discovering that I, too, was on an all-juice diet due to medical reasons spurred him to give me juicing recipes and advice.

After being told his cancer was incurable and he would die soon, Bill researched alternative medicines and began juicing every meal every day. The only meal he did not juice was Thanksgiving dinner. I could not fathom going years without a piece of food touching my lips. Yet his resolve encouraged me and drove me.

After his initial early morning phone call, which took me by surprise, I began to relish hearing his morning greeting. Soon I was asking him what he would like to have for breakfast. His response was usually "Coffee, bacon, ham and gravy."

We were two unlikely candidates to become friends—he reminded me of Colonel Sanders and I was a frail twenty-year-old. But the universal prospect of sickness, death, and recovery spanned the generations and miles.

Within weeks I was no longer dreading the various forms of juice that needed to be consumed, thanks to Bill taking time from his busy schedule to encourage a young girl in need. Years later whenever I would pull out my dusty juicer, I would remember Bill's kindness to this near stranger, and would remind myself that being positive amidst the trials of life can propel a person higher than the most advanced medicine.

Some people speak of taking lemons and turning them into lemonade. Only Bill spoke of carrots and celery as if they were country-fried steak. With Bill's positive attitude, even radishes and cabbage can taste like warm brownies with hot fudge and ice cream.

~Erin Fuentes

38

She Altered My Attitude

Attitude is a little thing that makes a big difference.
~Winston Churchill

My ninety-year-old grandmother rested quietly in her hospital bed after a visit from her heart surgeon. He explained that she needed a quadruple bypass and she clung to the only good news he delivered: she had the body of a seventy-year-old.

Grandma's vanity required that she still dye her hair and the brown curls framed her porcelain face, her warm eyes, and her thin-lipped smile as she asked, "What would you do?"

My grandfather had died nearly thirty years earlier and Grandma had independently made decisions ever since. I knew she'd made up her mind before she'd even asked, but she liked me to feel included in her life especially after my mother passed away.

"I'd have the surgery," I said.

She nodded and then softly said, "I don't want to go home and wait to die. Besides, I'll be fine."

She was right. A few days later, a post-op nurse allowed me to visit Grandma in the recovery room after her surgery, a rather unusual privilege in hindsight. I was relieved Grandma had survived the operation but had been strangely confident that she would. Surprisingly, she lay naked and unconscious on the gurney, not yet cleaned up or bandaged. She had yellow iodine smeared all over her upper body between her elongated breasts and I was impressed that her enormous incision was stitched together as perfectly as any seam she'd ever sewn.

The sight of her chest rising and falling was comforting, but if Grandma had been awake she would have been embarrassed for me to see her naked. I held her hand and pondered the point at which my body would look like her medically speaking "seventy-year-old" one and worried that given my stressful job, it would be by the time I was forty instead of ninety.

About a year after my Grandma's successful surgery, my partner Ann and I invited her to our house for barbecued ribs. It was one of her favorite meals. I thought she'd enjoy a diversion from the usual mashed potatoes and gravy fare served daily at her assisted living apartment.

That particular Thursday night, both Ann and I got stuck at work. We got home only minutes before Grandma arrived, which killed any hope of serving her normal early dinner. I bought some time by offering to show her my nearby office while Ann got dinner going.

I helped Grandma carefully lower herself into my sports car and then I drove the short distance to my company's headquarters. She almost gasped as I turned down the tree-lined driveway that framed the roadway to the front of the building. Her face was full of wonder, like it always was, and her bright eyes took in everything around her.

"It's so beautiful," she said. "It looks like a park."

I'd never really thought of the grounds that way. My mind was usually distracted by the latest project delay or staff crisis. I drove to the private driveway at the back of the building and used my security card to enter the underground garage. The automatic door slowly opened and I parked my car in my assigned spot and started her tour.

Grandma was impressed with everything: the pristine underground garage, the sheer number of cubicles that stretched as far as the eye could see, the variety of logo-wear for sale at the company store, and the smell of food wafting from the full-service dining room.

As we stepped into the cafeteria I asked, "Given your diabetes, should we grab something here to hold you over until we get home?"

She looked at the herbed chicken dinner, the salad, soup, and sandwich bars and said, "I don't want to spoil my appetite, but do they serve such extravagant meals every night?"

Again, through her eyes I'd taken the quality and convenience of our cafeteria for granted, but the aromas made me want to head home for our own dinner.

"Just one more stop on the tour, Grandma. I want to show you where I sit."

We walked to my office and we both plopped down in chairs around my small conference table. She stroked the mahogany and said, "This is really nice." Then she pointed across my office to the chair behind my desk and asked, "Who sits there?"

Grandmother had always gotten a glazed look on her face whenever I explained what I did for a living, but it seemed she thought I worked at the conference table while "my boss" sat in the big chair behind the desk. Knowing she had been impressed with even that, I giggled as I said, "Well, Grandma... I do... this entire office is mine. I usually sit there at the computer and use this table for meetings with my staff."

Her eyes flashed with astonishment and she looked around my office with a new appreciation. Her response struck me. She'd attended teacher's college—or normal school as she called it—but when she got pregnant with my father she gave up her career. The opportunities for women had expanded far beyond those available to my grandmother: teacher, nurse, secretary, or homemaker.

She went over and sat down in my desk chair. She spun the chair around and then, one by one, she stared at the photographs of Canyonlands, Zion, and Yosemite National Parks that I'd taken while on vacations.

I pointed to one picture on the wall entitled "Attitude." It had a rainbow stretched above a roaring mountain stream and William James' words embossed at the bottom.

"I bought it with your Christmas money last year."

She looked at the picture, drew in a deep breath and then read the words out loud, "The greatest discovery of any generation is that a human being can alter his life by altering his attitudes."

She said, "I like all your pictures, but I think that one's my favorite."

"Me too, Grandma. Are you ready to go home and eat?"

She nodded. As we left my office she stopped outside the door and looked back. She gestured towards my nameplate and said, "I didn't notice that when we walked in."

She touched the letters of my last name... of her last name... and then she looped her arm through mine, patted my wrist, and said, "You've certainly done very well for yourself. I'm so proud of you."

When we got back to my house, Grandma patiently waited for us to serve dinner. It was almost eight when we finally sat down for our meal. Grandma attempted to eat her plate of ribs, but the pork was tough as bricks. When she finished eating what she could, she wiped her mouth with her napkin and unwittingly summed up her philosophy of life: "That barbecue sauce sure was tasty!"

My employer's headquarters, my office, and even my job never looked as wonderful as they did, that day, through my grandmother's eyes—her glistening grey eyes that always sparkled with possibility and only lingered on the good, especially when she looked at me.

~Kris Flaa

Thank You, Mr. Flagman

It isn't our position but our disposition which makes us happy.
~Author Unknown

T he long line of rush hour traffic snaked its way down the rain-slick street as I glanced nervously at my watch. 5:30! It was the third time this week I'd been late picking up the children, and the babysitter would be unhappy. Well, she'd just have to be unhappy, I told myself. My being late couldn't be helped. Nothing had gone right all day, from the dead battery in the car this morning to the secretary's absence throwing the whole office out of kilter. This traffic jam seemed the perfect ending to a horrible day.

All I wanted was to get home and collapse in a tubful of hot, soapy water and enjoy some peace and quiet. But I knew the kids would be clamoring for supper the minute we walked in the door, and I'd left the house in such a mess this morning that I really needed to do something about it before my husband got home. Then after supper there'd be dishes to wash and tomorrow's lunches to pack and a load of laundry that really shouldn't be put off another day. After that, all I'd feel like doing was falling into bed, just like every other night.

I sighed loudly, though there was no one to hear. Lately my life seemed nothing more than a never-ending cycle of chores, work, and sleep, with nothing to break the monotony but weekends filled with more chores. Surely there was more to living than this. I guess I was simply too busy and too tired to look for it.

And then I saw him.

The lone flagman was standing, barely visible but for his blaze orange vest, in the middle of the street, patiently directing four lanes of traffic as they merged into one. But there was something unusual about this flagman, and as I edged my car forward waiting my turn to pass, I realized what it was.

Standing in the midst of dozens of impatient motorists, soaked to the skin and getting more drenched with every icy mud puddle splashed on him, he was smiling. And at every driver that passed, he not only smiled, he waved. Not many waved back, but some did. A lot of them smiled.

As I sat waiting my turn in my warm, dry car, I began to feel ashamed. If this man, who did nothing all day but watch one car after another go by, could stand in the cold rain hour after monotonous hour and still have a friendly gesture for every single person who passed, what right did I have to complain about my life? I thought again about what lay ahead of me tonight—a snug house, plenty of good food needing only to be prepared and, most of all, a caring husband and children who I loved more than anything in the world.

And tomorrow? Tomorrow I had the opportunity to use my skills and intelligence to perform useful, important work. What kind of life did I have? An absolutely wonderful one.

It was finally my turn to pass the flagman. As if on cue, we waved at each other.

"Thank you," I mouthed through the window. He smiled and nodded and I drove on, spirits lifted, attitude changed. And in the rearview mirror I could see him, raising his hand in greeting to every car that passed.

~Jennie Ivey

40

A Shining Star in the Midst of Darkness

If I could reach up and hold a star for every time you've made me smile,
the entire evening sky would be in the palm of my hand.
~Author Unknown

There are certain things that occur in our lifetime that are forever etched in our memories, and we can recall them as vividly as if they happened yesterday. May 29, 2009 is the date that I replay over and over in my mind because it was the day that we were told that my beloved niece, Cassy, was terminal and that her time remaining with us was limited.

"Three months at best," they said, and they would be dedicating their efforts to "keeping her comfortable" and "pain-free." I remember looking over at my sister, Cathy, and watching her face as the devastating news settled in and our fourteen-month journey suddenly veered off to an unwanted destination.

Cassy was diagnosed with Ewing Sarcoma, a form of bone cancer, when she was just eleven years old and she handled every surgery, treatment, and medical procedure with grace, bravery and a positive attitude that touched everyone who knew her. The roller coaster that our family rode during this time was exactly that, with highs and lows that kept us reeling with emotions that are hard to describe. There were many lessons learned as we tried to cope with the numerous doctor's appointments and hospital stays, while trying to maintain some level of normalcy within our lives. Cassy and our family worked very hard to keep this monster disease at bay, and no one would ever deny our tenacity and dedication to this cause.

When we were faced with the daunting task of telling Cassy the terrible news, we sat as a family and explained to her that treatments were being discontinued, and we were going to focus on helping her attain any wishes that she might have over the next several months.

Once again, we were amazed by Cassy's positive attitude and her acceptance of this unfair fate. She made a "list" of things that she wanted to do and places she wanted to go and our family set out on the mission of working through her wishes.

Her requests were so typical of a teenager that they made us smile when we read them. They were things that people take for granted, and yet they were incredibly important to Cassy.

She wanted to go to high school for a day, get a tattoo, get her belly button pierced, learn to drive, go on a trip with her family, go to her eighth-grade graduation (even though she was only in seventh grade), go to Prince Edward Island, and have a thirteenth birthday party with a Hawaiian luau theme. Well, over the next six weeks, Cassy did most of the things on her list… and we have lots of pictures that chronicle this last chapter in her life. It was a very special time for all of us, and we are thankful for those memories.

Cassy turned thirteen on July 8, 2009 and I remember struggling with what to buy her for her birthday and wondered… what do you buy a young girl who is not going to be with us very long? I decided to "name a star" in Cassy's name and I took the documentation up to the hospital on her birthday. Cassy was thrilled with the thought of having this special star named in her honour. She had lots of questions about where it was and how we would be able to find it. She found some solace in knowing we would have an ongoing connection with her, and we in turn, found some sense of peace in having this special symbol of our beloved angel.

When Cassy took a turn for the worse four days later, the family traveled to the hospital in the middle of the night to pay vigil with her as she made the difficult transition from this world to the next. My thoughts that evening drifted back to the night when she was born thirteen years earlier and I was called to the hospital to help coach my sister through the birth. I was the first one to hold her when she entered this world, and now I was watching her take her last breath.

It can be difficult to look back at Cassy's challenging journey, and think that there could be anything positive about it, but despite the heartaches and tears, there were definitely some life lessons learned. Our family learned the true value of friendship, community support and the love of family. We learned not to take the small the things in life for granted, and that perhaps we should all be a bit more spontaneous. We learned that you can influence people and leave an imprint on their heart, even if you are only here for a short while, and that memories provide us with the ongoing strength to keep going even when we don't feel like it.

Today we continue to cope with the loss of our precious Cassy, but we know her spirit is strong and her presence is felt daily through the subtle messages that she sends our way. We look up to the heavens and smile when we see the sparkling stars that have become our symbol of faith and hope.

She was and always will be our "shining star in the midst of darkness."

~Debbie Roloson

Think Positive

Counting Your Blessings

*The hardest arithmetic to master
is that which enables us to count our blessings.*

~Eric Hoffer

41

Counting Our Blessings

Why not learn to enjoy the little things — there are so many of them.
~Author Unknown

"We're not getting a paycheck this week."

I wasn't particularly alarmed by my husband's words. After all, he had gone without a salary in the past, and we had always made do. Mentally, I congratulated ourselves that we had no debt outside the mortgage on our home.

With two partners, my husband owned a small engineering firm. When times were tight, he and his partners went without paychecks, making certain their employees were paid. I was grateful to be married to such an honorable man.

Two weeks passed, then four, then six, all with no salary in sight. The bills arrived with depressing regularity, though, and we lived off our savings, a spotty food storage, and faith in the Lord.

The fall of 2008 marked an economic downturn for the entire country. Caught in the spiral, clients who had always paid on time in the past now failed to pay their bills.

Christmas approached and I wondered how we would find the means to buy even small presents. I didn't mention this to my husband, knowing he had worry enough on his mind. I searched bargain bins and put my creativity to work.

In the meantime, I joined freecycle.com, an international organization devoted to preventing more items from ending up in already overburdened landfills. As a freecycle member, I could post items online that I no longer needed or wanted and other members could respond. In the same way, I could answer others' posts if I saw something I needed.

Four weeks into our doing without a salary, I noticed two messages listing pantry items. I e-mailed back immediately, saying that my family could really use the food.

In freecycle, the first person to answer a listing is usually the one who receives it. When I noticed the time the listings were posted, my heart sank. Several hours had passed.

Surely the items had already been taken.

To my surprise and delight, both freecyclers e-mailed me, saying that the food was mine. They gave me their addresses, and we arranged a pick-up time.

I went through the boxes of food like a child opening presents on Christmas morning. Cans of vegetables. Potato flakes. A cake mix. Even fresh fruit. My husband, teenage daughter (the only child remaining at home), and I feasted that night!

A quick friendship developed between an older lady and myself. She gave me other foodstuffs when she had more than she needed. I drove her to various stores and did errands for her, as she was unable to drive. We sent each other inspirational messages and discovered we had much in common, including a deep faith in our Creator.

My membership in freecycle encouraged me to clean out clothes, books, and household goods that we no longer used. As I uncluttered my house, I felt as though I were also uncluttering my soul, ridding it of old grudges, resentments, and fears.

I wrote our four adult children, explaining our situation.

I also mentioned that we would be cutting back on Christmas presents that year and suggested they do the same. As a gentle hint, I told them that the best present they could give their father and me was to get out of debt.

In previous years, I had kept a gratitude journal. Every day I had recorded things, both large and small, for which I was grateful. As frequently happens with good habits, this one slipped away in the busy-ness of life. I revived it, listing five things every night as I wrote in my journal.

Small occurrences found their way into my gratitude journal. A shiny penny found during a walk. A letter from a friend. An unexpected phone call from a long-distance relative. A hug from my usually standoffish teenage daughter. The feeling of sunshine on my face.

Everyday things became a cause for rejoicing. When was the last time I had been thankful for a washing machine and dryer?

When had I last given thanks for friends who listened to my complaints without sharing their own? (Shamed, I resolved to mend that nasty habit.) When had I last thanked God for a strong body, even though it wasn't in the shape or condition I desired?

My priorities began to shift. I stopped thinking of what I didn't have and began to think more of what I did. At the same time, I looked around and realized that others were suffering as well. I took time to send notes to friends and church members who needed an extra dose of love. I prayed more and complained less. I counted my blessings.

Our financial situation hadn't changed, but my attitude had.

Nearly eight weeks had passed since my husband had received a paycheck and Christmas was upon us. I had managed to buy and make modest presents for family and friends. I refused to give in to the temptation to apologize for the humbleness of the gifts, knowing those who loved me would understand and accept my offerings.

One evening my husband returned home, a wide grin stretching across his face. "Money came in the mail." He went on to explain that one of his customers, also a victim of the slow economy, had sent a long overdue check.

We had gone nearly two months without a paycheck. Not only had we survived, we had thrived.

I took stock of our lives: we had friends, family, and faith. We were rich indeed.

~Jane McBride Choate

Getting Old Gratefully

To be interested in the changing seasons
is a happier state of mind than to be hopelessly in love with spring.
~George Santayana

When I turned sixty-eight, old age seemed to have arrived. Seventy loomed close, and felt especially ominous, as my mother died at seventy-two. My husband Tom, ever the optimist, reminded me that my father lived to be ninety-four—also, that I'm a lot more active and health-conscious than my mother was. After all, we stretch every morning before a breakfast of steel-cut oatmeal, take our vitamins and supplements, get plenty of exercise, and have meaningful days. Mine are filled with gardening and writing, Tom's with singing, playing keyboard and trumpet.

Still, sometimes it takes two of us to come up with an acquaintance's name, or the title of a movie we saw just yesterday! Once I could garden nonstop for six hours, but now I need a break after two hours. Then there are those startling moments when I turn the corner in a store to face an unexpected mirror. Who is that old person in the glass?

It's no accident that the three light bulbs above the mirror in my bathroom are now fifteen watts. I like that soft glow. Besides, without my reading glasses I can't see the wrinkles, although it does seem that my eyes are shrinking. Is it time for an eyelift? In a heartbeat, dread of surgery overcomes vanity. Then I think to myself that I've simply got to find a way to accept old age with all its changes. I'm making the last years of my life miserable with worry!

When I started to worry about aging, I decided to get some help from my friends in the Golden Years Gardening Group. We meet once a month to talk about our gardens and anything else on our minds. We're all women over sixty with a common love for plants. I proposed that our next meeting topic be "The Positive Aspects of Aging."

I worried that no one would show up. Why on earth had I suggested this topic? It might be too serious, too fraught with anxiety. So what a relief that most everyone showed up.

Gail Austin started the Golden Years Gardening Group a year after her husband Ken died. She wanted more time to spend with friends, to enjoy life—to work less and play more. As she began simplifying her large, high-maintenance garden, Gail realized that many older gardeners were struggling with a similar process and could use a support group to help them accept life's changing circumstances. We would share the adventure of letting go of stressful work and learn to enjoy less complicated gardens.

That afternoon Gail suggested we go around the room and give each person her turn to speak about the benefits of aging, without any interruptions. She began with a key statement.

"I don't worry about the little things anymore," Gail said. "Forty was the beginning."

This theme—the perspective we gain after experiencing many of life's changes over time—came up repeatedly. Hazel, a recent member, put a similar idea in her own words.

"Resilience," she said. "Life experience has given me that." There was a moment of quiet in the room as we all absorbed the importance of Hazel's wisdom. By now, some of us were nodding our heads in agreement, smiling in recognition of this big advantage of growing old.

Next, Lisa announced another common thread.

"My grandchild," she said. "I understand now why my grandmother meant a lot to me. I understand the love she was giving to me and can transmit it to my granddaughter." Some of Lisa's grandmother's love came in the form of discipline. Now Lisa practices that same tough love with her granddaughter, helping her set boundaries.

Jepi added another layer to the topic of family connections.

"I have a new relationship with my dad, who's eighty-nine," she said. "He became a gardener in his late seventies." Now they share that passion and spend time together in the garden. Her dad is slow, but that's just fine. What's important is that they're growing closer.

Dru reminded us about the importance of a positive attitude.

"I'm a 'cup is half full' kind of person, not a 'cup is half empty,' and I'm lucky for that," she said.

Ann echoed Dru's affirmation, adding more details.

"The cup is full, a new day is always wonderful. I feel appreciation to be here," she said. Ann practices gratitude each evening, reviewing the gifts of the day before she goes to sleep.

Diane reminded us about financial independence.

"I feel lucky to have retirement income," she said. "Now it's fun to get up at 6 AM!"

Renee piggybacked on that idea:

"I finally have my independence," she said. "I get to decide what I want to do."

By this time, I was feeling pretty good about growing old. I hadn't prepared what I'd say, but when my turn came I knew just what it was. Without any rehearsing, I blurted it out.

"I'm so happy to have found love late in life," I said. "I met Tom when I was fifty-eight years old, and we married five years later. After twenty-three years of being divorced, falling in love with a wonderful man was a great gift of older age."

I put my arm around Diana, who sat next to me in the circle of friends. We'd been gardening friends for many years, way before Golden Gardeners had been formed.

"Diana here was my role model—she encouraged me not to give up, to keep searching until I found the right man," I said.

Diana smiled and explained to the group that it took her five marriages before she found a lasting love. Both of us married younger men who would have been out of the picture when we were in our twenties—actually they would have been in high school! As we get older, ten years difference in age doesn't matter.

I thought more about how getting older helps us love more deeply. Tom is there for me when I'm sick, just as much as when I'm healthy. A natural-born comedian, he keeps me laughing every day, the best tonic I know. When I was younger, I never would have considered a short, bald man who'd been married and divorced three times. But when I met Tom, all I could see was his beautiful smile, warm blue eyes, and loving heart. I gave him extra credit for continuing to marry; I'd met so many men who'd become embittered after even one divorce. Tom's hopefulness gave me courage to marry again.

Our group had helped me more than I'd imagined. Not only were my worries about growing older quieting down—I was actually thrilled to be in this stage of life, now that I saw the big picture. Best of all, our circle had grown closer after sharing these intimate details of our lives. I looked around at my friends with greater understanding, respect and love. How wonderful to be part of this gathering of wise women, all of us lending strength to each other on such an interesting journey.

~Barbara Blossom Ashmun

Cancel the Pity Party

It's not the years in your life that count, it's the life in your years.
~Abraham Lincoln

I wasn't looking forward to my fifty-seventh birthday. The angst I felt when I turned the milestone birthdays of thirty, forty and fifty was nothing compared to the dread of the fifty-seventh.

Twenty-three years earlier, my mother had died at age fifty-seven of ALS—Lou Gehrig's disease. The shock of reaching the same age as my mother when she died hit me with the force of a locomotive crashing into my psyche. I could hardly believe mother was only fifty-seven when she died.

I wondered how many more years I had.

As a single parent, my four children had been out on their own for years, living in California, Arizona, and two of them eighty and one hundred miles away from my home in Wisconsin. I'd broken up with my last boyfriend ten years earlier, so there was no man around to orchestrate my birthday. I did spend the first half of the day with my daughter Julia and her three youngsters who had driven the hundred miles from their home in Dane, Wisconsin. This normally would have redeemed the day, but Julia was in the middle of an exhausting divorce and took a four-hour nap after lunch. Stress and tension seemed to ooze out of her pores and by the time they left I, too, was exhausted.

Alone again, I walked into my house and began a grand pity party. Did I do anything constructive or fun to pull myself out of the doldrums? Of course not. The pity party rules demand that you make yourself as miserable as possible.

No presents. No cake. The cards from my relatives and friends had all come in the mail a couple days earlier. My oldest daughter in California hadn't called. As in previous years, she thought my birthday was on the fourteenth instead of the twelfth.

My pity party continued, complete with tears and a bit of anger. I simply wished that those twenty-four hours would end quickly. I even started talking aloud to God, "Okay God, I'm a nice, happy, fun, pleasant person. I have lots of friends, great kids, wonderful relatives. Some of them must remember that it's my birthday. So why am I alone tonight? I do stuff for other people on their birthdays. Is there something you want me to learn from this dismal experience?"

In a last-ditch effort to find something productive to do that evening, I gathered the trash and took it out to the garage. On my way back into the house I spotted my old bicycle in the corner. My boyfriend had given it to me for Christmas twelve years earlier. I never really liked that bike. It didn't fit me right and the gears slipped like crazy in spite of a tune-up. I kicked the back tire and said, "You're about as worthless as I feel. I wish I had a new bike."

"That's it!" I practically shouted. "I'm going to buy myself a birthday present. A new bicycle! I'll go shopping for it Monday morning."

I'd wanted a new bicycle for three years, but when a single mom is in her sixteenth year of having kids in college without a break, one does not consider extravagant purchases for oneself. But my black mood pushed me over the edge of self-indulgence.

Having made the decision, I practically skipped into the house, feeling thirty years younger and filled with the anticipation of a brand new bicycle. I was a kid again, dreaming of a sleek new lightweight bike with shock absorbers and a comfortable seat.

That night, before bedtime, I was paging through the book of Psalms, trying to find a good definition of happiness. I found it in Psalms 144:12-15.

Sons vigorous and tall as growing plants.

Daughters of graceful beauty like the pillars of a palace wall.
Barns full to the brim with crops of every kind.
Sheep by the thousands out in our fields.
Oxen loaded down with produce.
No enemy attacking the walls, but peace everywhere.
No crime in our streets.
Yes, happy are those whose God is Jehovah.

The verse described my sons, my daughters, and my life perfectly. I was healthy, had plenty to eat, no enemies attacking my walls, no crime in my streets, and I had a wonderful friend in the Lord. This birthday was just another day. Most definitely, all was right in my world.

Monday morning dawned and my new bicycle excitement hadn't waned a bit. I drove to the bike shop and rode a sleek silver and white lightweight aluminum-framed beauty around the store. I felt as excited as I was at age seven when I got my first bike fifty years earlier. This dream-bike was even on sale because it was the fall season. I pulled out my checkbook and paid in full.

Since then, whenever I feel a little pity party coming on, I hop on my 21-speed beauty with the shock absorbers and a spring-loaded seat for extra comfort and head for the forty-nine-mile-long bike trail that is just two miles from my new home in Florida. An hour later, with another ten or twelve miles under my belt, my sunny disposition has returned. I've learned that when you're a big kid, every day can be a birthday celebration. Especially when you have a good bicycle with a nice soft seat waiting to take you away.

~Patricia Lorenz

Shiny Nickels

I don't think of all the misery but of the beauty that still remains.
~Anne Frank

She had no business being so cheerful. All over the country people were out of work, losing homes, and being pushed into social services or the streets. Young people in the college classes I taught were cynical and apathetic. Why study hard when there'd be no jobs? Was I teaching skills and work ethics that might be meaningless? Was I encouraging false hope?

Yet each day in the front row forty-five-year-old Betty smiled eagerly. She was a big woman draped in shapeless sweatshirts and baggy jeans, her gray hair hung straight to her shoulders, and she shuffled with the painful effort of someone with arthritis. How could she compete in today's dog-eat-dog job market? If anyone should be sour, it was Betty. But her homework was always done thoroughly, and she waited for class to begin like a horse fidgeting at the starting gate.

It wasn't just that she earned straight A's, jumped into every discussion, and did extra research. She accepted no cynicism or apathy. One time we discussed a story about a man who freed a bird from a zoo hunter's live trap so it could rejoin its mate that hovered in the sky overhead. Betty sighed, "I'm glad somebody does things like that. It's beautiful!"

A young man scoffed. "What's one bird more or less? It would've lived longer in captivity. Besides, they'll just catch another one. Do you know how much money people make capturing rare birds?"

Betty smiled. "That's true. But what counts is the moment when the birds meet again in the sky. Picture that and forget the rest. It doesn't matter if hunters catch another one, if the birds die, or if the world explodes. You have to live for those shining moments or why live? Life is full of loss and death. That's not news. You young people think the world is falling apart, but it's not. I know what real disaster is. My husband died last year. My daughter has kidney disease. We have no health insurance or income." The young man's face reddened. Betty smiled. "No, don't feel bad. How could you know? It's all right. Just because bad stuff happens doesn't make life bad. It should teach us to love what's good now. Don't wait for money and success to light up your life. You've got to grab the little shiny moments that come to all of us while they're here."

Yes, I thought. That's what I ought to be telling my students — and myself.

A week later I saw someone bending deep into a trash bin in the student union. It was common these days for homeless men to comb the college trash for beverage cans redeemable for five cents each. But when this person straightened up with two cans, it was Betty. I hesitated to greet her. Being caught raiding the trash by her professor might be embarrassing. Heck, it embarrassed me. As I tried to slip by, she noticed me, and her face brightened. "Professor!"

"Hello."

"I collect cans between classes. It's my bus fare! It's amazing what people throw away, even in times like this." She dropped the cans into a bag. "Actually, it's wonderful. I come to college each day with an empty purse. Not a cent sometimes! But I always find enough cans for bus fare and sometimes lunch too. They're waiting for me every day."

"Suppose you can't find enough?"

She laughed and shrugged. "I could hike home if I had to, I guess. But they just keep coming. What a person needs is usually there if you search hard." I told her that if she ever fell short, to stop by my office. She smiled. "See? Now I have bus fare insurance!"

I drew her aside from the streaming crowd. "You know, what

you said in class last week really hit those young people hard. They've been writing about it. You made them see things differently. Me too," I admitted.

"I'm glad. Maybe even suffering can do some good."

"I'm so sorry about your husband."

"Oh, I won't lie. For a long time I was broken without him. Broken in pieces. And it's been horrible trying to survive. He died two months before qualifying for his pension and of course the health insurance expired when we needed it most. I'm lucky I still have him to hang onto."

"What do you mean?"

She smiled. "I love him so much, just like always. Every night I think about how we'd lie in bed and read and talk, sometimes until 3 AM. We owned a rickety old house, but we had dreams. Oh, such shiny dreams! You can't ever take that away from a person who wants to hold onto it. I'm alone in an apartment now, but we're still in love and married. It's just that he's dead. We'll meet again someday, just like the birds in the story."

"What will you do about your daughter?"

"The doctor says her kidneys might last another five years. I'd give her one of mine, but we don't match. We'll just have to see what happens. I can't control what fate brings. I can only control how I respond to it. So why choose misery? Isn't it wonderful enough just to have lived? To have felt and seen and tasted life? Bill and I made sure our daughter did that. She won't die without having lived."

I suggested several agencies that might help with her daughter's medical bills. "Oh, I know them," she said. "We're working on that. And here I am at my age starting college to get a decent job!" She laughed. "Bill would love that! Those young people don't think jobs are out there. But you can find one if you look hard and aren't afraid to get dirty. There's a job out there that I'll find." She shook her bag so the cans rattled. "These aren't garbage. They're not recyclable aluminum. They're shiny nickels."

~Garrett Bauman

Power Out

My riches consist not in the extent of my possessions,
but in the fewness of my wants.
~J. Brotherton

I awoke to a silent chill. In my cottage, no clocks blinked, no refrigerator hummed. In this rural Oregon coast area, power pauses are frequent: a minute, an hour, sometimes three. Then, eventually there's that cascade of welcome sound—buzz, blink, hum and whirr—as radio, refrigerator, clock, computer, TV, heater and answering machine snap back to life.

I've made it through numerous power failures. No light, no heat, no sound—all that I can handle. But I can't function without morning coffee. I could have built a fire on the stone patio outside my back door and heated water. But it was pouring rain. I could have hiked up the hill to my neighbor's, to see if Jenn had coffee perking on her camp stove. But wind whipped through tree branches. At least the phone was working.

I telephoned my boss. "It's going to be a long time before the lines are repaired," she said. "Hunker down. Work's cancelled. There's emergency food and shelter in town at the Methodist Church." Groping in the dim morning light, I excavated a lantern and my down sleeping bag from the back of my closet. I set the lantern on the kitchen counter, reread the instructions, struck a match and lit the mantle.

Blessings to Coleman for inventing this marvel. The metal top heated quickly. Maybe coffee was possible after all. But what balances on a conical lantern lid? I attempted to heat water by balancing a thick-bottomed saucepan, then discovered a tomato sauce can from my recycling bin worked best. After rinsing and filling the can with clean water, I put on potholder mitts and steadied the tin with two plastic chopsticks. Soon a mini-cup of instant coffee steamed fragrantly. Four tins later, I'd enjoyed a jolt of caffeine and even had a half-cup of hot water for a spit bath. I relished the simple pleasure of a warm washrag on my face. It would ready me to cope with the powerless day.

I put on an old feather parka and sheepskin booties. Gathering several books from my bedside stand, I zipped up the parka, tied the hood tight and crawled into my sleeping bag. I adjusted the lantern and snuggled in to read. Descriptive passages from *Under the Tuscan Sun* transported me to sunny Cortona with Frances Mayes while outside my window the thermometer read thirty-four degrees. Poorly insulated, my old cottage was chilly and damp. Turning pages, my fingertips grew numb. I wiggled out of my down bag to search for wool gloves. I was mentally listing friends with wood stoves, yet I relished the thought of some solitude. Then my neighbor Jenn drove up. "I'm going to my boyfriend's," she said, poking her head inside my door.

"That's seventy miles and mud slides along the road." I was concerned.

"Lucky man has power. Lucky me. You're welcome to stay in my house, use the wood stove, except I'm out of wood. Keep company with my Lab and kitty. They'll keep you warm."

Walking back toward her vehicle, she added, "Oh, there's brandy left from the party. Help yourself to anything." My vision of a warm wood stove was about to become a reality.

I assumed there would be no problem finding wood. We live in a forest. Branches and twigs litter the ground. I scoured the yard, gullies and roadside, but found only water-soaked wood. Chopping branches kept me sweating for hours.

That night the temperature plummeted to well below freezing

With a barely smoldering fire, I needed multiple layers of clothing and three sleeping bags to keep me warm. The cat and dog curled up with me. We survived. The next day was much like the first: hunting for wood, chopping branches, feeding the fire torn cardboard and scrunched up newspapers—anything to get the wet wood to burn. Outside the window, fir trees thrashed in the wind. While I watched the storm, the aroma of spicy lentil soup simmering on the stove wafted in the air.

On the third morning without electricity, I was desperate for dry wood that could fit into the stove without hours of chopping. I walked back to my cottage and hunted in closets, in cupboards and under the bed for wooden objects to burn. I scanned the walls, shelves and tables. In desperation I grabbed the engraved plaques from Toastmasters, the wooden clock my ex-husband had made, a redwood jewelry box, garage sale picture frames waiting for family photos, knickknack shelves that needed glue.

At first, it seemed like a crime to burn my teakwood tongs and salad bowls, but I rarely used them. Torching Grandma's rolling pin struck me as taboo, but it was moldy and missing one handle. I wrestled with the idea of burning my walnut bookshelf. No way! Instead, I stacked wet branches on Jenn's porch, getting them out of the rain, then sawed them into stove lengths and brought them in to dry near the fire. Who knew how long the power would be out?

I'd always intended to purge my cottage. Now, desperation pushed me past intention into action. For each wooden item, I quizzed myself: "Do I love this? Do I need this?" Soon objects were heaped by the door: the driftwood lamp, the myrtle wood bread-box, the dilapidated three-legged plant stand. As I whacked each item apart with a hammer, I began to feel a sense of inner strength. I hauled the wooden pieces up to Jenn's house. After I shoved the forlorn keepsakes and family artifacts into the wood stove, I realized the power outage had filled me with intent and courage—a ritual release of my past.

While the crackling fire in the stove cranked out heat, I peeled off parka, sweater and turtleneck, rocked in an overstuffed easy chair and sipped apricot brandy, while snuggling with the pets. A pot of Swiss fondue bubbled on the stove and my cup steamed with hot coffee. Looking around, I appreciated Jenn's simple décor and reflected on how her energetic spirit seemed rarely weighted down. I picked up my pen and wrote Jenn a thank-you poem and decided that next Christmas I'd tell her boyfriend to buy her a mini chain saw.

Having to survive without electricity for eighty-four hours I developed a new appreciation for light, heat and an electric stove. I was also grateful for the experience. I'd burned relics that had cluttered my life. Thanks to the blackout, to Jenn, and to fire, the great purifier, I felt empowered and warm all over. My possessions were fewer, my blessings greater.

~Shinan Barclay

One Hundred Blessings

If you count all your assets, you always show a profit.
~Robert Quillen

One day, while I was going through tough times, I read a book that challenged me to stop feeling sorry for myself and instead, list one hundred blessings in my life. Since I was wallowing in my dark mood it seemed like an impossible task. But as soon as I began to randomly write down the positive things in my life, I was amazed how quickly one hundred blessings spilled onto the page. Soon my furrowed brow disappeared and I began to smile.

Afterwards, when I read though my long list of blessings I realized... I could easily add a hundred more.

Life is good.

100 Blessings

1. Being alive
2. Being healthy
3. Being able to exercise
4. Being an American
5. Having enough money
6. Husband Jim
7. Married for 47 years
8. Daughter Betsy

9. Daughter Lori
10. Son Steve
11. Grandchild Rachel
12. Grandchild Adam
13. Grandchild Kyle
14. Grandchild Sarah
15. Grandchild Emma
16. Grandchild Amy
17. Grandchild Anna
18. Grandchild Ava
19. Grandchild Andrew
20. Son-in-law Geoff
21. Son-in-law Matt
22. Daughter-in-law Stephanie
23. Writers
24. Writing group
25. Writing talent
26. *Chicken Soup for the Soul* books
27. Editors publishing me
28. Beautiful home
29. Courtyard
30. Decorating talent
31. Waterfront view
32. Dolphin encounters
33. Little boat
34. My car
35. Music
36. Flowers
37. Good food
38. Sale of farm
39. Memories
40. Computer
41. Cousin Lyz
42. Clothes
43. Parties

44. Good books
45. Backrubs
46. Holidays
47. Good teeth
48. Shopping bargains
49. Laughter
50. Hanging out with my kids
51. My kitchen
52. My laundry room
53. Antiques
54. Christmas trees
55. Freedom
56. Mild climate
57. Coconut palms
58. Healing
59. Travel
60. Kindness from others
61. Stimulating conversations
62. Walks in the neighborhood
63. Sunrises and sunsets
64. Birds at birdfeeder
65. Deck
66. Comfortable bed
67. Antique bedstead
68. Fireplace
69. Education
70. Retired from teaching
71. Interesting TV
72. Peaceful beach
73. Good tenants in our rentals
74. Family adventures
75. Church
76. Safety from harm
77. Comfort
78. Quiet neighborhood

79. New job in retirement
80. Beauty of nature
81. Precious moments
82. Glad I lived this long
83. Special friendships
84. Free time
85. Gardening
86. People who respond to me
87. A good doctor
88. A future
89. Smiles from others
90. Forgiveness
91. Praise
92. A teaching career
93. No major disasters in life
94. Free of cancer
95. A good night's sleep
96. Relationship with God/Christ
97. Two Bible studies
98. Electricity
99. Air conditioning
100. That I have 100 things to be grateful for

~Miriam Hill

47

Life Is Not an Emergency

The cyclone derives its powers from a calm center. So does a person.
~Norman Vincent Peale

I was privileged to be at an event with both Mark Victor Hansen and Jack Canfield. Jack was speaking when suddenly a cry came from the crowd indicating that one of the attendees needed medical attention. A handful of medically trained attendees emerged from the crowd and went right to work attending to the lady who needed their help. Jack quieted the audience and asked that we direct our thoughts to healing the person. A quiet calm came over the audience. There was a feeling in the room of such compassion and stillness that it made an indelible mark upon my memory that I would carry with me always.

I remember thinking how the serenity of the room was in stark contrast to the busy hospital where I worked the night shift and where calls for help were often so stressful. In that moment, at the conference, I made a mental note that "life is not an emergency." I decided that when an emergent situation in my life arose, I would meet it with the same peacefulness that I felt in the conference. Little did I know that a few weeks later I would put that lesson to the test.

It was a Saturday that started out like any other Saturday, filled with the activities of a busy family. Ken filled his morning in typical fashion, working at our rental properties to ensure that our tenants were well taken care of. His to-do list could have been completed within a few hours except that he loved to spend time with each family, catching up on their activities and listening to the adventures of their children.

We met up in the afternoon at a family birthday party. Then we returned home where Ken worked on our own projects, including painting our bathroom. When we realized that it had been quiet overhead for a while, I went upstairs to find Ken slumped over on the floor and barely breathing.

My own first aid training kicked in and as I called for help, I remembered the moment at the conference when a similar call for help was made and the incredible feeling of calm that accompanied it. Those feelings of peaceful calm washed over me.

At the hospital, after many tests, we learned that my forty-four-year-old sweetheart had suffered a severe stroke. We began to form a plan for this unexpected new chapter in our lives. I realized that our lives would never be the same.

I'm not sure most people would view their most difficult and tragic times as miraculous, but that is how we chose to view our circumstance. We determined that we were being given a great test, one that as a family we would need to endure together, and as we lived through the test we knew that we were experiencing a true miracle.

Five long months and many sleepless nights later, after rejecting the suggestion that Ken should live out his life in a nursing home, he finally returned home. This once strong, independent man had to rely on us for his every need. My kids were stellar in attending to their dad as he struggled to do even the most basic things for himself.

He received therapy for a short while until it was determined that he had come as far as he would ever come and would not get any better.

The last day of therapy was the day I bought Ken watercolor paints and brought him home to our own brand of therapy. Though we aren't trained in physical therapy, we worked Ken's muscles and his mind. Each family member shared in the responsibility of providing Ken with the attention and stimulation he needed to improve.

The greatest ingredients in home-style therapy have been patience, creativity, and lots of love.

Over the course of the past few years, Ken has made monumental progress. He can walk using a cane when he was once wheelchair-bound. Where he was virtually blind in one eye, he now can see. He can say about thirty whole words, with "I love you, forever" and "thank you" at the top of his list. He can sing the songs that have been the soundtrack in our lives together. He gives us hope that we can do anything we set our minds to doing. His determination teaches us never to quit. Ken's courage inspires us to better our lives and to reach for impossible goals. We don't take even a single breath for granted. He is our own living miracle.

Our lives have been so richly blessed in the midst of this most difficult time. Our family has received such strength as friends and family have supported us and cheered us on. Though we wouldn't wish this on anyone, we can see that in the moments of deepest despair we have been given the comfort of peace. In the dark nights of doubt we have been given the light of optimism. We have come through the storm with a calm that I learned to draw upon in a moment when I learned a most valuable lesson, that "life is not an emergency."

~Debbi Stumpf

48

Death Star

If the skies fall, one may hope to catch larks.
~Francis Rabelais

The Ides of March is layoff notice day. As a teacher and the teachers' union representative, it is a day I dread. It is the day the victims get their notice. The meetings are brief and wretched. It is hard to shake the gloom.

After the painful meeting, I rounded a corner to return to my classroom and bumped into a former student's father. His daughter had been in my class the previous year. Three months earlier, he had been shot by a gang member—a fourteen-year-old who had been in my fifth grade class. A boy who had written to me twice from prison, most recently that Friday. It was jarring to see the man stand a foot in front of me and know that at home I had two letters from the student who had shot him.

What do you say to someone who's been shot? I opened with, "So, I heard you had some troubles."

The man lifted his draped black jacket and showed a bandaged shoulder, "Got shot, lucky to be here."

"What did you get hit with… a 22, a 38?"

"25 caliber."

"Good luck. Got to go."

I left and shook my head in disbelief. It was turning out to be a dark and very strange day. Layoff notices, I get a letter from a teenage shooter and then I see the victim. What else would go wrong?

I later ate lunch off campus with a fellow teacher and when we crossed the road a car screeched to a stop. Someone lowered the passenger window and a face beamed at me. "Hey, Mr. Karrer. I got it. I got it two weeks ago!"

The boy in the car, Zavier, was my former student. He'd been on dialysis for most of his twelve years, slept at death's door, and had lucked out finally getting a kidney transplant two weeks ago. His mom, the driver, said, "Show him."

Zavier opened the door, climbed out, and lifted up his shirt.

A nasty, six-inch horizontal scar started near his belly button, then made a vertical ninety degree upward turn for another six inches.

"Best scar I've ever seen," I said.

His mom, still sitting in the driver's seat, held up a huge plastic container filled with prescription drugs. "He needs thirty pills a day for the rest of his life."

The boy stepped closer and gave me a hug. He beamed and I couldn't help but notice his red cheeks and healthy skin. Last year he held his head low, his skin was gun-barrel blue, and he grimaced most of the day.

He stepped back in the car. "You got a second chance kiddo," I said.

"Same exact thing I told him," his mom said. "We didn't think he'd make it past last year and now he's twelve."

"Yeah and remember I almost killed him too."

We were all quiet for a second. THAT had been scary.

• • •

Last year, in the teachers' lounge, a fellow teacher had asked, "Mr. Karrer, would you like some star fruit for your kids?"

She smiled and sliced pieces of fruit one-tenth of an inch thick and tossed them into a huge green, plastic container.

"Sure. Where are they from? So I can tell the kids."

"Taiwan."

"Okay." Taiwan?

I gave a piece to each kid but the supposed Taiwanese origin bugged me. I booted up the computer to Google star fruit.

"Star Fruit—Carambola

Originally from Sri Lanka... blah blah blah...

IMPORTANT NOTE:

Star fruit causes several symptoms in patients with chronic renal failure or end-stage renal disease. The symptoms include insomnia, intractable hiccups, agitation, muscle weakness, confusion, consciousness disturbances of various degrees, seizures, and cardio-respiratory arrest. Because no effective treatment is currently available, patients must be warned not to ingest star fruit, even in small amounts."

I stared at Zavier Mendoza. Renal failure meant failing kidneys. I stood and looked at Zavier. He caught me, smiled and licked his fingers.

"Zavier." I tried to remain calm, "Where... is your star fruit?"

He smiled and pointed at his stomach. I turned pale.

"Zavier. You and I need to go to the office, now!"

We made it to the office. He sat and I shut the door behind him. I cornered a secretary. "Get the principal ASAP."

Long and short of it, we called Stanford—the kidney center where Zavier went every single week—and they said they didn't know about star fruit, but watch the kid like a hawk, and they'd call back in a minute. In less than one minute Stanford called back. "You taught us something today. Star fruit can kill him. We have a helicopter on the ready. Keep an eye on the kid. We're in the air if he starts hiccupping. Can we land in the school ground if we need to?"

Zavier Mendoza never hiccupped. The helicopter never needed to come. He was fine. He came to school the next day with a big, fat grin on his mug. But I didn't sleep too well. Apparently there are different kinds of star fruit. That had been a year ago.

•••

Zavier put on his seatbelt and looked at me. "Mr. Karrer? You know when we went up to the office last year cuz of the fruit? I never seen you run so fast. Even when we did laps."

I shook my head. "Well, promise me no more star fruit for you — EVER!"

"Duh... Mr. Karrer. Duh.... Cuz YOU might get a heart attack and you'll need the chopper to Stanford."

We all laughed. They waved and I did the same.

Some terrible days can end very, very well.

~Paul H. Karrer

49

From Nuisance to Blessing

A dog is one of the remaining reasons why
some people can be persuaded to go for a walk.
~O.A. Battista

From the first, I thought of him privately as Natty the Nuisance. My husband had picked up the puppy as a freebie from the Flour Mill, a local feed and hardware store where people bring unwanted litters. He'd been advertised as a Great Pyrenees mix, but he looked more like a Heinz 57 to me.

"Look, isn't he a lively one?"

Ken set the black ball of fur on the floor and our usually aloof adult female Akita bounded over to nuzzle him. She immediately flopped on the floor and rolled over on her back so that he could pounce on her belly and gnaw on her ankle.

"I just know this mutt will be a great companion for her," Ken said. "She's been lonely."

I just stared at the rollicking seven-week-old pup. That's just what I needed... another creature to pick up after, and a shaggy one, too. What a nuisance!

Besides the dogs, three cats also shared our house. I liked animals in theory, but Ken had been ailing for years, so feeding, grooming, walking and cleaning up after all of them fell on me.

I muttered through the weeks of mopping up messes until Natty was housebroken. I grumbled until he finally learned to lap water out of a bowl without tipping it over. He sensed I was not his fondest fan, and spent most of his time curled up in Ken's lap. When he got too big for that, he settled for resting his nose on Ken's knee as my ailing husband idled away his days watching reruns of *Gunsmoke* and *Cheyenne*. Whenever I walked into the living room, Natty would cast me a mournful glance, and then bound over to Ken's recliner to snag some petting.

The only time Natty ever came near me was when I ran a comb through our Akita's coat or cuddled a cat. Then he'd scamper over and nose my hand away from the other pet. If I ignored him and continued to groom or caress, he'd whine and whimper, and then poke my hand again, harder. A total nuisance, I'd say to myself, the world's biggest pest.

"I've never seen an animal that craved so much attention," I'd complain.

"Oh, he's just a puppy," Ken would say. "He'll outgrow it."

But he never did. Then last spring my husband died. In the days that followed, Natty's neediness quadrupled. He'd avoided me before, but now he wouldn't let me out of his sight. He'd track me from room to room, and if I settled down to read or to work on the computer, he'd immediately sidle up and start nudging my arm.

I felt sorry for him. Ken had been his constant companion. I know dogs mourn loss just as we humans do. Nonetheless, I didn't appreciate the annoying interruptions. I wondered vaguely if I should find another home for him, one where he could get all the attention he hungered for... maybe a family with children to play with. I had my Akita as a guard dog, so I couldn't figure out what purpose Natty really served.

Nearing his sixth birthday, which should be middle age for a dog of his size, Natty suddenly seemed to be sliding into an early senescence. I noticed that he spent most of his time in the backyard just lazing on the grass, watching the birds and occasionally barking as a truck passed the house. Where he used to shoot back and forth from the patio to the apple tree, now, if he even bothered to get up, he'd plod slowly across the lawn.

Kind of like me, I thought. But I'm well into my seventies and this dog was far too young to have severe arthritis as I do.

When I took Natty in for his annual checkup and shots, the vet didn't pull punches.

"No arthritis. He's pretty healthy. But he's overweight, and should lose around twenty-five pounds. I know it's hard, but see if you can walk him more."

I sighed. I needed to lose twenty-five pounds, too. I'd packed on weight during my husband's decline. In grief, I'd comforted myself with creamy casseroles and carrot cake. And though I lived on a country loop frequented by walkers, joggers and bikers, I found endless excuses to avoid walking that mile-long course myself. It was too hot. It was too cold. I was too tired. I was too old.

Twice daily I'd been taking the leashed Akita for a brief stroll up and down in front of my property, with Natty trotting along beside us. But I hadn't walked the mutt around the loop since his puppyhood.

The next morning I dragged out Natty's old leash. While I snapped it onto his collar he thudded his tail against the front door. At least one of us was excited. I put on my jacket and mittens and the two of us set out.

To my surprise, Natty confidently lead the way, keeping a steady pace, not stopping to sniff at every twig the way his Akita sister does. He marched ahead, tugging me in his wake, not even pausing when neighbor dogs scrambled to the front of their owner's property to growl their territorial rights.

To my surprise, I enjoyed breathing in the scent of lilacs on the fresh spring air, feeling my heart beat a little faster from the mild exercise, even running my fingers through Natty's coarse fur when I reached down to pat him in approval when he heeled rather than strained to chase a passing car.

The next day we did it again. Then again. Soon we settled into a routine. If I grow too engrossed in catching up on my e-mail correspondence, around 10 AM Natty will be at my side, shoving his snout under my arm. Or if I become too distracted by household chores, he'll plant himself by the front door and rumble until I remember it's time for our walk.

Nowadays I see Natty as a blessing rather than a nuisance. Though the Akita remains my bodyguard, my elegant and diligent protector, scruffy Natty has become my personal untrained therapy dog. Together we're striding into shape.

He's nudged me into a new lease on life.

~Terri Elders

Living in Barbie's Dream House

The man who has no inner-life is a slave to his surroundings.
~Henri Frederic Amiel

Years before treading the murky waters of our dismal American economy, my husband and I challenged ourselves to seek the positive side of a simplified lifestyle. With eyes wide open we made a conscious choice to live within our means rather than kill ourselves living beyond them. Simplifying in many ways means doing without. For us the bottom line translates to a positive outcome though I must admit, it's not all sunshine and rainbows.

The house we've lived in for the past twenty years is a pretty good example of real estate with no bells or whistles. Most people refer to it as quaint, but frankly I've seen phone booths with more square footage than our living room. One or two things out of place in this small house and all of a sudden it looks as if I haven't done any housework since the Reagan Administration.

If you're trying to picture our humble abode, it's not exactly Barbie's Dream House. It's probably the same size, but I imagine Barbie has better plumbing. We don't let it bother us. I'm confident it's only through the Grace of God that we enjoy indoor plumbing in the first place. So what if it's not possible to take a shower and run the dishwasher at the same time without risking a scalded appendage or two? Maybe the guy who invented paper plates suffered from the same problem, and look what it did for him!

Our "Graceland" was built 140 years ago on ground originally used to stable horses. About 141 years ago the horses left town, and I know why. The draft that blows through our living room in the winter could knock a Clydesdale off its feet. I'm the only person I know who dresses according to the wind chill factor—in the living room. As you might have guessed, I've amassed quite an extensive sweater collection, and there are days when I wear them all at the same time. If it's cold enough outside, I end up looking like the Michelin Man. But, it beats having to work sixty hours a week just to afford the mortgage payment on one of those houses with the newfangled, double-paned, insulated, energy-friendly windows I keep hearing about.

Over the past twenty years we have discovered what makes a house comfortable and it has nothing to do with acreage, inground pools, or multi-car garages. We have none of the above, unless you count the moat around the sump pump as an inground pool of water. Yet, people often remark about the cozy and inviting atmosphere that flourishes here. A home is comfortable and inviting when the occupants are relaxed and content. It's just that simple.

We don't watch our DVDs on a TV the size of a roadside billboard. Of course, we don't have a room large enough to accommodate one of those things anyway, but we do sit down together every night and relish each other's company over a home-cooked meal. Neither one of us is ever in a rush to get out the door to a second job.

On Sundays we savor a pot of coffee and the Sunday paper. We read it all afternoon if the mood strikes us. Well, the truth be told, it is a bit of a squeeze finding a spot on our downsized coffee table for the coffee pot and that big fat newspaper, especially if the idea of bagels and cream cheese enters the picture. Somehow we juggle things and make do.

We make no pretense of striving for the good life. We enjoy the good life every day. Free from the financial burden of keeping up with everyone else allows us time for laughter and fun. I imagine it's not easy to relax by the pool when you are robbing Peter to pay the pool man.

The price paid in time alone (not to mention stress and aggravation) to support state-of-the-art home theaters, flashy cars, and overpriced real estate, along with countless other so-called amenities is staggering. Without a doubt it quells the occasional twinge of envy I have over the luxuries of others. Our luxury is having no worries about how to pay for big-ticket toys.

We spend a great deal of time at home, cramped quarters, drafty rooms and all. I don't mind a bit when we are snuggled together on the couch under a cozy afghan enjoying an old movie, or out on the side porch sipping iced tea and basking in the beauty of a summer sunset.

Oh, we occasionally grumble about how grand it would be if we could take a shower and run the dishwasher at the same time, but we get over it.

Especially when we consider that at the close of last year we made our final mortgage payment on this little house, many years in advance of the scheduled payoff date. I'm positive we were not expecting this outcome when we made our decision to live a simplified life. It just turned out to be one of the perks.

~Annmarie B. Tait

51

Pressed, Stressed and Blessed

There are no menial jobs, only menial attitudes.
~William J. Bennett, The Book of Virtues

I once saw a bumper sticker that read, "Too blessed to be stressed." I snorted, "Yeah, right. It's more like 'too stressed to be blessed.'" I was fifty-eight and heading to a job interview that paid a whopping eight dollars an hour and involved some lifting, mail sorting and conveyor work. I had planned to be semi-retired by this time, living off the benefits of a lovely investment—one that had unexpectedly gone south along with our economy. I had to give up health insurance and my body was beginning to tell me things I did not want to hear. I wallowed in my own pity party, remembering nostalgically how I once co-owned an export business that paid well, afforded me good vacations, international travel and a primo health insurance policy.

My body protested loudly for the first couple of months on the job and I was known to spit out an occasional expletive under my breath when a fifty-pound bag of mail got the best of me. I was determined to show the owner that this "old broad" could perform. I did everything and anything, usually before I was asked. This behavior sparked the "youngsters" on board to up their performance levels and the operations of the plant actually improved. My rah-rah attitude and outward appearance of boundless energy came at a price. I came home exhausted, whining and moaning for Bengay. My husband would disappear when he heard my car in the driveway. But eventually a transformation took place. My quads and biceps toned up and those flabby thingies on the backs of my upper arms disappeared. I lost weight and my back toughened up once I taught myself how to bend at the knees. And that blessed, sweaty little job not only helped pay bills but brought me at least two life-changing opportunities simply from chatting with clients who came by to drop off their orders.

The first was a writing contract that I landed from one of the clients who hired us to print and mail her marketing brochures. I noticed the text was a bit weak and unappealing from my point of view. I decided to approach her when she came by. After admiring her artwork I gulped down my fear and offered her a couple of suggestions to make the text "pop" a bit. She looked at me and asked, "What do you do here?" I stammered, "Well, I work here part-time doing this and that, but I also write." She gave me what I thought was an odd look and left. She must have thought I was an idiot, a presumptuous one at best. I was immediately immersed in self-doubt wondering if I had overstepped my bounds. Would I be fired? About a month later she came back in to talk to me personally. She told me she was impressed with my ideas and asked if I would consider doing some independent work helping with the text of her website and her bio. And I could work from my computer at home. Wow! I was being paid to write something and my hourly rate just tripled. Was it my imagination or did my body suddenly feel more energized and less tired?

The second opportunity came from the owner herself. Noting how much I took on and the way I worked with some of the clients, she nominated me to join an organization called Women of the Year in our community. She added, "It's a year-long commitment and you will meet some wonderful people." She was right. I did meet a woman who told me about a national organization called eWomen Network. I thought the initial fee a bit pricey, but within the first year I had ten new clients. It was at one of these eWomen Network monthly events that I spoke to the featured speaker, LeAnn Thieman, a wonderful, vibrant woman who was a nurse earlier in her career but is now a professional writer and public speaker. She also co-authors books for Chicken Soup for the Soul. "I love those books!" I gushed. I asked her if anyone could submit a story. She in turn asked me, "Do you have a story?" I responded yes and she told me how to go online and find instructions for making a submission. To my surprise and joy, my story was later accepted and published. Who would have thought that my personal experience with hot flashes would become a story that someone else might find interesting enough to publish?

Eventually, I quit my job sorting mail and lifting bags. The owner offered me a fifty-pound mailbag when I left, joking, "Here, I don't want you to get out of shape." I grinned at her but declined. I did thank her for the opportunity of working for her. It had been a blessing in disguise.

Today, as I sit here typing, my fountain bubbling in the background, my legs pumping away at the portable pedal cycle (much better than the mailbag) beneath my desk, I am smiling. Hindsight is an amazing tool to rethink my abundant blessings and how they came to be. Yes, I admit I feel pressed at times about a deadline or finances. Yes, I sometimes allow myself to worry about something that, in the long term, is not worth the effort. And we all know that worrying puts deep creases into the face right between the eyes, something I definitely do not need. If I am going to have lines in my face let them be from smiling in joy and gratitude. My husband says those lines are kind of cute. Does he know what to say, or what? Oh yes, indeed, I am blessed — too blessed to be stressed.

~Linda L. Leary

Think Positive

Overcoming Adversity

*Man performs and engenders so much more
than he can or should have to bear.
That's how he finds that he can bear anything.*

~William Faulkner

52

From Fear to Joy

There is no hope unmingled with fear, and no fear unmingled with hope.
~Baruch Spinoza

Tears ran down my cheeks and into my ears as I lay on the exam table in the dimly lit room. My husband Patrick stood beside me squeezing my hand in support. The ultrasound tech gave us a sympathetic smile as she prepared my belly for the transducer. She placed a small amount of ultrasound jelly just below my navel and sat down on her stool to begin the scan. I looked at the ceiling and prepared to hear the worst. After experiencing a miscarriage a few months earlier I was worried it was happening again.

Ten years earlier, my three daughters had been killed by a drunk driver while driving with their father. After leaving his friend's house, the drunk driver turned onto the highway going the wrong way. He crashed head on into the car, driven by my ex-husband, carrying our four children. Katie, Miranda, and Jodi, ages eight, seven, and five, never made it to the hospital. My ex-husband died a few hours after he arrived at the hospital. Jodi's twin brother Shane survived the car wreck with a slight concussion and a broken leg.

Going from four lively children to one very quiet little boy was almost more than I could bear. Before the wreck my days were filled with gymnastics, piano, and baton twirling lessons, not to mention all the other chores of motherhood. Shane was an easygoing kid; once the visitors stopped coming and things settled down, the house was eerily quiet. To be honest, I didn't feel like a mother anymore.

I wavered back and forth about having more kids. Just when I thought I was ready, my sister-in-law's niece was killed in a car wreck. I was shook up and the whole thing unnerved me, enough that as we drove home from the funeral, I told my husband that I had changed my mind. I did not want to have more children. Unlike the labor pain that you forget once you hold your new baby, the pain experienced after the loss of a child continues to pierce the heart. I knew I could not take the chance of going through that again. We bought a little sports car and attempted to move on with our lives. I busied myself with my job at the local hospital and with Shane's activities. Though I tried to put the thought of another child out of my mind, the longing never quite went away.

Six years passed before we were finally ready to add to our family. Because of the tubal ligation I had after the twins were born, we needed to find a doctor who could perform a reversal, called a tubal reanastomosis. I didn't necessarily feel it was a coincidence, more like a nudge from God, when late one night I was watching television and saw the end of a surgical show on The Learning Channel. It was an outpatient tubal reanastomosis performed by a doctor in North Carolina. I frantically looked through the television guide for the next showing and set the VCR. Within six months we were sitting in his office for a pre-surgery interview. I was pregnant within a month. Unfortunately, our joy turned to sorrow when I miscarried a week later. After one more miscarriage, Landry joined our family. He was perfect in every way; his brown hair and brown eyes looked remarkably like his big sister Katie's. There were two more miscarriages before our son Kelley was born. When I peered into his clear blue eyes, I was reminded of Miranda.

Kelley was eighteen months old when I realized that I wanted a little girl. But I was torn—should I chance it one more time? At nearly thirty-eight, it was hard not to be concerned about risking another pregnancy. Again, I got pregnant but it resulted in another miscarriage; this one took its toll. I wondered if I could emotionally sustain another miscarriage. That is when I decided, just between me and God, if I was not pregnant by my thirty-eighth birthday I would be happy with the children I had.

Two weeks before my birthday, my mom and I were taking the kids for a visit to my sister's for the weekend. The morning that we were to leave, I took a pregnancy test out of the bathroom drawer, turning it over and over in my hands, I weighed the pros and cons of finding out my pregnancy status. Deciding not to ruin the weekend fun, I threw the test back in the drawer, slamming it shut. "It'll wait until I get back," I said to myself. I grabbed my purse and keys, put the kids in the car and off we went. By Sunday evening when we arrived home, my hopes were high. The next morning, I used the pregnancy test and confirmed my suspicions. The answer became apparent well before the minute was up. I left the stick on the counter, as was customary, to tell my husband that we were expecting. Knowing the pattern was two miscarriages for every full term pregnancy I remained cautiously optimistic.

One of the advantages to working in a hospital is the ultrasound techs. They like to practice their craft, and pregnant women like to see the life growing inside, it's an arrangement that is mutually beneficial. I was in the ultrasound room with my very pregnant friend who wanted to have her baby measured one more time before her due date. While the tech finished up with Bobbi, I asked, "Hey, can we look and see if we can find a heartbeat? I think I'm about five weeks along."

"Sure," she responded, "hop up on the table."

I pulled up my shirt and pushed the top of my pants down. I wanted to give her the clearance she needed to move the wand around and find the blinking light that would confirm for me that all was well. I stared at the screen; I could easily see the dark circle portraying the yolk sac that held the baby.

"There it is," she said.

I looked closely. Bobbi leaned in too. Then she pointed at a tiny, flickering lima bean. I was overjoyed. I knew that once a heartbeat is established the risk of miscarriage is less likely. I went back to the pharmacy and called my husband. "There's a heartbeat!"

Always more reserved, I could hear the hesitation in his voice. "That's great, let's hope this one sticks."

A few weeks later, I was in the mall shopping for maternity clothes and when I got home I discovered that I was spotting. Trying my best to be brave, I found Patrick working outside; I slid the door open and told him what was going on. We quickly dropped the boys off with my mother and rushed to the hospital. I tearfully answered the questions from the triage nurse and then the doctor. He used a Doppler to find the heartbeat and when we heard the whoosh, whoosh sound I felt a little better. But when the doctor tried to send me home without an ultrasound, I balked at the idea. "Please," I said, "I just need to know what is going on in there." He nodded and said he would call in the ultrasound technician.

So, there we were, waiting for the ultrasound tech to begin the scan. She swiped the transducer across my belly and my husband began to shout, "There's two, there's two, there's TWO BABIES!" Fresh tears begin to flow.

Our twin daughters arrived six months later: twenty fingers and twenty toes, two healthy babies.

~Brenda Dillon Carr

53

We Go On

Feed your faith and your fears will starve to death.
~Author Unknown

'm glad I found out in the summer. I wore sunglasses a lot and could cry without being noticed.

I would go on my daily walks.... and cry. Mow the lawn... and cry. And no one ever knew. Twelve years later they still don't know. Oh, I've broken down and told a few people. And have been sorry I did. No one can really help. They can't keep up the day-to-day care it takes to support someone who lives with AIDS that long. Especially when that someone looks perfectly normal.

When we found out, I thought I would be a widow in a year. His CD4 count was as low as it could go — zero. And his viral load so high! 880,000! I remember holding his hand tightly when the doctor told us the counts and seeing the rims of his eyes turn red with suppressed tears.

It was our twentieth anniversary. We were leaving for Jamaica in two days and I had to be tested before we left. I wouldn't get the results until we came back. It was a long ten days. The first time I ever went to an all-inclusive resort and lost weight! Food had no appeal or taste.

I went to the library before we left and checked out a book on the immune system and read it by the pool on our vacation. My husband slept a lot. I latched on to anything positive to tell him.

One day we were sitting by the pool and a little group of Jamaican singers was performing. They strolled up to us and sang "Don't worry. Be happy." The group leader was a tiny old man, his only tooth gold, and I stared into his eyes wondering if God was sending me a message through him that it would be okay.

When my test came back negative I told my husband that I would be able to put all my strength into fighting for him. We realized that his one-time exposure had happened fourteen and a half years prior. During that time we had had our only child! Thinking about it I began to clearly see God's protecting hand. If we had found out earlier we would have never had her. Unimaginable! If condoms hadn't been my chosen form of birth control (something I have since heard is unusual for married couples) I might have gotten it. We used to joke when we decided to have a baby that it took one try and I was pregnant!

Also, he didn't find out until the AIDS "cocktails" were developed, so he didn't have to go through the trials and errors with drugs that people in the 1980s did, who then built up resistance. The combination he started on almost immediately brought his viral load to undetectable and is slowly but steadily raising his CD4 count. And the doctor told him since he was only exposed one time and so early in the history of the disease, his infection was probably a more pure strain. Multiple partners pass on built-up resistance to various drugs. It can get very messy.

And somehow I knew immediately where to turn for information—not only on the disease and drugs, but natural healing and vitamins and herbs. He actually takes more vitamins and herbs than he does pills. And he gets fewer colds and illnesses than almost anyone we know!

So he's doing well twelve years later. But, of course it has changed him. It has changed us. I latch on to articles that say AIDS is becoming a chronic illness, but still feel sick to my stomach when I read, "AIDS, always fatal."

God got our attention all right!

For a long time he woke up in the middle of the night and he would go down to his keyboard and write music. Beautiful music.

Christian songs. He's in two praise bands and people come up to him after they hear one of his songs and tell him the words spoke to them: "show me Jesus Your sweet way, guide me through another day, walk beside me hold my hand, make me humble, help me stand..."

I got into a seven-year Bible study and almost immediately began to teach a couple of adult Sunday school classes. In one of my studies I read the verse Deuteronomy 8:3 "He humbled you, causing you to hunger and then feeding you with manna" (the word of God) and I realized with a jolt that's exactly what happened to me. I really do thirst for His word. I learn so much every day that not only helps me endure, but takes me beyond our situation. I listen hungrily to Christian radio programs. All of the programs about trials speak straight to me.

I've learned from the story of Jacob that there are consequences to actions and while God will almost never take the consequences away, He can turn them into a blessing because "all things work for the good of those who love Him."

I've learned that it glorifies God when we can praise Him in the midst of our trials. This is harder for me since most people don't know what I'm going through. It sets me apart from people somewhat, but makes me more dependent on God. I wonder maybe if He's setting me apart like the Israelites in the desert until I learn what He is teaching me.

I am learning to ask, "What does God want me to learn from this?"

It's not easy. You would think something like this would make you appreciate every minute. Not sweat the small stuff. It does for a while. But then you sort of get used to it.

I would say to my husband, "I'm so afraid that you will live to be ninety and look back and say I wish I had realized at age forty I wouldn't die young and not have worried so much."

All life is temporary.

So we go on.

~Jo Weinert

54

World Travel with Asperger's

*You gain strength, courage and confidence by every experience
in which you really stop to look fear in the face.*
~Eleanor Roosevelt

London, England, Late April 1998: My first full day in a
foreign country. It was the first of many Western European
countries I'd visit on my group tour. I ventured out a few
blocks from my hotel and came upon an Underground (subway) station that could take me virtually anywhere in the metropolitan area.
How I wanted to go to Parliament to watch the House of Commons
debate! I approached the Underground entrance, but then I suddenly
froze: the steps that most people would simply descend in order to
get from Point A to Point B were for me synonymous with being
confronted with a million things to juggle simultaneously.

A condition that I live with every day made it almost impossible for me to satisfy my desire. It's a neurobiological disorder called
Asperger's syndrome. Those who have this condition experience a
wide range of symptoms and behaviors, like taking in every little bit
of stimuli that their surroundings emanate. So when an environment
isn't familiar, it can be too overwhelming to handle, which is what I
was experiencing at that moment.

I struggle with my condition but I have learned to overcome it
in order to pursue my passion for world travel.

I went on that group tour thinking the itinerary would fill my time with all the sightseeing and exploring I could ever hope for, along with the security of traveling with others. I quickly discovered this wasn't the case. Free time for exploring on our own was often scheduled for the group. As a result of my condition, I restricted myself to exploring only those areas that were within walking distance of my hotel, which made me feel very cheated: London was beckoning and here I was clinging to sites around Hyde Park!

My first trip abroad progressed southward over the next few weeks all the way to Athens, Greece. My poor sense of direction, also inherent in my condition, almost got me into dire straits on more than one occasion. As with London, I was only blocks away from my hotels in the cities of Brussels, Belgium, and Innsbruck, Austria. Yet I found myself wandering aimlessly through the night in those two cities, asking myself how I would find my way back to the hotels where my tour group was staying. Only with the help of the police and/or very conspicuous landmarks did I manage to return to the hotels… eventually. On rare occasions, I would hang out with one or two people in the tour group during our free time to do some off-the-beaten-path exploring. I relied on them to get us where we needed to be, and thus my sense of inadequacy was only heightened.

When I got back to the USA, I knew that something was going to have to change. I knew deep down that my love for traveling and exploring was stronger than the handicaps of my condition. For almost a year and a half, the debacles of my first foreign trip would haunt me. By the autumn of 1999, I felt compelled to go back to London, vowing to travel independently on the subways and buses to all the parts of the great city no matter how scary that seemed, no matter how lost I would get.

I knew that for me to become the independent traveler that I wished in my soul to be, I would have to compensate for my natural shortcomings with two things. First, I would have to study extra hard the detailed maps provided by tourism departments and the Internet before embarking, using positive visualization of finding my way around. Second, once abroad, I needed to acquire the gumption to go up to complete strangers to ask them if I was on the right path to one of London's icons even if that meant doing so every other block along the way. This would keep my sense of direction in check. For many people with Asperger's syndrome, going up to the locals to interact is also a challenge, as we are not generally the most sociable folks in the population. The bottom line was that in order for my aspirations to be realized, I had to seize my Asperger's syndrome by the horns.

My friend from Virginia would accompany me for the first part of the trip. We'd be together, but I'd act like I was alone while trying to figure out how to get to a certain destination. He'd only interject if I began to take a wrong turn. This technique proved to be very effective. He headed back to the States a few days before me, but I survived being totally alone in the metropolis. Consequentially, I developed a new confidence in trekking the world independently.

A year later, in October of 2000, it was I who would play tour guide, so to speak, as I took another friend of mine all over London and its surrounding areas. Sometimes, my sense of direction resulted in some minor inconveniences for us, but I persevered. The end result was a trip full of sightseeing successes!

Since that first fateful trip abroad in '98, where I let my disability diminish my sense of adventure, I have taken even more trips to Western Europe, China, South Africa, and Panama, mostly on my own. I've secured hotel reservations, train and bus tickets, etc., all over the world. I've challenged myself even further via my journeys to Spain, Panama, and Italy. I had to be even more resourceful while visiting these countries, given that I am not fluent in Spanish or Italian. I got around fine with the aid of really detailed and user-friendly phrase books. The locals in those countries appreciated my attempts at using their language to communicate with them.

By 2004, I had enough travel experiences to feel confident in submitting travel articles to various publications. I've now had many of them published in various magazines and online sites for pay. Globe-trotting inspired me to confront my Asperger's syndrome in a way that I wouldn't have done otherwise, and ultimately led me to a new career as a travel writer.

When I look back at my initial reactions on that 1998 London trip, I am amazed at the changes and the consistencies. The difficulties remain, but now I know I can deal with them and I have a backlog of memories and techniques for dealing with my disability. I may still feel hesitant about putting myself into a situation where I'm unfamiliar with the environment and feeling overwhelmed with the sensory overload, but I also know I can control my reaction and draw on my past experiences to get through the moment in order to fulfill my desires.

The key to overcoming obstacles is having a desire that is stronger than the reality of the obstacles. It is that inner quest which will lead one to find ways of overcoming!

~Roy A. Barnes

55

Life View

Never, never, never give up.
~Winston Churchill

I t was Easter vacation and I was home from the university for ten glorious days. I knew how much my mother missed me while I was at school and I knew she was going to cook all of my favorite foods and spoil me rotten.

I was an art student and would graduate with my degree in two months and I had just been given a scholarship to attend a university in England for two years. I'd never been happier.

Friday night I stayed up late to watch a funny movie on TV with my mother and older brother and we laughed until our sides ached. It was good to be home again.

Saturday morning I woke up and couldn't see out of my right eye.

"Mom, something is wrong with my eye!" I said. I wasn't too scared because I thought it was a simple infection or allergic reaction to something.

My mother took me to an eye doctor and he took one look at my eye and ordered us to catch a plane to get to a hospital hundreds of miles away. He said he'd call ahead and make arrangements for a specialist to examine me. He wouldn't tell us what was wrong. My mother said maybe a sliver of glass or something had gotten into my eye and they'd have to remove the splinter and I'd be fine.

A few hours later, after five doctors had examined me, one of them told us the bad news.

"You have histoplasmosis. It's fungus, a disease that eats the blood vessels behind your retina. It's untreatable and incurable. You could be blind or dead in a week."

I started shaking from shock. My mother put her arms around me and I could feel her shaking too.

"My daughter is twenty-two years old. She's an artist. She can't go blind or die! I'll give her one or both of my eyes for a transplant," my mother said.

"They can't do eye transplants," the doctor said. "All we can do is some laser treatments to try to stop the bleeding in her retina."

I was rushed to the emergency room for a painful and prolonged procedure, one that I would have to endure fifteen more times. I was sick, in pain and had to remain in a completely dark room for seven days.

It seemed I was doomed to go blind or die.

I wouldn't graduate. I wouldn't go to England. I'd never paint again. My life was over.

My mother and I called my oldest brother, Aaron, from the hospital and told him the bad news.

His first words were, "Can I give you one of my eyes for a transplant?"

We told him they couldn't transplant eyes.

We called my middle brother, Shane, and told him.

"Can I give you one of my eyes?" he offered.

When we called my youngest brother, his immediate response was the same.

"Can I donate one of my eyes to save your sight?" he asked.

My mother and all three of my brothers, on hearing the news of my possible blindness, without hesitating, had offered to give me one of their own eyes and go through life with only half of their sight.

I'd always known my family loved me but I was overwhelmed.

"I guess I should drop out of the university here," I said, "and notify the university in England that I won't be coming."

"You still have one good eye and you're still breathing," my mother said. "Don't give up. Fight! It won't be easy for you—you'll have to find the courage to try harder than anyone else. You're an artist. I don't know what the future holds but you have to live every minute of every day. You can't give up, roll over and die the first time life knocks you to your knees!"

Ten days later, I returned to the university and graduated. I went to England and attended the University of Sussex and earned a Master's Degree.

My vision is permanently damaged. My disease is not cured, but it is in remission. It could flare up tomorrow and I could be blind or dead in a matter of days or I could go years without further damage to my sight.

Seven years have passed since the day I found out I had histoplasmosis. It was the worst day of my life. It was also the day my entire family offered to sacrifice half of their vision for me. It was the day I found courage I never knew I had and found my family's love for me had no limits. I found a dream was worth fighting for. I have less than half the vision of most people, but that doesn't mean I can't be an artist. It just means I'll have to try harder.

Since that day, I've painted hundreds of pictures. My paintings have won recognition and awards in dozens of art shows and exhibits. I have designed my own line of greeting cards.

At one art show, every one of my paintings sold, giving me an unexpected windfall of cash. "What should I do with the money?" I asked my mother.

"Use the money to go to Paris and see the paintings of the greatest artists in the world," she said.

I did. I stood in awe as I was surrounded by the beauty and genius of Van Gogh, Monet, Leonardo da Vinci and others. For me, it was a miracle.

I never take a single day for granted. Before this disease took half of my vision, I was an artist.

I'm still an artist.

~Spring Stafford

56

I Can Get Through This

We acquire the strength we have overcome.

~Ralph Waldo Emerson

Sprawled across the front seat of my car, I taste it. Blood. A mouthful of it. Suddenly, someone taps on my shattered driver-side window. "Miss, can you hear me?"

I try to respond, but I can't seem to make myself do so.

"No, no, don't move. We're coming in to get you."

I finally put it together that my Good Samaritan is a police officer, and that I've been involved in an accident. My rescuers are now trying to cut me out of the car, the rear of which is smashed into the front, rendering the doors inoperable and the backseat destroyed. "Wait," I cry, panicked. "Where are my sons?"

The officer appears confused, and that's when I remember: I'd been on my way to work and had just left my two young sons with our babysitter. Relief pours through me as I relate this now to the officer. "What a blessing," he says. "If they'd been in the backseat, they'd be gone."

His observation is sobering, and I panic anew.

"Hey now, you're okay, and so are your boys. You can get through this."

I nod, managing to thank him, even though my face feels so crooked I can barely speak. As I'm loaded into the ambulance, I notice that it's the kind of day to rejoice in, a beautiful blue Indian summer day with Thanksgiving a mere week away, and I offer my own tearful prayer of thanksgiving. I'm so grateful to be safe, and so much more, to know that my boys are safe.

What I can't know in that moment, however, is just how long my injuries will affect me. In the first years after the accident, I undergo extensive dental work, a bone graft to my fractured maxilla, and some sixteen root canals and implants to repair my damaged teeth. I begin suffering sometimes agonizing face, neck, and ear pain, and my mouth opening starts to decrease, making dental work hard to accomplish. It disrupts the "little" things too—eating, kissing, brushing and flossing, even talking. My oral surgeon suspects temporomandibular joint disorder in my jaw joints, and MRIs and a painful procedure called an arthrogram confirm his diagnosis.

The temporomandibular joint is that little unassuming bump in front of each ear that joins the lower jaw to the temporal bone of the skull. It's a complex joint in that it enables the mouth to move both up and down and from side to side. A normal mouth can open to forty-five millimeters; mine gets down to four at one point. My doctors try to stabilize things with splints and non-invasive "stretching" procedures, but finally, five years after the accident, my surgeon performs two open-joint surgeries, which, unfortunately, provide nominal relief. I continue to struggle with eating and a limited opening. Liquids and soft foods are all I can manage, and to "crank" my mouth open, my doctor tries an apparatus that resembles a hefty eyelash curler. But even this I can't accommodate, so he resorts to tongue depressors, forcing one flat stick into my mouth atop the other. This keeps the joints moving and breaks scar tissue, but the pain it causes nearly lifts me out of my chair. "One tongue depressor at a time, Theresa," he encourages me, wiping away my tears. "You can get through this."

I nod, conveying my thanks with my eyes.

Eighteen years after the accident, my jaw has deteriorated to such a point that the joint bones have fused, leaving virtually no movement. Heat pads, ice packs, and medication have become constant companions, and the pain often sends me to bed. It takes a toll on my work and family, and it's increasingly hard to think positive.

My doctor believes that the only thing left for me is total joint replacement, a very specialized undertaking. Of course, I worry. How pervasive will my scars be? With such a limited opening, can I even be intubated safely? But I have every confidence in my new surgeon. In a thirteen-plus-hour procedure, I am fitted with prosthetics made of titanium and screwed into bone. After surgery, my mouth is wired shut for three long months and I must learn to eat through syringes. I "shoot" Ensure and other liquids into the tight open space between my cheek and clamped teeth, dreaming of a day when I might chew.

When bandages are removed, I get a first good look at my face, and I tremble in awe when I see it. For so long, I'd feared this would end badly, but thanks to my surgeon's artist's hands, my scars, once healed, will be minimal and mostly hidden in my neck and hairline. One complication arises, however: I can't close my eyes. This is due to nerve damage, and it makes for a blurry, no-blinking world. By day, I can scarcely see, and by night, I tape my eyelids shut to sleep. With my mouth that can't open and my eyes that won't close, I feel trapped inside my body, wondering if I'll ever truly be "me." To rejuvenate the nerves, I use a daunting device that my husband lovingly calls "the stun gun," and slowly, with this electrical stimulation, the muscle movement around my eyes returns. After the wires come off, I embark on nearly two years of physical therapy with a therapist who must manually manipulate my jaw. He is gentle and strong in equal measures, and, knowing I can get through this, I vow to follow his lead.

Today, twenty-seven years after my accident, I keep in mind just how much I've been blessed. I've doctors who still greet me with hugs, family and friends who have been with me every step of my journey. The accident and its aftermath have taught me that with a little faith and a lot of determination, I can get through anything. Yes, I still live with chronic pain, and I know that because the prosthetics degrade over time, I will face at least one more replacement surgery in the future. But it's also because of that surgery that I've now achieved real quality of life. I may not be able to eat salad or meat or popcorn at the movies, but I can still go to the movies. I may use baby toothbrushes and sleep propped with pillows and heat pads, but I can still wake to welcome the dawn. And yes, I worry that all the surgeries, all the years of medication and less than optimal diet could shorten my lifespan, but I've learned that life is meant to be lived a moment at a time. For we are not, praise God, like jigsaw puzzles. Our pieces don't necessarily have to be interlocking and uniformly cut for us to feel complete. I look in the mirror and I say to myself: this is what I have; this is who I am. I am strong, and I am here. And no matter what difficulties life might bring, I know I've stared fear straight in the eye before and I can do it again, emerging proud and shining.

~Theresa Sanders

57

There's Always an Exception... I'm Usually It

We shall draw from the heart of suffering itself
the means of inspiration and survival.
~Winston Churchill

I was born two months premature with underdeveloped lungs and a heart condition. The doctors told my mom that I wouldn't live long enough to make it out of the hospital. I was hooked up to half a dozen different machines that did everything from breathe for me to notifying the nurses when my heart rate dropped too low.

As the days went by, doctors couldn't believe I was still alive. They told my mom I was defying the odds. With each new day came new struggles and challenges, but also more hope. Everybody began to see that I was a fighter. After about a month, the doctors took me off all the machines to see if I could breathe on my own, and more importantly, survive. I exceeded their expectations and was released from the hospital two days later.

A nurse was sent to my home every day to help show my mom how to care for me. After a week, my mom was able to do everything on her own. I had breathing treatments and medicines I had to take every day, but I was always a very content baby. Then, one day things took a drastic turn. I began crying uncontrollably and turned purple.

My mom took me to the emergency room. My doctor came in and told my mom there was a blockage in one of my valves and I would need heart surgery immediately to release it.

My grandparents sat in the waiting room with my mom while I was in surgery. The surgery took four and a half hours, but they were able to clear the valve completely. The doctor said I was strong enough to go home after just two weeks, on Christmas Eve. Everybody agreed that was the best Christmas present ever!

Years went by and I was pretty much just like every other kid. I did still have to take medicine for my heart every day, but only had to do breathing treatments when my inhaler didn't work. I went to the doctor once a month for checkups and that became part of my normal routine. I was sometimes hospitalized for days at a time, but I was so used to the place it didn't bother me much. Plus, I had other kids in the ward to talk to. I sometimes got tired much faster than the other kids at school and couldn't always play as long, but in the hospital, those kids were just like me.

When I was in eighth grade, things started to go downhill. I had a constant pain in my chest and couldn't figure out why. After a couple of days, the pain became unbearable and I had to tell my mom. She made an appointment for the next day.

At this point, I had had the same doctor for about nine years and was very comfortable with him. Doc—as everyone called him—made it a point to tell me things straight out and not beat around the bush, so I was confident I'd get the answers I needed and be on my way in no time. Boy was I wrong! He couldn't tell me what was causing the pain because he had no idea what it was.

Over the next week, Doc performed test after test trying to determine what was causing the pain. I'd never been poked with so many needles in such a short amount of time. I was ready for this to be done and over with. When I was just about to say "Enough," Doc finally found the problem. It wasn't good and I'd have to start a treatment program for it right away. That meant missing quite a few days of school though. The number of days I would miss would determine whether or not I would be able to graduate with my class.

The decision was up to me. Should I do the treatment right then and chance not graduating, or should I put it off till the summer and possibly cause irreversible damage? This was not going to be the easiest decision because my head was saying one thing while my heart was saying the opposite. It was definitely something I had to sleep on. After talking it over with my grandpa and mom, I decided to go through with it and worry about everything else later.

The treatment program was very similar to the chemotherapy cancer patients go through. I wasn't looking forward to it, but if it was going to help I was all for it. After the first week of the treatment, I realized I wouldn't be going to school for a while. I was physically ill many days and just completely drained both physically and emotionally.

I was out of school for about a month when the counselor called and told my mom there was no way I'd be able to catch up on all the work in order to graduate with my class. I lost hope at this point. Not only was I in pain from the treatments and too ill to go to school or hang out with my friends, but now I wasn't going to be able to graduate. What was the point in doing all this?

After a couple of days feeling sorry for myself, I realized it took too much energy. I thought back to a saying my grandpa always used to tell me: "There's always an exception, and you're usually it." I thought about all the stories I was told about the first few years of my life and how hard I had to fight just to stay alive. I realized that if I was able to fight that hard at such a young age, I could surely get through this. The only difference was that when I was that young I didn't know all the odds were against me; now it was all too obvious. I couldn't give up just yet though... not without giving it my all first.

I had my mom go to school and get all the work I had missed so I could catch up on it while I was stuck in bed. I sat there for hours on end doing assignment after assignment until I had it all finished. I continued getting work brought to me and was able to finish it pretty fast. I was out of school for two and a half months, but wasn't a day behind any of the others by the time I went back. Not only was I able to graduate, but I was also valedictorian of my class.

I had succeeded in accomplishing what many thought was impossible. Once again I defied the odds; I was the exception to the rule. Although I had my doubts and thought it was a hopeless cause at times, I was able to stay positive enough to finish what I had started. Just like that baby in the hospital all those years ago, I continue—even to this day—to have that same fight in me... that will to not only survive, but to succeed in everything I set my mind to as well.

Just remember: if you believe in yourself hard enough you can accomplish anything!

~Grace Gonzalez

58

Positively Uncertain

It is a mistake to look too far ahead.
Only one link of the chain of destiny can be handled at a time.
~Winston Churchill

Have you ever tried giving your medical history while breathing through contractions that are five minutes apart? Add to this that you've already answered this same questionnaire three months prior and that the information gatherer resembles Hospital Admissions Barbie, and you have my entrance into motherhood. As soon as she finished, an equally teenybopper-looking doctor on call came in and hooked me up to a fetal monitor. After watching it for a minute and doing a brief exam, she announced "We're sending you home."

My response? "I don't think so!"

My pregnancy had brought on so many physical experiences and emotions. The nausea was alleviated by the notion that a healthy baby was forming. The excitement of becoming a mother overrode the fear of psychologically damaging my future offspring. But there was one feeling that becoming a mother cemented in me that no other milestone in my life had yet achieved: trust your instincts.

"There's no reason for you to stay here," insisted the medical expert. "You're only one centimeter dilated. If you're in too much pain to go home, I'll admit you, but it's going to be at least twenty-four hours before you deliver." I was admitted at 6:00 AM. At 1:53 PM my son was born.

Two days later my husband Aaron and I brought our firstborn home and we began adjusting to life as a family. I half-heartedly joked that we were in P.O.W. mode; everything revolved around the will of Joshua Berger and he alone determined when we ate, slept and showered. And though exhausted, overly emotional and worn out, I did my best to remain positive.

As time progressed, so did Josh. He was a happy, good-natured baby who made eye contact, rolled over and smiled. He was gaining weight and gave us the gift of sleeping through the night at five months. He loved music and being read to, and his disposition and babbling charmed everyone around him.

All was developing fairly normally with the exception of a few red flags. I mentioned these concerns to his pediatrician, since he was a little late in walking and his first words were atypical. Instead of the standard firsts of "mama," "dada" and "baby," Josh's first words were "cat," "cow," and "goat," all of which are harder sounds to pronounce and none of which force your lips to touch upon utterance. She had told me not to worry, despite Aaron's family history of autism. Josh was making eye contact and talking. "If autism were a factor, it would have shown itself by now," she assured me.

But when the time came for Josh to eat solid foods, my warning bells clanged full-force. He gagged on Cheerios. He refused to eat anything but puréed food and though he took himself off his baby bottle, he refused to drink anything but water from an eight-ounce water bottle. Certain temperatures and textures seemed to offend him. I brought him back to the pediatrician and demanded scripts for special education, occupational, physical and speech therapy evaluations. Granted, she treated me like a hysterical mother, but humored me enough to hand them over. I was positive that this was something that needed to be dealt with; the sooner we did, the better off my child would be.

The evaluators came and observed Josh. At fourteen months, he was cruising, but his grasp and sitting stance were considered "immature." All agreed that it was better to be safe than sorry, and Josh was granted early intervention services. I was lucky to be a stay-at-home mom, which allowed me to work closely with all of Josh's therapists. And while he was eventually eating solids of various textures, he wasn't making progress at the rate he should have been. He lost his language skills and became fixated on specific pictures in books. He would endlessly twirl without getting dizzy and didn't respond to his name. At the recommendation of Josh's occupational therapist, I requested a neurological evaluation. My pediatrician agreed, but not without saying "I really don't think you're going to find anything."

It was at this evaluation that I received confirmation of what I had been afraid of long before becoming pregnant. I didn't even wait for the diagnosis. When I finished answering the neurologist's questions, I simply asked, "Is he on the autistic spectrum?"

"Probably," he answered "but I've seen a lot worse. The goal now is to get him more therapy."

"And the prognosis?" I croaked through tears.

"There's no way to know. All I can tell you," he advised, "is to remain cautiously optimistic." Aaron and I walked out of that room devastated. Josh was twenty-two months old and all we knew for certain was that he had been diagnosed with PDD-NOS (Pervasive Developmental Disorder, Not Otherwise Specified).

I allowed myself two weeks of mourning the loss of the child I thought I had. I cried, ate chocolate and avoided dealing with people. After that, I realized one thing. I couldn't control what had happened to Josh, but I could control what I was going to do, how it was to be handled, and my attitude in how I approached this situation. I could focus on the uncertainty of the diagnosis, or the fact that there was reason to hope. Nobody had told me that Josh would never again speak, play with toys functionally or attend a regular school. These were things still to be determined. It was clear that I had one of two choices: I could remain at a standstill, or do everything that was humanly possible for my child.

Since receiving Josh's diagnosis, my husband and I have pushed ourselves into full-throttle work mode. While Josh attends a special education preschool in the morning, I research programs and learn all I can about different modes of therapy. When Josh comes home,

I actively observe and participate in the methodologies that help my wonderful son achieve the goals that have been set out by his incredible therapists. Aaron, though a full-time pharmacist, is always there to lend a hand when he can and takes an active, loving interest in Josh's progress.

This summer we will mark the one-year anniversary of our son's diagnosis; and though he isn't a typical two-and-a-half-year-old, he's come a long way. He is far more aware of his surroundings, communicates with some language, and approaches the front door whenever he hears a knock or the bell ring. He has begun saying "Mama" and "Dada" when he wants us and knows how to manipulate us to get what he wants.

Can I be absolutely certain that Josh will be able to overcome all of the obstacles that autism brings with it? No. But I do know that Josh has parents who see him as more than a diagnosis, are dedicated to getting him what he needs, and who love him unconditionally. And as long as these things are granted freely and generously, I don't think any one of us will suffer any lack in the end. Of this I am positive!

~Jennifer Berger

59

No Complaints

A woman is like a tea bag.
You never know how strong she is until she gets in hot water.
~Eleanor Roosevelt

Macular degeneration didn't sound scary when Mom first mentioned it. She told me her cataract surgeries the previous fall had been successful. Her eyesight had grown worse over time though, not better. Her ophthalmologist had referred her to a retina specialist for more tests. She'd let me know what happened. No big deal.

Two months later, Mom called to share the test results. She'd been diagnosed with age-related macular degeneration, or AMD as it's known in medical circles. Her macula, the central part of her retina responsible for detailed vision, was deteriorating.

"Remember I told you about the two types of macular degeneration, dry and wet?" she asked. I remembered; I'd researched the condition online.

The "dry" version of AMD moves slowly. People with dry AMD may retain good vision with no other symptoms, or their central vision may gradually start to blur. The "wet" kind of macular degeneration moves fast. Abnormal blood vessels in the retina begin to leak and bleed, usually causing visual distortions and rapid vision loss.

"I've got the dry kind," Mom said, "so there's good news and bad news. Here's the bad news: Doctors have no viable treatments for the dry kind. There's nothing I can do about it. But the good news is I'll go blind less quickly."

Blind? I couldn't imagine my mother blind.

Images from the past raced through my mind. Mom devouring a new book with a mug of hot coffee in her hands. Mom reading her Bible in the early morning light. Mom glancing at a recipe card while she stood over a mixing bowl. Mom and Dad on the couch watching a football game. Mom reading a story to her grandchildren. I wondered what images the future would hold.

"I'm so sorry, Mom. I'm sorry you have to go through this."

I didn't know what else to say.

"Oh, sweetheart, you don't need to feel sorry for me," Mom replied. "God has blessed me so much. I've seen a world of beauty with these eyes. I've seen sights I never imagined I'd see. If I go blind, I'll have nothing to complain about."

Mom may have said more, but I heard nothing else for a few minutes. I was replaying her last four words: nothing to complain about.

Mom told me later she chose her response to AMD ahead of time—before she received the diagnosis. She knew the choice would be harder if she waited to see how the condition might change her life. And she wanted to focus on her blessings, not her losses.

When Mom's macular degeneration moved from dry to wet a few years ago, she didn't grumble. When her doctor recommended monthly eye injections, she took the plan in stride. She's received twenty-eight injections in her right eye so far. They're not fun, but they haven't slowed her down.

I can't imagine someone sticking a needle in my eyeball, but my mom handles the process with humor and grace. Her attitude isn't surprising, I guess. Why would you whine about a needle in the eye if you were okay with going blind?

~Donna F. Savage

60

Beyond the Diagnosis

Those who wish to sing, always find a song.
~Swedish Proverb

I didn't expect to laugh so much. I didn't expect to hear so much spiritual wisdom or to be so inspired during my visit with the Early Stage Alzheimer's Support Group.

I attended the group because I wanted to understand what it was like to receive and live with a diagnosis of Alzheimer's. Years ago, when my mom was diagnosed with dementia, I was too scared to think about such questions. Even though being around my mom and other people with Alzheimer's had lessened my fear, still, when I had one of those "senior" moments, I worried: Is this normal or is this Alzheimer's?

Now I was in a room with people who had a label to go with their memory loss and lapses. Instead of looking gloomy and stricken, they were laughing.

The facilitator, Michelle, invited people to go around the circle and check in.

Barb was sad because she could no longer drive.

"I have lost my independence," she said mournfully.

"It's not about who's behind the wheel," Michelle told Barb. "It's about how you see yourself as a person."

As Michelle was speaking, Larry walked in.

"Sorry I'm late," he said sheepishly. He was a handsome man in his early fifties. He looked like he'd do a fine two-step in his cowboy boots, western shirt and jeans. "I got lost. I know where I am but I don't always know how to get from one place to the other." Just days ago, he told us, he got confused in the parking lot of a local mall and had to have a security guard lead him out.

"I know what you mean. My inner maps have disappeared," Louis said. "Now I have to use MapQuest and really plan how I'm going to get someplace."

Louis, who was in his early sixties and had a Ph.D. (which he described as "piled high and deep") had a lot of places to go. He volunteered five days a week at a local charity and refereed soccer games most nights. He played bridge. And in the middle of all this he still spent an inordinate amount of time looking for "things that were there just a minute ago."

"I function almost normally, but I am not normal," Louis said and everyone nodded. They all knew the inner slips and slides that could accost them at any minute.

Around the circle people reported feelings of both harmony and frustration.

"Some days, time moves along but I don't," Charlie, who was newly diagnosed and in his mid-fifties, said. People murmured their understanding.

"I am at peace," Sherry said. Also in her mid-fifties, she was one of the youngest people in her assisted living facility.

Dick, a former attorney, said he felt better now that he was back to tennis and physical activity.

"Then some days, I'm out of it." He shook his head. "Well, I just have to laugh."

"I am a positive person," Bob, one of the newer group members, reported. "I like to have a lot of experiences and this is one of life's experiences."

Michelle asked the group what kinds of messages she should put on the signs for them to carry at the upcoming Memory Walk fundraising event.

"We never give up!" Sherry said.

"We're still the same," someone else suggested.

"We have Alzheimer's, not leprosy," Bob offered and everyone cheered.

The group ended. The caregiver's group, which was meeting in the next room, also ended and family members reunited.

I felt exhilarated as I walked to my car. I had expected to attend a group glumly talking about coping with a dreaded disease. Instead I encountered people who were determined to embrace their challenges and live life to the fullest. Their sense of hope and optimism in a daunting situation reminded me that anything was possible.

~Deborah Shouse

His Badge of Courage

I not only bow to the inevitable; I am fortified by it.
~Thornton Wilder

The clicking of my fingers on the keyboard is the only sound in the house. I am working during these few precious moments of peace I have dug up from the chaos that has become my everyday existence. In between doctor's appointments and a strict medication schedule, I rarely have a moment to myself. I have a deadline to meet because life doesn't stop for surgery and yet, after all we've been through in the past three weeks, deadlines don't seem that important anymore.

My husband, Mike, shifts on the bed that used to occupy the bedroom of our small apartment. The bed is now the centerpiece of our living room and the centerpiece of my world. It no longer is a place for rest. It now serves as a prison of sorts for Mike. His antibiotics, given intravenously, tie him to it.

When I envisioned my life, I saw myself living in happiness, complete with matching dishtowels and a home that came straight out of a Pottery Barn catalog. I saw myself as a successful career woman, a successful wife and the envy of my friends. I didn't see myself as this weary woman who is barely holding onto her sanity.

As I sit, pretending to be productive, I wonder if we will ever be able to go back to how we were before this happened, before Mike was hospitalized for sixteen days, before we found out about his heart defect, before he had open-heart surgery. I don't think it's possible, but I need something to hold onto because the man trapped in our bed seems so different from the man I married and I am desperate for a glimpse of his former self.

Mike's face is an unhealthy shade of white. His lips are cracked despite my efforts to make him put on lip balm. His previously muscular body, toned from years of playing basketball, has been reduced to a pile of skinny limbs attached to a scarred and stitch-filled torso. All of this is distressing, but nothing is as disturbing as the look in his eyes. They have lost their light and he rarely smiles anymore. Instead, he constantly wears a worried look that makes him appear older than his twenty-six years.

I walk over to the bed to check on him. I have run out of comforting words to say, so I gently squeeze Mike's hand three times instead. It has been our quiet way of saying "I love you" since we started dating. He squeezes back, but it is barely detectable. He just doesn't have the strength. He is trying to be brave for me and I am trying to be brave for him and neither of us is doing a good job.

Mike doesn't feel like talking or watching a movie so I leave him to stare at the ceiling. I briefly mull over taping posters to the ceiling, like in the dentist's office, to give him something to look at. As I consider this, I realize that the only poster I own is an old *Finding Nemo* poster and I actually consider it for a minute.

"You're getting pretty desperate if you think Nemo will make this any better," I say to myself.

I chuckle a little at the thought of Mike lying in bed with a school of cartoon fish staring at him.

No, that won't help, I decide.

At 6'3", Mike is too tall for our bed and I can see his mint green hospital socks sticking out from underneath his blankets. The socks are a staple of hospital attire and are covered with white plastic stars that keep patients from slipping when they walk. At first we laughed at the idea of Mike having to wear the star socks, but not anymore. He is so weak that I fear he will fall every time he tries to walk. The socks are added insurance that he won't. They remind me of the socks that my one-year-old niece wears. She is just learning to walk, but right now she is steadier than Mike. His socks are a little dirty, but I don't want to wash them. The dirt shows that they have been used. It shows that he was once up and out of that horrid bed and it gives me hope that he will be again.

I can feel tears stinging my eyes and I quickly turn away from him. One of us has to be strong. I say a quiet prayer under my breath, asking for strength for the both of us. I pray for strength because, more than his body, I can see his spirit wasting away, a fact that scares me more than I am willing to admit.

"How are you feeling?" I ask for what seems to be the hundredth time today.

"Okay."

"It's time for your shower. Can you walk to the bathroom by yourself or do you need help?"

"I'll do it myself. Just give me a minute."

I walk back to the bathroom to make the necessary preparations. Even something as simple as a shower has become a big production, complete with multiple towels and plastic wrap used to prevent infection in his arm where the IV attaches. I can hear him struggling to walk down the hall. Everything in me wants to help him, but I know I shouldn't. He needs to do this on his own. He needs to feel like he can still do things for himself.

"Ready?" I ask.

"Can you help me take my shirt off?" he asks quietly.

As I gently lift his shirt over his head, I notice that he is intently staring at his reflection in the mirror.

"What are you doing?"

"I'm looking at my scar," he says without emotion.

As he stands in front of me, half-dressed, I take stock of how his body has changed. He has wasted away to almost nothing. His neck is dotted with scars from his central line. His arm has bright hoses dangling from it. His stomach has two slits in it from chest tubes and a bright red incision measuring more than six inches glares at me from his chest. It makes me feel sick.

"I can't look away either," I say. I hate the sight of his incision and I'm sure that he is thinking the same thing, but I am wrong.

"I know." He pauses. "It's kind of cool."

I look at him in surprise and I see his eyes flash with unmistakable pride.

"Wait. What? Why is it cool?" I ask.

"Because it's my badge of courage."

I am awed as I realize that my husband has chosen to embrace what others would surely try to hide. For the first time in weeks, I feel a sense of hope. The man standing before me reminds me of the man I first fell in love with. I squeeze his hand three times as we stare at our reflections in the mirror. I remind myself that tomorrow will be a better day. He squeezes back, a little bit stronger than before.

~Jessie Miyeko Santala

Think Positive

Attitude Adjustments

*The greatest discovery of my generation
is that a human being can alter his life
by altering his attitudes.*

~William James

Word Gifts

As we express our gratitude, we must never forget
that the highest appreciation is not to utter words, but to live by them.
~John Fitzgerald Kennedy

Shortly after the death of my twenty-one-year-old daughter, Kristen, my military husband received orders that would move us from our home in the desert to Verona, Italy. We were a family grieving. My children, Kate and Nicholas, soon began having problems in school, and I began to experience some strange physical symptoms that the doctors here in the United States could not diagnose. Once or twice a week my blood pressure spiked and I was admitted to the hospital for tests. I soon developed debilitating chest pain and muscle spasms that swept through my entire body. Traveling across the Atlantic Ocean to our new home was almost an impossible feat.

Three weeks after arriving in Italy and settling into our hotel in Verona my health problems came to a peak. Life should have been exceptionally wonderful for us at that time. We were living in an exquisite part of the world with so many new things to explore. However, I slipped further into my illness. In the early morning hours, I was rushed off to an Italian hospital. I was in severe pain and could barely move. Every test that they performed on me came back negative. Finally, after three weeks of excruciating tests, my diagnosis was Post Traumatic Stress Disorder.

Because loud noises and the rumbling sounds of the busses and cars on the cobblestone streets outside our hotel bothered me, we made a family decision to move away from Verona to a small medieval village by the name of Montecchia di Crosara. The village was everything I had ever read about and watched in movies. It was serene and set among the rolling hills of the Soave vineyards. I was certain I would heal there. I needed to resume being the happy mother and loving wife that I had once been. As is so often the case in this type of life scenario, there was a glitch. My psychiatrist and doctor, an army doctor, was transferred back to the United States six months after I had begun therapy. I was on my own!

Because my family left each day for long hours to attend school and work, I enrolled in a mind/body correspondence class with the very brilliant Jon Kabat-Zinn. I learned to practice Hatha Yoga and to meditate. Although these things were very helpful, something was still missing and my progress toward health was slow.

Then one day, while shopping at the local *groceria*, I met a neighbor who could speak a bit of English. He was a gentle *signore* who always smiled and waved as I passed him each day while I walked through the village.

"Buon Giorno, Signora," he said. "I hope you are feeling good today!" I answered with a curt nod. He grinned and looked deep into my eyes. "Be well," he said. "Be well." If only it could be that easy, I thought.

The following day, while deep into my meditative state, I felt myself slipping into something that I had not experienced before. A small child approached me in a wonderful and glorious mist and handed me a piece of paper. It was folded in two. When I opened it, I saw that it had just one word scribbled on it. It said "dance." I placed the piece of paper in my pocket. As I returned to reality I felt alive and refreshed. I wanted to dance, and I did. I danced while doing the dishes; I danced while I prepared dinner. In fact, I danced whenever I could and the feeling was one of elation. What was happening?

The following week, I went into the same meditative state that I had enjoyed when the young girl gave me the folded piece of paper. Here she was again. She handed me another piece of paper with the word "kiss" on it. As you might expect, the entire week after that I kissed my family whenever I could. It was not automatic at first. I had to push myself in that direction, but it was something I had not done in a very long time. After just a few days, I was actually compelled to kiss them. I was rewarded by warm smiles and fun stories about their days at school and work.

Upon meditating the third time, I received the word "laugh." I had not been able to laugh and felt that this might be the hardest of all the words to accomplish. But it was not. Again, laughter slipped through me and I found myself enjoying the antics of my family, as well as the people who lived around me in the village.

"Hope" was the next word. There would be no way! This was something that I knew that I would need to practice, but practice it I did! Within only a few days, I began to look forward to a life that could be interesting and fun. I began to attend all of my children's functions on the base in Verona, as well as entertaining some friends in our villa in Montecchia.

The last time that I saw the little child she gave me a piece of paper with the word "joy" inscribed on it. Although I was still in depression and mourning the loss of my daughter, I found that I was able to allow joy into my life again. By this time, I was dancing, kissing, laughing, and now had joy in my life. My old, Italian neighbor was onto something that day he leaned into my face and told me to "be well." He knew the positive words could change a person's life. They were beautiful and powerful gifts.

Now, fifteen years later, I am a happy and productive author who has learned the power of positive words. I call them "word gifts."

We are a family that has managed to rise above the tragedies that life sometimes throws our way. My children are married with wonderful lives and children of their own. My first granddaughter, although diagnosed with leukemia at the age of five, is now in remission. Throughout the entire ordeal our word gifts were called to task many times. They always worked their magic. Why? Because we know how truly precious they are in making a difference not only in our own lives but also in the lives of others.

~Janet K. Brennan

63

Choice

Anywhere is paradise; it's up to you.
~Author Unknown

My lungs hurt as I struggled for breath. I had been crying so hard that I hadn't noticed the woman who had entered the clearing with her small dog. I stopped sobbing long enough to mumble something about how refreshing it is to just come out to the clearing and think. Then I walked away before she was able to read the pain on my face.

The source of my pain stood a hundred yards away. Tucked in beside the other motor homes, my RV should have been a source of fun, excitement, and adventure. The park housed what Florida refers to as "the snow birds," people who were escaping the cold of the winters up north. It was mid-December. I looked down the row of trailers lined up in the Florida sun. Many of those sun followers had decked out their motor homes with Christmas lights, statues, and trees covered with seashells and wind chimes.

I gazed at the twelve-inch Christmas tree I had placed in the front window of our motor home. Again, I began to cry. This was not how things were supposed to be. I heaved another sigh, and decided I needed to walk once more around the park. My husband seemed content enough, and I hated to have him see me like this—tears streaming down my face, broken spirit. So I walked. I knew every step. For weeks, I had paced the paths up and down the rows of the motor homes. I knew which one had the birdcage with two loud cockatiels that squawked most of the day. I passed row three that had the cat that liked to lie in the sun in the middle of the small road that led through the park. Going all the way to the front brought me to the office where there was always a group of laughing, smoking, talking people. Their routine was so established; their pace slow, deliberate.

They chose this life. With foresight and planning, they deliberately packed up their belongings and headed for this small park. I couldn't identify with that. I preferred to relate to the ones I called the one-nighters…. people who came in with a car packed full of belongings, pitched a tent, used the showers, did laundry, and the next day they were gone. I used to sit and weave stories in my mind — where they were going, what had brought them to this place. I was convinced that they were gypsies, or homeless people, and honestly, as much as I felt their pain, it made me feel better.

My husband and I had not planned to be "snow birds" or even to be in Florida. Only a couple of months before we were living in a large suburban home outside Charlotte, North Carolina. Life was good. I traveled for my job, often running through airports and texting while I waited to catch a flight for my next assignment. My husband worked full-time in a field he'd been in for years. We spent our weekends driving around the eastern part of the state looking for property to purchase. Our dream was to own a large place where we could settle down, plant gardens, perhaps raise a pony that my granddaughter could come and ride in the summers.

As I passed the park office that morning, I saw the notices for the annual Christmas dinner on the board. A man who looked like Santa asked me if I would be attending the dinner. I mumbled something about not being sure what our plans were. In my mind Christmas was not going to be a happy day. My husband's unemployment check had not arrived. Our food stamps were almost gone, and the money we had borrowed from my daughter was a memory.

I stopped in the office and asked for the mail. Each day there was a moment of hope — maybe some money had come in.

I wondered if anyone could sense my pain and disappointment as I left the office. As I rounded the bend and saw my motor home at the end of the row, I realized I needed to walk one more loop around. Questions swirled through my mind—Why had we gotten ourselves into this mess? How could we both get laid off the same week? And why was everyone else so happy, living in those small metal boxes they call recreational vehicles? I felt as if the place where I laid my head each night was a jail cell. It was a motor home, but we had nowhere to motor to. What used to be a weekend trip of camping and s'mores had turned into a grim daily reminder of things lost.

Over the last month, I'd done more than my share of praying. Having nothing else to do, my husband and I spent our days reading the Bible, praying, and talking about God's promises. He seemed to have a firm grip on his faith, while my daily prayers often turned into sobbing and fear; I called it my crisis of faith.

One foot in front of the other, I made my way toward my home on wheels. As I opened the door, I heard the sounds of music playing, eggs frying. The little lights on the tree twinkled. The cats stretched out on the bed, not having a care in the world. My husband turned, looked and flashed a smile—"Hi, how was your walk?" I thought for a moment. I was in a place that most people spend a lot of time and money to get to, in a motor home that many would love to have. My healthy husband was glad to see me. And the tears stopped. I realized that each day is a choice. We often don't get to choose what happens to us, only how we react to it. My crisis of faith really wasn't a crisis at all—it was a decision. At that moment, I knew that my God had heard my prayer, and reminded me that He is often found in the little things. I reached out and smiled at my husband—"It was good, it's gorgeous out. They are having a potluck at the park clubhouse for Christmas. Do you want to go?"

~Cindy Gore

64

When Health Fails, Paint Nails

Your attitude is like a box of crayons that color your world.
Constantly color your picture gray, and your picture will always be bleak.
Try adding some bright colors to the picture by including humor,
and your picture begins to lighten up.
~Allen Klein

Over and over again I heard from people that I was just too young to have diverticulosis. I was in my mid-thirties, but I did indeed have it and I had a very bad case too, one that required surgery.

I had rarely been sick in my life so the idea of being in the hospital and spending hours on an operating table and then days in recovery frightened me. I liked knowing what was going to happen; I liked being in control. There was nothing I could do to control this disease or the treatment I had to undergo to be healthy again. I just had to trust that things would go well. The alternative was unthinkable.

A few days before the surgery, I was in the bathroom picking out the things I would need to take with me to the hospital. I knew showers would be out for a while so I packed ponytail holders and barrettes to keep my hair off my face. As I rummaged in the drawer for a few extra barrettes, I saw a bottle of rosy pink nail polish.

The color of the nail polish reminded me of climbing roses my mother used to have in her yard. I knew following the surgery

I would be bedridden for a few days while my incisions healed and that it would be a long time before I could bend again to touch my toes to paint them.

Putting my packing aside, I set to work on a first-class pedicure for myself. If I was going to be staring at my toes for days on end, I wanted them to look good. Even though the inside of me looked bad, at least I could have pretty feet. I took great care to do a neat job and when I was finished I had to give myself credit—my toes looked wonderful.

The morning of the surgery, as I lay on the gurney in the hallway next to the operating room, my father stood beside me looking nervous and scared. Carefully, so as not to bump the new IV in my hand, I pulled back the sheet covering my feet and said, "Look Dad, I painted my toenails."

He was surprised and said, "I never knew you had such pretty feet" and he began to point my toes out to every person who came to check on me. Nurses, surgeons, anesthesiologists—and even one man sweeping the hallway—all got to see my rosy pink toenails as my dad tried to take the edge off the fear we both had by focusing on my toes and not the surgery.

It worked. We were laughing and not thinking about what was going to happen to me. When they finally came to take me into the operating room my dad no longer looked nervous or scared; he was smiling. The last thing I remember before the anesthesia took me under was my surgeon saying how great my pedicure was and asking whether I would do her toes when I got better.

The surgery went well, though it took longer than they expected, and soon I was in recovery coming out of the anesthesia. I was still a little groggy, but understood the nurse as she uncovered my toes and said, "Can't cover up those pretty pink nails." It made me smile. My toes and I had made it through.

All those long days of recovery, my pink toenails continued to delight the hospital staff and the people who visited me. It was one small thing that shined a positive light on an otherwise painful experience.

If I ever face a hospital stay again, you can be sure I'm going to round up a bottle of bright pink nail polish... or maybe I'll try red next time.

~Shawn Marie Mann

Weeds

There are no seven wonders of the world in the eyes of a child.
There are seven million.
~Walt Streightiff

My four-year-old daughter Kristina and I were late again. I had our faded blue minivan going as fast as our town's streets allowed, but we still got stuck at every red light and didn't make it through the final intersection in time to beat the school buses exiting the high school parking lot. So there we sat for a long time.

The grassy field beside us was a sea of dandelions—not the yellow flowers, but the white fluffy ones.

I said, "Oh Kristina, that poor yard... look at all those weeds," to which she replied "Oh, Mommy, look at all those wishes!"

~Kathi Lessner Schafer

Magic

Happiness is an attitude. We either make ourselves miserable,
or happy and strong. The amount of work is the same.
~Francesca Reigler

'm tired of being a tragedy-oriented person. So I decided I was no longer going to always assume the worst. That said, a few weeks ago I was cutting pears for dessert. I heard the buzz of my husband Bob's chainsaw.

"He's cutting down a tree," I said to myself. "He's fine." I kept slicing.

"Fine, fine, fine, fine." I heard the tree fall. "I'm not checking on him." I took a little sliver out of my thumb. During this bloody episode, my "normal" self had a minute to slip in, accompanied by all of the sirens of the Goddess of Neurotica.

"A limb went through his heart," the sirens informed me.

I answered, "No. He's fine."

"He sawed into a killer bee hive and they've sucked out his eyes."

"No." I continued with the pears.

"He's DEAD!"

Okay. That did it. I looked out the front door but couldn't see Bob. And that was because he was lying on the ground... under the fallen tree... with a broken leg.

I ran to him and cradled his head in my arms as he tried to speak. He opened his tear-filled eyes, looked up at me while in agonizing pain and whispered, "Please don't write about this." I promised I wouldn't. When people are in shock, they forget everything so you can promise anything you want.

So now Bob's in a cast and can't do much. But that's okay, because I won't let him do anything that requires lifting heavy equipment, such as spoons. Judging from something he said last night, I think I'm really getting on his nerves.

He said, "You're really getting on my nerves," and hobbled off to the kitchen, where he got the can opener for the coffee. I grabbed it. "I'll do that."

He took it back. "I'm nearly helpless and you're making it worse."

I pried it from his hands. "It's good to share your feelings, Bob." I opened the can. "Getting rid of pent-up emotion is good for the colon, and aches and pains in general."

"Well, I do have one big pain… in the neck."

And so, we haven't been able to do things together like take long drives or go hiking. Last week, we went to an ice cream shop and shared a hot fudge sundae in the front seat of our car.

We giggled while having the delightfully forbidden ambrosia. Later, I e-mailed my pal Deb, and told her that we didn't do anything today because of Bob's broken leg. We just had ice cream. She replied, "I hope your ice cream was magic."

I told Bob about her message. He was on the couch, trying to scratch under the cast, but he couldn't. Then he was having a hard time, I could tell, asking me to do another favor for him that day. He wasn't even able to get his own Kleenex or play tug-of-war with our dog and her favorite stuffed hedgehog. And he was obviously so sick of this.

I sat by him and massaged his foot. "Hiking in the woods would have been a lot more magical than ice cream," he said.

But then, as I often do, I pretended to look down at this scene from above. I saw two cranky people cloistered inside, not enjoying the gorgeous autumn day. And then, a new scene slowly washed over. I saw a tender moment in time with me scratching Bob's leg as we sat quietly in our home. I saw the vibrant colors of the bittersweet, in full bud right outside our window. I saw a man with a broken leg that would surely improve with time. And I knew how lucky we were to be together, on this day that dreams are made of, when we joyously shared an ice cream.

If that's not magic, I don't know what is.

~Saralee Perel

A Positive Step

The first step binds one to the second.
~French Proverb

"I don't want her to come," I whispered conspiratorially to my brother. At fourteen, he was three years older and, from my eleven-year-old perspective, much braver than me. Not only did I look up to him, but I trusted him to stand up for me, and to speak for me when I was too afraid. And he did.

"Dad," he said to our father from across the tiny apartment. "We really just want it to be the three of us."

It was Fourth of July weekend, and we were heading downtown to watch the fireworks. Me, my brother, my dad, a blanket to sit on, a cooler filled with soda pop, and fireworks to light up the sky were on my agenda. My dad's girlfriend was not part of my plan.

My father was angry. And hurt. He had been dating Mary for several months and he wanted us to accept her. We saw her as competition. What little time we had with him, we didn't want to share. Not only was I protective of my time with my dad, but I worried about my mom, too. In my own mind I thought that if I let myself like Mary, I'd be hurting my mom. My dad had already decided that he liked her better than my mom. What if my mom thought we liked her better, too?

Dad remarried a few years later, but it took me much longer than that to even give Mary a fair chance. She was always kind to my brother and me. But, I think I held back from a false sense of loyalty to Mom.

Twenty years later, while my husband and I were in the midst of our own divorce, my boys, nine and seven, came home from a visit with their dad in tears. They confided in me that their dad had sat them down earlier in the day and told them he had a girlfriend. Patty, he told them, would be spending quite a bit of time with them. I knew the boys thought she was nice. I knew that if they decided not to like her, it might be because they somehow felt that they needed to, out of loyalty to me. I didn't want my kids to make the same mistake I did.

You see Mary has been like a second mother to me. She takes nothing away from my mom, who is wonderful in her own right, but Mary has been another person in my life who I can lean on. Technically, I am Mary's stepdaughter. But when she looks at me, she sees no "step"—she sees someone she loves, someone she'd do any-thing for—and she has. She has been there for me through thick and thin. And she loves my kids the same way their biological grandparents do.

So when my boys looked at me that night and told me about Patty, I thought about all the years I'd wasted being angry with Mary. I could finally see some good coming out of that difficult time.

"Guys, listen," I said to my boys. "I know exactly what you're going through." They both rolled their eyes. "No, really." I tucked a foot under me and leaned forward. "After my mom and dad got divorced, my dad got a girlfriend."

"Papa had a girlfriend?" asked seven-year-old Jack. Now they were both interested.

"Yep. And I didn't like her at all. I was afraid that she would try to be my new mom. And I already had a mom I loved very much. I was scared. And I thought if I liked her it would make my mom sad. And she was already sad."

They both nodded, completely familiar with the emotions that I had gone through all those years ago when I was eleven.

"Well, I guess I just wish my mom would have told me it was okay to like my dad's girlfriend, because it turns out she was a really neat person and I wasn't nice to her for a very long time, because no one ever told me it was okay."

The room was quiet. My boys looked at each other and then at me.

"Guys? Do you know who that girlfriend was?" They both shook their heads.

"Your Grandma Mary." Nine-year-old Connor looked at me with big, round eyes.

"Grandma Mary?" exclaimed Jack. "Wow!"

"Yep. Can you even imagine your life without Grandma Mary in it?"

"No," they said in unison.

"So," I said, taking each of their little hands in mine. "I want to tell you right now that it's absolutely okay for you to like Patty. You are not going to hurt my feelings. And you are not going to make me sad if you enjoy your time with her and your dad. She's a nice person, and as long as she's nice to the two of you and your little sister, then that's all I care about. Okay?"

I got big hugs that night. As a child going through the pain and sadness of my own parents' divorce, I couldn't possibly have imagined that one day I would actually be grateful for that experience. But, all these years later, it turned out to be a wonderful gift that I was able to give my own children. Everything happens for a reason, and now I finally understood that what I had gone through as a child had given me the tools to help my own children when they needed it most.

~Beth M. Wood

Seeing the Good

If we shall take the good we find,
asking no questions, we shall have heaping measures.
~Ralph Waldo Emerson

No matter how many TV images, Internet videos, or snapshots I view, a location never possesses authenticity until I'm there. So it was with Turkey. I had always pictured the place as a third world country with roaming camels.

I couldn't have been more wrong! It's thriving, bustling, and jam-packed with the entrepreneurial spirit. When we landed in Istanbul in the summer of 2009, I sought a shuttle to take us from the airport to the hotel. After I located the bus stand, I turned to see Byron talking to an Antonio Banderas lookalike, only Turkish. The young Turk wore a white shirt, black trousers, and a name tag designating something regarding tourism. Byron motioned me to return inside the terminal, but I had already exited and was on the other side of guarded doors that didn't allow reentry. To enter again would necessitate walking a long way round so I signaled him to join me outside. He obliged. My husband and his new acquaintance picked up the luggage and stepped out the door.

"This fellow can get us a shuttle to our hotel," Byron announced, pleased.

"But, I see the bus right over there." I pointed.

"No, No. You don't want that!" the young Turk said with a dismissive gesture at the shuttle that I now noticed was surrounded by protesters carrying signs.

"Follow me," he said with a strong accent. This stranger led us into a stairway, down dark corridors, and into a deserted parking deck.

"A shuttle comes here?" I said. My voice dripped with skepticism.

"Yes, madam. Here."

"You mean a taxi?" I asked cautiously.

"No. No. My friend." Before I could interrogate him further, a white subcompact whipped up and another attractive Turk in pressed white shirt and black pants hopped out and popped his trunk. With no fanfare, he began throwing our suitcases in. "Get in," our new companion advised.

We hunched over and squeezed into the back. Our escort jumped in, next to the driver. They spoke limited English. I wasn't sure how much they understood so I felt unable to communicate my concerns to my husband. My mind raced: We are now hostages in a car driven by two foreigners in a nation where we know no one and not a word of the language.

I stared at my husband who was grinning about his good luck finding us transportation. I elbowed him and mouthed, "Is this safe?"

He nodded yes. And, he began asking the fellows questions. They pointed out the fishermen on the bridge. Byron inquired about the kind of fish they were catching while I busily memorized the route and desperately tried to recall kickboxing moves. Then, I punched hubby in the side again and lip-synched: "Are we being abducted?"

He leaned over and whispered, "They are respectable young men—entrepreneurs."

I rolled my eyes.

Defeated, I slumped back, resigned to my fate, and tried to picture myself in a burka. The young men asked if we'd like to drive past the Blue Mosque. "Sure!" bellowed my protector, who seemed to be enjoying this sightseeing escapade, while I was secretly formulating my escape plan. We stopped the car near an alley. Wide-eyed, I stared at my husband.

"Would you like to go inside the mosque?" our self-appointed guide asked.

My husband turned to me. "How 'bout it?"

"No! Just want to go to the hotel!"

They started the car, and the driver asked if we'd mind if we drove to his pal's house first. His pal would then drive us the rest of the way in his car. I looked over with narrow slits for eyes at my husband.

"Are you comfortable with that?" the driver asked us.

"Sure," said my husband sealing our fate as fish bait at the bottom of the Bosporus.

As we were stuck in traffic, I commented on how some women dressed in black burkas and how awfully warm they must be on a day like this. "Fanatics!" our friend in the passenger seat exclaimed, disgusted. I relaxed.

They rode along the river and showed us where our cruise ship would be stationed the next day. At some point, the driver must have changed his mind because he drove us directly to the front door of our hotel and gave us his card and said he'd love to chauffeur us around tomorrow if we had time. I bit my lip. My husband paid them the agreed fare and gave them each a healthy tip. They acted happy and thanked us profusely.

"I would never have gotten into a car with strangers like that," I said after their departure.

"They were professionals. I saw their nametags. Nice boys trying to make an extra buck," responded my husband.

I've travelled ten times more than my husband and should be more comfortable in the presence of exotic tongues than he, but he correctly sized up the Turks as young men trying to earn a little cash at the end of their workday by ferrying tourists to their hotel and giving them a taste of hospitality along the way. My husband wasn't suspicious, mistrusting, or guarded. He welcomed the helping hand.

Turks, I found in our few days in Istanbul, Kuşadasi, and Bodrum, will go out of their way to be cordial. They'll offer you Turkish coffee or ouzo on the house; they'll take you on a walking tour of the Blue Mosque just in the hope you'll stop by their carpet shop afterward; they'll negotiate with you on prices and throw in an extra embroidered towel if you've bought other wares. They are welcoming. They are polite. The men don't gawk at women or make lewd remarks. They are persistent businessmen, but they are not too pushy.

Because Turks long ago conquered Greek civilization, I think I always harbored resentment toward them. Since I was a schoolgirl, I've been enamored with the glory of Ancient Greece. But, seeing modern day Istanbul with its clean streets, friendly folks, and fabulous vistas and parks, I now reassess what I used to believe. I am filled with wonder. I wish I'd studied more about Turkey when younger. Yet, learning is a lifelong process and with so much media at my modern fingertips there's no excuse for not redressing prior gaps in my education. Tonight I'll watch *Gallipoli*.

For a better world, we need to trust a little more, assess people individually, and when given a chance, travel far and wide while always keeping an open mind. Those entrepreneurs taught me something. And so did my husband! Think positive and give people the benefit of the doubt.

~Erika Hoffman

Survival Steps

Courage is fear that has said its prayers.
~Dorothy Bernard

Nine hundred pounds of frantic horseflesh tossed me into the muddy water, struggled up the steep riverbank and then raced off down the dirt trail. The animal's hooves barely missed my head as they flashed by. Standing up, dripping wet, I wondered again, "How did I end up here?"

"Here" was by the side of a swollen river in the jungles of southern Mexico. Never the outdoor type, I had asked myself over and over how I came to be in the second month of a survival training camp, with three more months yet to go.

Before leaving the safe haven of an ivy-covered university dorm in New York, I had pondered the skills I would need to survive these months. I, who never did anything more handy than change a light bulb, would have to build my own home using vines, branches and logs harvested from the rainforest. I, who swam laps in a carefully chlorinated pool, would be crossing rapids and paddling a half-ton wooden canoe. I, who studied the Spanish of literature in high school, would learn an indigenous language so full of foreign clicks that it sounded like a pile of marbles rolling around in a glass jar. Yet all of these skills would be required as I followed my career path doing language research in remote villages far off the Pan-American Highway.

In my anxiety, I wondered if God had made a mistake by leading me in this direction. I could imagine a smile on His face as I questioned His vast wisdom. A psalm expressed my fears: "Show me where to walk… I run to You to hide me." Given my future plans, I might have changed it to read, "Show me where to hike."

The first weeks at the training program did not bolster my confidence. In woodshop, most of my team made three-legged stools. I would have too, except I kept trimming the legs shorter and shorter to make them even. The end result looked more like something used to scrape boots than to support feet. My experience in metal work was no better. Excess solder flowed down the sides of my metal pipe faster than wax dripping on a candle standing near my campfire. And in the kitchen I scored another defeat when I substituted tablespoons for teaspoons when measuring salt into the breakfast oatmeal. Not even the mules would eat it.

As I moved through the program, I discovered a method to cope with my fear of the unknown. A voice inside my head told me to take only one step at a time. Instead of quaking in terror and thinking about the twenty-five-mile single-day trek that loomed ahead, I concentrated on the task in front of me. Instead of worrying about the three-day survival hike scheduled for the second phase of the training, I focused on learning how to give injections in the first aid class. I let concerns about the upcoming canoe trip wash downstream as I shampooed my hair in a bucket.

Over the weeks, yes, I managed to build my own hut, complete with a latrine. I coped with poisonous spiders, snakes and army ants. When flames leaped five feet into the air and threatened to set the thatch roof ablaze above my head, I grabbed a damp towel and smothered the fire. I hiked, I swam, I survived.

At the end of the program, the staff called each trainee in for a personal assessment.

"Come in, Emily," the director began as he thumbed through a sheaf of papers on his lap. He made a few polite introductory comments before getting to the point. "We noticed that you seem to lack some of the basic pioneering skills."

With a grin, I replied, "Hey, I could have told you that on Day 1 and saved everyone a lot of trouble."

The director smiled before going on. He asked me where I planned to do my fieldwork. I mentioned an area of the world that, while remote, still had access to highways and small planes. He nodded his approval.

The staff was right. On the one hand, I would never stand out as a carpenter or welder, but on the other hand, they forgot to ask me what I learned during the training. You see, I discovered during those five months of jungle training how to substitute native plants like yucca for familiar friends like apples and potatoes, but I also learned a far more important lesson about myself. I found that when I trusted my God and moved forward in faith, I could reach my goals. I just had to keep moving forward step by step, one step at a time, even when some of those steps included climbing up a muddy river bank after being thrown from a horse.

~Emily Parke Chase

Moving Forward

We can destroy ourselves by cynicism and disillusion,
just as effectively as by bombs.
~Kenneth Clark

Our old neighborhood had been like modern-day Mayberry. Neighbors chatted over fences. Newcomers were welcomed with chocolate brownies and butter-braid bread. It had been easy to find friends there.

Our new community was different. It seemed that family roots grew deep. Deep as the Mississippi River that flowed past the tiny river town. Breaking in was tough.

We'd moved to decrease my husband's commute to work. Only thirty miles.

I wished that I could erase each one.

After living there for six months, I was ready to pick up tent stakes and move back home. I was lonely for a friend. My three boys were lonely. My husband, Lonny, fared okay, but he spent his days at work.

"I'm so alone here," I said to Lonny one evening. "I don't see my old friends much, and I can't seem to make new ones." We were sitting on the front porch of our old Victorian. Our three young sons kicked a soccer ball around the side yard.

Lonny is a good listener, but he also has an engineer's brain. He's a problem solver. "What have you done to meet people?" he asked.

"I go to story time at the library every week. I initiate conversations at the park. I even stalked a lady at a garage sale. She had two boys and looked like someone I'd want to be friends with. But she was more interested in that old vase she was looking at than chatting."

"Sounds like you're doing the right stuff," he said. "Keep at it."

And I did. I tried to be open and friendly. It wasn't that people were unkind. They just all seemed established.

A few more months passed and winter settled in. It was harder than ever to meet people. I admitted that we had a few obstacles. We homeschooled our boys and still attended church in our old community. But I'd never had trouble making friends before, and I started to develop an attitude. Who needed a friend? I was tired of trying to fit in a place it seemed that we didn't belong.

Grey winter days eventually gave way to fresh spring color, but my attitude stayed dark and gloomy. I began to feel bitter. I still went to the library and park, but I didn't start conversations. I didn't invite anyone over. I wanted to move back to our old neighborhood.

Lonny noticed my sinking disposition.

"Shawnelle, you look unapproachable," he whispered in my ear one afternoon. He and I were sitting in lawn chairs at our son's first-of-the-season Little League game. Samuel, our three-year-old watched the game from his own little Scooby-Doo chair.

"What do you mean?"

"Body language. Your arms are crossed. You placed our chairs fifteen yards away from everyone else."

"It doesn't matter. I'm not going to have friends here."

"You sure won't if you stop trying," he said.

Just then Samuel looked up. He must've heard our whispers. "Mom's right, Dad. We'll never ever have friends here. And we just want to go home."

I sat there and looked at my tiny blond son.

His words mirrored my attitude. And I didn't like the murky reflection. That's when I knew that I needed an adjustment. I didn't want my boys to learn that the way to work through a tough time was to wield a wounded and bitter attitude.

Over the next few months I worked very hard. I smiled when I didn't feel like it. I joined conversations at the ballpark. The boys and I baked cookies for our neighbors. It's going to be great when I find that friend, I told myself. I'll appreciate it even more than if I'd made friends right away. I stopped talking about moving back home. We signed up for reading programs at the library and frequented parks and the bike path along the river. I was still lonely, but some of the frustration slipped away. At least I wasn't sitting home stewing. And it was harder to grumble when I was smiling.

I went forward each day. Doing the things I could do. Trying not to look back.

One afternoon Samuel and I clambered up the stairs to the library activity room. We'd signed up to attend a craft class, and I was going to sport my improved attitude. As we rounded the corner, I made sure that I looked approachable. Arms uncrossed. Wide, bright smile as we walked through the door.

A blond woman who I hadn't seen before sat at an oblong table with a tiny, redheaded boy. She smiled back. I noticed her deep dimples and kind, blue eyes. The little boy was about Samuel's age.

There were empty chairs beside her. I decided to walk closer.

"Hi," she said. "I'm Tammy. This is Chase. Do you need a seat? There's one right here."

I sat down next to Tammy. The boys delved into their craft and Tammy and I delved into conversation. Soon class was over, and we still had a lot to say. "Why don't you come over later?" Tammy asked. "I live on a farm. There's plenty of room for the kids to run."

We went.

And since that day, we've been back a million times. Tammy and I became the best of friends, and that farm is like a second home to my boys.

When I look back, I'm grateful for that lonely, tough time. I learned to persevere. I learned to hold my attitude in check. A new sensitivity was born in me—I'm always on the lookout for newcomers. And I was right—I do appreciate my friendship with Tammy. My family has broken into this community, and this little town is where we want to be.

I'm glad I didn't give up.

And as for my boys, they learned a lesson too. A valuable lesson about tough times.

"Keep moving forward," is what I tell them. "Your heart will follow."

And once in a while it leads you.

Straight into the arms of a friend.

~Shawnelle Eliasen

71

Half Full

Every day may not be good, but there's something good in every day.
~Author Unknown

My middle child, Jacob, was intelligent, resourceful and good-looking. Despite all he had going for him, he possessed the disturbing tendency to constantly see the cup of life as half empty. Every day when he came home from school Jake would list everything bad that happened that day! Despite my best efforts, I couldn't convince him to lose the negative attitude and choose to count his blessings.

On his ninth birthday, we saved enough money to take the family to Disneyland for two days. His dad and I didn't make much then, so it was a considerable sacrifice, but we felt Jacob's birthday was worth it. After doing Disneyland to death, we collapsed in our hotel room and I asked the birthday boy, "Did you have fun today, Jake?"

All my faultfinding son could say to me was, "Pirates of the Caribbean was closed!"

"Jacob Marshall," I chided, clearly unable to contain my exasperation, "we stood in line for an hour and a half to see The Haunted Mansion. We rode Space Mountain three times. We walked in the park for two solid days, and all you can say is, 'Pirates of the Caribbean was closed?'" Clearly, something had to be done about his negative attitude, and I was going to be the one to do it!

I approached my mission with the determination of a battalion commander. I read every article, bought every book. If the Internet had been available then, I would have Googled for weeks to find the ammunition I needed to defeat his negativity.

With the help of great resources, I developed my strategy. Several books I read identified my son's temperament as melancholy: He was sensitive, artistic, deep, analytical, and able to see the worst in every situation. That described Jake all right.

My research informed me that people with the melancholic temperament have an emotional need for order and sensitivity. That meant I needed to listen patiently to my son's daily pessimistic litany. My usual reaction was to try to talk Jake out of his negativity, but that wouldn't satisfy his need for sensitivity. I had to let him finish his lament and ask, "What good things happened today?" Then I needed to wait until he could tell me—wait for as long as it took. This would help Jacob realize that good things really were happening to him, despite his woeful perspective.

The day came when I was ready to put my new tools to work. Jake came home from school, flopped down on his bed as usual and again began to tick off his list of the terrible things that had happened at school. I listened attentively, making eye contact and nodding with empathy, before I asked, "What good things happened today, Jake?"

His response was what I expected, "Nothing."

"Something good had to happen. You were there for six hours," I encouraged. Then I waited. I waited fifteen long minutes that first day, determined to stay there all night if that's what it took to shift his paradigm.

At last he admitted, "I did get to dust the erasers."

"By yourself?"

"No, with Brandon."

"Your best friend?"

"Yeah."

"You mean you got to leave class and dust erasers with your buddy? You're one lucky kid, if you ask me!"

"Yeah, I guess I am," Jake remarked with his head back and his shoulders squared.

This began a daily exercise for us. I lost count of how many times we repeated this ritual. Jacob came to understand the power of a positive perspective, but the path to get there seemed to escape him at times. Then I would encourage him to see things differently, and he would get back on the track of choosing to see the positive and losing the negative attitude. It was a struggle, but he was making headway.

The school year was winding down and Mother's Day rolled around. Jake's dad took him to the store for a Mother's Day card. Next to the cake he and his sisters had prepared was the card he had chosen by himself. Grinning from ear to ear he presented it. On the front it read:

"The pessimist sees the cup half empty.

The optimist sees the cup half full."

I opened the card and read inside:

"But Mom sees the cup as one more thing someone was too inconsiderate to put in the dishwasher! Happy Mother's Day."

Jake and I laughed until we cried, and in that moment, I was convinced my hard work was paying off.

~Linda Newton

72

Drops of Inspiration

When you feel dog-tired at night,
it may be because you've growled all day long.
~Author Unknown

I made my way to one of our local medical complexes for an appointment. The day was beautiful, and the afternoon sun and warm breeze seemed to be intentionally mocking our local forecasters, who collectively had predicted a gloomy, cloud-covered, "still-waiting-for-spring" type of day.

Upon entering the complex, I prepared myself for the almighty waiting room. I was, however, pleasantly surprised when I walked into a virtually empty room. I almost felt guilty, if not foolish, for imagining that I might get in at my actual appointed time. But it happened, and I'm sure the grin on my face left the nurses and attendants wondering just what sort of mental disorder I was seeing the doctor for. I was whisked into the weigh-in stall and given all the preliminary once-overs, which, as everyone knows, have to be done before your regular tune-up.

The doctor entered, the conversation was meaningful and informative, and my concerns were promptly addressed. Solutions were agreed upon, and before I knew it, I was checking out and in the hallway, finished and wondering what time warp I had just stepped through.

At that point, I found myself in the middle of the building's foyer, dressed in rumpled clothes, jacket in hand along with my checkbook, medical paperwork, prescription information, and a new doctor-recommended diet plan.

Looking around, I couldn't find a table or chair to set everything on so that I could get myself organized. So, I calmly laid the paperwork on the ground in front of me, along with my other belongings.

As I started to slip my jacket on, I felt a distinctive "bloop" on the back on my head. I immediately turned and spied a boy, eight or nine years old, sitting with his mother in the attached pharmacy's doorway. He laughed at me while sporting a toothless grin and cherry Kool-Aid stained lips. Mom was engrossed in the latest *People* magazine, oblivious to the one-sided hysteria beside her.

I stared, giving the boy a parental look of anger, concluding that he must have obviously been responsible for this little incident.

I turned to pick up my things from the floor when "bloop" again, to the back of my head.

This time, I heard the boy giggling even before I turned around.

He was making a fool of me and feeding my frustration by the second. His mother broke her trance and looked at him. Following his gaze, she noticed my displeasure, and attempted to stop the boy from laughing at me, although she didn't know why.

Silently repeating a few choice words, I was ready to walk over and let her in on her son's activities when "bloop," a large drop hit the paperwork I was holding in my hand.

Instinctively, I looked up. "Bloop" right between the eyes.

The boy erupted, and his boisterous laugh echoed through the foyer, drawing attention from everyone within hearing distance. The mother worked hard to suppress her laughter, turning it instead into a shy grin, which she tried to hide under the palm of her hand.

My frown slowly turned to a grin also. The misplaced ceiling tile overhead revealed evidence of a minor water leak, providing the aforementioned "bloops," which came regularly as I stood there gazing upward.

I nodded apologetically to the boy, feeling like I was shrinking under those drops of water.

As I was leaving the complex, I wondered how I could've let a possible childlike prank ruin the otherwise perfect day that I had going on.

Then I realized how this happens.

It's just how we are, meaning "we" as a society. We let the slightest things get to us, causing us stress, anger, and resentment. I merely reflected that in this situation. From my simple example, through our society's increased violence toward each other, we collectively seem to have less and less tolerance for views, opinions, or actions that deviate from our own. Obviously this type of behavior toward one another is very destructive and just plain wrong, but how can it be corrected?

That question has been debated long and hard, with as many solutions being thrown around as there are opinions. But we can make a good start by stepping back, taking a deep breath, and laughing at ourselves once in a while.

And if need be, even splash a bit of cold water in our faces.

~Gerald L. Dlubala

Think Positive

Silver Linings

Clouds may come,
but clouds must go,
and they all have a silver lining.
For behind each cloud you know,
the sun, or moon, is shining.

~Author Unknown

73

Sudden Clearing

As each day comes to us refreshed and anew,
so does my gratitude renew itself daily. The breaking of the sun over the
horizon is my grateful heart dawning upon a blessed world.
~Terri Guillemets

t was a true leap of faith on my part. Moving from the populated, civilized suburbs we'd always known to a secluded home in the country had always been my husband's dream, not mine.

But when two people are in it for the long haul, their dreams merge just like their CD collections and their grandmothers' china. So on the day he told me he'd found paradise—a house for sale on a ten-acre lot fifteen miles away—I knew my life was about to change.

"It's perfect," Jim said, his voice full of hope and longing. "There's plenty of room to put in a garden, plus it already has a hayfield, a pole barn and lots of evergreen trees for privacy."

When we toured the property together I saw that he was right about everything—including the enormous evergreen trees. While some politely edged the driveway or marched along the distant property line, others loomed just a few feet from the front door and windows, dark and imposing. They formed an impenetrable green wall that blocked both the light and the view.

"You can't see the front yard from the house," I pointed out, "or even a car coming up the driveway."

"Don't worry," he assured me. "If it really bothers you we'll cut some down. But maybe you'll end up liking them."

I could see that he had his heart set on the place, and months later I found myself living five miles north of a one-stoplight town. But it didn't take long for me to get used to the solitude. I began to appreciate the peace and tranquility of country life, falling asleep to the sound of crickets and waking up to birdsong. From the backyard I could watch the ripening hay rippling in the breeze, the deer that cut across the field, the sandhill cranes that nested in our wetlands. I felt grateful to have found something I didn't know I'd been missing.

But those trees! I just couldn't get used to that dark wall of evergreens towering over the front of the house. It made me feel claustrophobic. I longed to look out the windows and see the wide, sunny expanse of lawn stretching down to the road. I also worried about our safety—every time the wind blew I wondered if a limb would come crashing right though the window.

Jim's promise that we could simply cut them down had been sincere but naïve. We'd learned that trees of that size were very expensive to remove, requiring a lot of specialized equipment and manpower. And the trucks were so heavy that the company could only schedule the job during the late winter, when the ground was still relatively frozen.

So we waited, putting money into the "Tree Fund" whenever we could. Knowing we could afford to have only a few removed, we walked the property over and over, looking at the house from every angle. We solicited opinions from family, neighbors and friends. In fact, every guest who visited us in our new home got the same interrogation: "So, should we take out every other tree, or maybe a grouping on just one side, or...?"

Finally, on a chilly day at the end of February, the experts pulled up in their oversize trucks. By late afternoon they'd cut three trees down to the stumps, punching a pretty good-sized hole in our tree wall and letting some weak winter sunshine through. I was grateful that we'd been able to begin the project, but wished we could have done more.

I had no idea then that a twist of fate was about to help that wish along.

On a muggy Sunday afternoon just a few months later, Jim and I were outside when we noticed the wind picking up. Then the sky began to darken with ominous and fast-moving clouds. I grabbed a few flats of flowers and raced with them to the shed, just before the first raindrops fell.

I was watching from the back porch when I realized that this was no ordinary storm. The rain fell in torrents, pushed nearly sideways by a wind shear that charged across the field, heading straight for the house like a freight train.

"Hurry!" I called to Jim, who had gone upstairs to close the windows. I had to shout to be heard above the roar of the wind. "We need to get to the basement!"

I went in search of our cats, knowing they'd be terrified in whatever hiding place they were cowering. I could hear the rain pounding against the house, then a loud crack that could only mean tree limbs breaking. The lights went out, signaling that we'd lost power for everything from the refrigerator to the well pump.

By the time Jim grabbed a flashlight and met me at the basement door, the roaring had stopped. The rain dwindled to a sprinkle. As quickly as it had begun, the storm was over.

Fear making our hearts beat faster, we stepped outside to survey the damage. In the backyard, small branches littered the soaked grass, and some lawn furniture had been tossed around like beach balls. That didn't seem so bad.

Then we went around to the front, where we stared in amazement. The pear, cherry and maple trees were all intact. But the huge evergreens, which must have been standing for at least thirty years, had not survived. Some had snapped in half like toothpicks. One had been ripped out of the ground by its roots and had fallen against another tree, missing our house by inches.

Unbelievably, miraculously, not a single tree or branch had fallen on the house. I blinked back tears of relief and sent up a prayer of gratitude that the home we were building our dreams on was still standing strong.

Cleaning up the mess took several months of work with a chainsaw, plus a return trip from the tree removal guys. In all, six trees had been lost, with our homeowners insurance covering most of the cost.

So in the end, what could have been a devastating experience turned out to be a blessing. Our months of planning and agonized decision-making had been swept aside by Mother Nature's awesome power—in just ten minutes, the wind had accomplished what would have taken us years to do.

Thanks to those storm clouds, and their beautiful silver linings, our country home is now our haven, a place filled with peace, contentment... and light.

~Carol A. Grund

74

Walking Wounded

Things turn out best for the people
who make the best out of the way things turn out.
~Art Linkletter

I didn't even make it through the first day. Less than twenty-four hours after my arrival on Maui, I was in the ER. My daughter and I had been boogie boarding for about an hour in front of our condo on the beautiful south shore of the island. Smooth sailing and having a blast. But on the south side, conditions can change like flicking on a light switch. The wind comes whipping in and the surf gets high and rough and breaks close to the shore.

A "killer wave" came roaring in, but my timing was off. It flipped me over and slammed me into the shore, dislocating my left shoulder for the second time in my less than illustrious career of board sports. (The first was skiing, twenty-two years previously.) I knew immediately what the damage was.

I made it off the beach up to the lawn in front of the condo complex where my wife was relaxing with a book. With my arm jutting out above my head like I was hailing a taxi, I calmly (at least for the situation) said that I was going to need some medical attention.

"Is there a doctor around?" my wife yelled out, just like in the movies. "Or a nurse... anyone who can help us?"

Well, it just so happened, there was a doctor around. Two in fact. They were brothers who were vacationing together with their families. And one was an orthopedic surgeon. What luck!

Not so fast. They gave it a good try, they really did. But without painkillers, there was no way they could pop it back in without excruciating pain.

Okay, Plan B. My wife and daughter strapped me into our compact rental car, my arm still extending straight out, and headed out for the hospital, a mere twenty-five minutes away, or three hours in extreme-pain time. Fortunately, it was still early in the day and the waiting time to be seen in the ER was only another half hour. (Again, see above for discomfort conversion).

"Don't worry," said the ER nurse as she administered my long overdue dose of Demerol. "Dr. Smith is very good at this. He does these all the time."

"I did three yesterday," the shaggy-haired, surfer-dude type in the white coat announced proudly as he approached my bed. "You're my first today. But it's still early!"

Lucky me, I'm Number One!

The goofballs kicked in, I passed out, and the shoulder was popped back in. I came to, and my wife and daughter led me out to our rental car on shaky getaway sticks. Ten more days of vacation and my grand plan of days filled with water sports and frolicking in paradise were literally dashed on the rocks, much like my broken body.

We stopped at a grocery store for supplies on the way back to our condo. I needed beer, lots of beer. As I had declined the offer of prescription painkillers, I was going to have to self-medicate. Not feeling like strolling among the aisles of the store, I let the girls do the shopping while I settled in at an outdoor table at the bar across the street.

I was sipping my beer when I noticed the first one, the lady at the far table with the leg boot, drinking a mai tai.

I felt her pain. I glanced at the table at my right, and there was a fellow beer drinker with an arm cast. I finished my beer and on the way out noticed two more—a neck brace and... another sling!

I went to meet the girls and noticed even more casts, slings, braces, boots, crutches and canes.

Suddenly, I felt better. Yes, my shoulder still throbbed. I was facing several months of physical therapy. My vacation plans were severely altered. But… I wasn't alone! I had company! There were others like me, who had scrimped and saved to come to paradise for their dream vacation, only to wind up bent, folded, spindled and mutilated.

Yeah, I probably wasn't going to be as active as I had wanted to be. I would have to adapt. I could still hang out in the pool and snorkel in the shallow water by the reef. I would have to walk the beach for a few days instead of my daily run. But that next morning as I cracked open a beer on a chaise lounge, under a palm tree, a panoramic ocean view in front of me, it hit me.

If you're going to have to convalesce, this was a great place to do it.

~Lee Hammerschmidt

75

Working Out for the Best

Angels deliver Fate to our doorstep — and anywhere else it is needed.
~Jessi Lane Adams

Second semester junior year was tough. I was an economics major at the University of Redlands and had to take an art class to fill a graduation requirement. To make matters worse, the only one that fit my coursework schedule was three hours once a week, on the same night as Intervarsity Large Group Bible Study.

Intervarsity Large Group was more or less my whole social life. I was a double major with a minor, worked two campus jobs, and went home every weekend to take care of my grandmother. I didn't have much time for the friends I so desperately wanted. This weekly fellowship was all I had, and the thought of missing it made me feel completely insecure.

Unfortunately, I had no choice. I needed the class to graduate, and I had no guarantee there wouldn't be a worse schedule conflict the following semester. I had no legitimate reason not to take the class. Besides, surely my friends wouldn't forget me completely. Just because I couldn't go to Large Group didn't mean I wasn't a part of Intervarsity, and I could catch up with everyone at the annual retreat the first week of summer vacation.

Every year the Intervarsity group had a retreat to Catalina Island, off Newport. Everyone always had such a wonderful time, bonding within the fellowship, growing in their faith together. I had always wanted to go, but never could. This year was different. I was going to have the money for the trip. I was going to be a part of that group, making real interpersonal connections with others, in faith. I was going to belong.

The semester went on, and I rarely saw my friends. Every so often a student Bible study leader would drop by my dorm to visit me and keep me abreast of upcoming events. After a while, the Bible study leaders stopped coming by. I didn't mind too much. I was busy with everything else going on.

About two weeks before the end of the semester, I called one of the group leaders to ask about details for the retreat. Slightly startled, she told me she didn't know that I was interested in going. I conveyed with enthusiasm how much I was looking forward to it.

"Oh, I'm so sorry. Registration closed last week."

Silent mortification. It had happened. They had forgotten me. After three years of being a part of the fellowship, not a single person thought to call me about the retreat. I was so insignificant; my insecurity swelled.

Hurt and with a bitter heart, I wondered how I could be so easily dismissed by these Christians. Could it be that these people, striving to live the word of God, couldn't find any value in me? Did they even notice when I was there? Was my existence truly so inconsequential?

Then the anger came. Anger at the fellowship for forgetting me. Anger at myself for being vulnerable to the pain. Anger at God for letting it happen.

If God is in control, and all things happen for "the best," what could possibly be "the best" in being completely forgotten by my friends? How does "the best" end up with me being cast aside by my fellowship, and not being allowed to go on retreat? Why would God not desire me there? Am I so despised that God Himself doesn't want me?

The semester ended. Envious and sorrowful, I watched my former friends pack up their cars and start out for the retreat. Continuing to feel hurt by the situation, I headed home to take care of my grandmother. The wound continued to fester for the entire first day of vacation.

The second day of vacation, my grandmother died.

Around two in the morning, there was the familiar sound of her getting out of bed. It was the usual ritual. Many nights she would wake up with some type of stomach pain and sit in the living room until it passed.

Dragging myself from my warm bed, I followed her out to the living room. We both sat in silence. I felt my eyelids gaining weight. I might have fallen asleep for a moment, but then she suddenly began gasping for breath.

Only half alert, my eyes opened to take in the situation. There she was, sitting in a blue overstuffed chair, her eyes bulging, her mouth open, her body heaving as she gasped for air.

"Are you okay?" I asked like an idiot. She couldn't even catch a breath to answer.

"I'm going to call 911," I said as she gasped more violently.

By the time the ambulance came, she had already died. It was a heart attack.

While it was obviously painful, it was over quickly. She knew I was there, holding her hand. She died in her home, knowing I was with her, and that she was loved.

If I had gone on the retreat, she would have died alone. No one would have even known until I came home the following week to find the body. I would have never been able to live with myself if that had happened and was suddenly so grateful that I hadn't gone.

God does use everything and everyone to His greater glory. Even when it seems we have fallen out of favor, and He is turning things against us, it is part of His loving protection.

My grandmother and I were both blessed by His use of a silly university graduation requirement, and the turning of the hearts of my friends to forget me when it was time for retreat registration. He further blessed me, after I was left alone by the death, by stirring the hearts of my friends to remember me once more. The discomfort I felt from Him turning my friends from me for this short period of time was minimal compared to the pain both my grandmother and I would have suffered if she had died alone.

God is in control, and things do happen for "the best." It's just hard to see what "the best" is before it happens.

~Mei Emerald Gaffey-Hernandez

76

Writing a New Story

Keep a green tree in your heart and perhaps a singing bird will come.
~Chinese Proverb

" 'm sorry we don't have anything suitable for you," said the receptionist behind the desk as she handed me my résumé. I felt the now familiar feeling of despair. I counted off mentally—this was the fifth "no" I'd received over the week.

It had been four months since my husband's transfer brought us to this small town and I felt like a fish out of water. Life seemed to have come to a standstill after the hustle and bustle of vibrant Mumbai. I missed my work, my colleagues, my friends. God, I even missed the overcrowded Mumbai locals. My job with a large financial corporation seemed like a distant dream. Back in the 1990s, smaller Indian towns had barely any financial activity. For someone used to spending over twelve hours at work, sitting home was punishment. I needed to work.

I went to the few placement agencies in the city. Not satisfied with that, I went to the business hub and dropped off my résumé at all suitable offices.

No luck! Either I was rejected for being "over qualified" or the jobs just didn't excite me. Now, after almost a month of serious job-hunting I was still jobless.

I pored over my résumé looking for other qualifications I could use. I had a dual specialization in marketing and finance... so if finance wasn't working out maybe it was time for a marketing job.

Every city needed people to market something, I reasoned. I had no experience but I had to give it a shot.

Soon I was back at the offices with a new résumé highlighting my marketing qualifications, back to the placement agents telling them I was okay with a marketing job.

Then followed another wearisome round of interviews and the "no-thank-yous" really hurt. There were times I had a brusque "no vacancy" flung at me heartlessly. Sometimes people would glance at my résumé and dismiss me with a curt "but you have no experience." Other times the reasons were bizarre. "You are an MBA but you will be reporting to a college graduate; it won't work." Or even stranger, "we have an all-male team; you're a girl so you just won't fit." I'd have laughed if I hadn't been so miserable. Worse, there were times I couldn't even get past the receptionist. I'd plead with her to let me meet the management. But they were always "busy."

It was frustrating and I despaired. Was there really nothing I could do? I felt worthless. My self-confidence, always a tad shaky, took a deep plunge. My husband was busy with the demands of his new assignment and I felt well and truly alone.

Then one day a neighbour dropped in. While I brought her water she idly flipped through the "crib diary" I'd left on the table. This was an informal journal where I'd often pour out my anguish after tough days of job-hunting. "You write quite well," she remarked casually, even as I took the journal from her, terribly embarrassed about my private ramblings. She left, but the thought remained. After months of rejection the compliment felt good. I was good at something... or was she merely being polite? I dismissed the thought and tried to busy myself with the housework.

That evening over dinner I mentioned the incident to my husband. "I know someone at the local newspaper. Why don't you check with him? Maybe they have something suitable for you," said he. Newspaper? No way. My only relationship with the entire publishing industry had been that of an avid reader. It was uncharted territory.

However I did make an appointment with the shift in charge. I had nothing to recommend me — no qualifications, no background, no experience. However I firmly pushed back all my anxieties. I tried to concentrate on what I DID have. My convent education and love for books ensured that I was fairly well acquainted with the intricacies of written English. That was what I had.

The next morning, armed with the shreds of my confidence and my résumé, I went to the newspaper office. I had nothing to lose—perhaps it was that thought that gave me courage. I told the shift in charge I had never worked in publishing before. He silently handed me a copy and said, "Edit it." When I finished, I handed it back to him. I waited with bated breath for the dreaded "you won't fit" line.

"This is not bad," said he, "but you realize you'll be starting at the bottom of the ladder?" Bottom of the ladder? I was being offered a job! I stopped myself from whooping with joy and managed to reply with a serene "Yes, that'll be fine."

"Well then, go down to the Personnel Department and work out the compensation," said he. I tripped out feeling suddenly light and euphoric.

That's not the end of my story, though. Each day I was assailed with doubts. I made mistakes and got laughed at. But I learnt. I learnt the intricacies of news reporting, of conducting interviews, of scanning pictures, of dummies and layouts, of ads that came in at the last moment and upset my careful space calculations. Each day was a challenge and I fell in love with it all. I'd never enjoyed work so much before.

Ironically enough, a year later I was approached by the financial corporation I had been working for in Mumbai. They were setting up office in our city and wanted me to head the operations. And guess what, it was my turn to say "no thank you."

~Tulika Singh

Downsized Dad

We must be willing to get rid of the life we've planned,
so as to have the life that is waiting for us.
~Joseph Campbell

The phone call came late on a Friday afternoon. I listened to the cryptic voice mail message from my boss telling me to meet him at the airport on Monday morning. Though he regularly traveled to my sales territory to tour stores and meet with me, never had such a trip been sprung on me like this. They were scheduled weeks in advance and involved lengthy itineraries. This time it was different and I knew instantly what was coming.

After nine years with my company I had seen many employees let go. They never told you over the phone. I drove a company car and carried a laptop and cell phone that were company property. It was too much for them to risk. The pink slip always came via a short-notice visit from your regional manager.

Call it downsized, laid off, let go, fired, it didn't really matter. What did matter was that in forty-eight hours, I was going to lose my job of nine years—a job that I had sacrificed so much for in an attempt to provide the best life I could for my wife and eventually, for our family.

I pulled the car over and sat on the side of the road. I was numb. I wanted to cry. I wanted to scream. I wanted to call my boss and beg for my job. Instead as I sat there I wondered how I was going to tell my wife Amber that just three months after bringing our first child home from the hospital, I was out of a job.

The weekend was a blur. I didn't sleep. I couldn't eat. I was sick to my stomach. Amber and I sat up long into the night trying to plan for what was coming. We had minimal savings and lived in a city known for its weak job market. I wondered how we would make it. I was scared. Actually, terrified would more aptly describe my state of mind.

It was during one of those late night conversations that my wife gave me a great piece of advice. It not only got me through the darkest days of my life, but also turned what I saw as the worst thing that could ever happen to me into something that I now view as an incredible blessing.

"Hold your head up high, be proud of what you have accomplished, go in with dignity and leave the same way," she said. "This is happening for a reason, and eventually, you'll know what it is."

I woke early on Monday and put on a crisp shirt and tie. I organized my files, and took my name badge, cell phone, extra car keys, and other materials and packed everything into a large manila envelope. I got to the airport early, bringing my wife and daughter with me for support (and a ride home once my car was taken from me).

I saw my boss crossing the terminal toward me. I felt my chest tighten as I rose from my seat. My legs were rubber and I was sure I was going to collapse as I followed him to a corner table. Most of what was said was a blur, but once the ax was officially dropped, I handed over my corporate possessions, stood, shook his hand and thanked him for the opportunity he had given me.

As I turned the corner and walked away, tears began to well up in my eyes as the gravity of the situation hit me. For the first time since I was thirteen years old, I was unemployed.

I spent the next week in a haze. Since I was married to a teacher, my wife had the summer off. While she stayed home with Zoey, I hid out in matinee movies, unsure of what to do while everyone else was at work. I did my best to get lost in whatever was on the screen, hoping to dull the pain that was eating away at me while I tried to reconcile what had happened.

I had spent a lifetime being identified not as the smartest, the best looking or the most talented person in the room, but always as the hardest worker. It was who I was and without that security blanket, I was lost.

No longer able to afford the daycare we had planned for Zoey, it would be up to me to assume the role of stay-at-home dad. My wife returned to school, and in what seemed like a blink of an eye, I went from managing a sales territory with twenty employees and millions of dollars in annual revenue, from a cell phone ringing off the hook and a calendar filled with appointments, to finding myself changing diapers, washing bottles and singing lullabies. Little did I know that what at first seemed so devastating would turn out to be an incredible blessing.

As the days melted into weeks, the depression faded, and I realized, like it or not, I had a responsibility to be the best stay-at-home dad I could be. The problem was, I didn't know what to do with a baby. I had never had one and never spent much time around any babies. I had no idea how was I supposed to occupy her time. So I did the only thing I knew how—I made it up as I went along.

Soon Zoey and I were taking day trips to the mall and drives to the lake. We became regulars at the local bookstore, attending readings and book signings. Sometimes, she would fall asleep and I would sit and read the newspaper, but most of the time, she was attached to my side, and soon, we were inseparable.

She became my lunch date, my confidante and my best friend. Even more than that, I became a dad. Not a father, not a dutiful breadwinner, but a dad. I was there for her first word and her first bite of solid food. I watched her take her first steps. It was incredible. I understood her various cries, I learned her quirky personality, and she and I developed a bond that four years later is unbreakable.

Though the fat salary, the bonuses, the company car and all the other perks of corporate life are long gone, I wouldn't change a thing. What was so dark and devastating, what caused such financial hardship and strain in our lives, left me a new man. There isn't a job in the world worth giving up the time I spent with Zoey, and with a new set of priorities, I eventually had the courage to change careers and pursue my dreams.

Today, I am back at work, in a job I love, doing what I always wanted to do. The money will never be what it was, but the satisfaction, the peace in my heart, and most importantly, the relationship I have with my daughter are all things money could never buy.

~Matt Chandler

78

Everything Happens for a Reason

A person often meets his destiny on the road he took to avoid it.
~Jean de La Fontaine

The first time I saw my twelve-year-old son blinking unnaturally, I thought he must have gotten an eyelash or a piece of dust stuck in his eye. Every few seconds, he blinked his right eye—more like an extended wink, which he held down tightly. But even after washing his eye and examining it thoroughly, there was no evidence of any foreign body trapped inside.

"I don't know what's wrong with me," he told me with that worried voice that kids reserve for their moms. "I have this sudden urge to blink, and even when I try not to, I can't stop it from coming." When I looked at him with confusion on my face, he tried to explain. "It's sort of like when you have to cough and you can hold it in for a little while, but then it has to come out."

Little did we know then that Craig's blinking was just the beginning of a continuing and challenging journey that would take us from doctor to doctor, and bring a diagnosis of Tourette syndrome.

"Tics," the neurologist called his uncontrollable urges. When his blink tic finally disappeared, as abruptly as it had started, it was replaced by a continuous sniffing. Other tics followed: grunts, snorts, throat clearings and head twitches. Some were little more than an annoyance, others more intrusive. But when loud noises began to erupt from him — a cross between a bark and a yelp, he became the object of curious stares and cruel comments, leaving him overcome with shame. My son was trapped inside a body that had developed a mind of its own.

Tourette syndrome, we learned, is a neurological disorder characterized by repetitive involuntary movements and vocalizations. It is estimated that 20,000 Americans have the most severe form, and as many as one in 100 exhibit milder and less complex symptoms, such as chronic motor or vocal tics.

During Craig's adolescence, tics came and went. My smart, popular, well-rounded teenage son became a recluse, escaping at every opportunity to the privacy of his bedroom where his body could release the uncontrollable yelps and barks and snorts without embarrassment. His only peace came when he fell asleep and his tics finally stopped. The years that should have been filled with the most carefree fun were instead ones of loneliness, confusion and anger over having a disorder that most people didn't understand.

As his mom, I became his health advocate, searching for information about Tourette syndrome and possible medical treatments, while helping him to accept "being different." My greatest challenge was trying to answer his most painful question: "Why me?"

"Everything happens for a reason," I repeated to him over and over, hoping that I could convince him — and myself — to believe that. Meanwhile, I prayed silently that before too long, we would find the reason why my son was tortured by a body he couldn't control.

Then one day, Craig had an amazing discovery. While we were testing out our new video camera, he and his sister were fooling around, entertaining us with their own renditions of scenes from some of their favorite movies. When we played back the video, we couldn't believe our eyes... or our ears. In front of the camera, all of his tics suddenly disappeared. No blinks. No grunts. No yelps or barking.

He soon learned that when he was totally focused and deep in concentration, his tics were suppressed, at least temporarily.

As Craig continued to recite movie monologues and improvise

comedy sketches in front of our camera and his own mirror—savoring his tic-free moments—a dream began to form: to become an actor.

In spite of his self-consciousness, he enrolled in acting workshops and took the Long Island Railroad into Manhattan every Saturday. His determination helped him to ignore the stares and comments, to focus instead on his goal. While I worried constantly about my son, the knot in my stomach began to loosen as I watched him develop a new sense of self-confidence. Encouraged by his acting teachers, he began to believe in himself. He made new friends and re-invented himself—not as a victim, but as a strong, perseverant individual. And as he did, his tics became less important. Understanding what it felt like to be "different," he has also become more sensitive and compassionate than most people his age, not afraid to reach out to others who face their own challenges.

Craig managed to get into an Ivy League college despite his Tourette syndrome. By the time he graduated from Cornell, Craig knew that he—tics and all—was ready to turn his dream into a reality. Moving across the country, 3,000 miles from his family, was not an easy decision. Torn between his drive to pursue a career as an actor and his fear that his body wouldn't cooperate, he discovered courage within him that he never knew he had. His journey over the following months included many bumps: health setbacks and moments of loneliness, frustration and embarrassment. But it was also filled with achievements, triumphs, empowerment and ultimately, acceptance.

I will never forget the night he called home to tell us that he "booked a job" as a guest star on CSI. And how ironic: his character was a guy with Tourette syndrome!

I could hear the excitement and pride in his voice as he reported the details of his successful audition. After so many years spent trying to hide his tics, he had gotten a role on the most widely watched TV show in America, and the part called for him to twitch, snort and show as many tics as he possibly could!

Before we hung up, he gave me the sweetest gift of all.

"Thanks, Mom, for repeating the same words to me so many

times through the years, until I finally started to believe them. Now I know that you're right; everything happens for a reason."

~Linda Saslow

79

Unexpected Rewards

We cannot direct the wind but we can adjust the sails.

~Author Unknown

Four years ago I flew to New York City for a business trip—another in an endless series of meetings. I took a taxi from LaGuardia to the National Coffee Association meeting, and after the hours-long affair where I barely said a word, I wheeled my suitcase into the November evening. "You can catch a cab right outside, no problem," the staffer had assured me.

And I tried, I really did, in my tentative, Central Illinois way. Of course, to the city dwellers, all hurrying home from work, carefully avoiding eye contact, I'm sure it looked like I was waiting for my chauffeur.

First, I stood at the curb and stared, brow furrowed, down the street. As the first taxi approached, I held up a finger, emulating the wave perfected by farmers where I grew up: one finger raised from the steering wheel for a moment, then a quick downcut. That was a more than sufficient salutation. When this was ignored, I tried waving, and even ventured a timid "Taxi!" to no avail. Cabs rushed by, all occupied by businesspeople more important than me. Safe and warm—doubtless being taken to dinner.

I crossed the street, walking as fast as I could, but still not quickly enough to get all the way across before the light changed. My knee buckled at odd moments, such as in the middle of the street, and I had to pause to get it to lock in again.

I tried my technique on the other side of the street. I was getting cold and the wheeled suitcase and laptop were heavy. It occurred to me that if I sat down on the sidewalk in despair people would just walk around me. The idea of perishing on the streets of New York didn't appeal to me, so I looked around and spotted a Sheraton with a taxi stand up the street. Desperate, I dragged my suitcase toward the hotel, where a suited gentleman was just emerging from a cab. I threw myself in front of a couple who were approaching the cab, and applied a little New York finesse to the situation: "I need to go to Brooklyn. Can you take me?"

Not waiting for an answer from the cabbie, I collapsed in the backseat and prayed he would put my suitcase in the trunk. He did. As we sped toward Brooklyn, I called my business friends already at the hotel. "I had some trouble catching a cab," I told them.

I arrived at the hotel, checked in, and rode the elevator upstairs, exhausted. Room 440. I gazed at the floor plan and realized that my room was at the other end of the floor. Facing a long hallway lined with closed doors, I summoned up my remaining strength and pulled my suitcase toward the room, silently cursing my lovely pointed-toe pink shoes that fell off at least five times during the long trek.

I unpacked my meager business wardrobe, set up my laptop on the desk, ordered a sandwich and a glass of wine from room service, and began to answer e-mail.

I had seen my doctor the previous week for an MRI after almost two years of medical postulating at what could possibly be wrong with me. The nurse had called with the results of the MRI—they hadn't found any problems—so I had e-mailed my doctor to ask if I needed to keep an upcoming appointment.

The waiter knocked at my door and deposited my salmon sand-wich on a nearby table, waiting solicitously for me to sign the receipt, including a generous tip. I sat back down at my computer, opened up my e-mail and saw, to my surprise, that my doctor had responded almost immediately.

Yes, the MRI had not shown any lesions, her e-mail said, add-ing a proviso: "Your history of progressive neurological dysfunction and abnormal spinal fluid is compatible with a diagnosis of Primary Progressive MS."

I sat back in my chair gazing out the window over the dark square facing the hotel. At that moment my life changed forever. Not all at once, but slowly, irrevocably. And it is still changing as this insidious disease slowly destroys the myelin surrounding nerves that enable me to walk, write, and speak.

The diagnosis jolted me into action. Always a voracious reader, my greatest ambition was to write a book. Now, my decreasing mobility made it possible for me to devote hours to writing. Just as many people make big changes when midlife hits, I decided it was now or never.

Fortunately, I had an idea. Since 2003, my husband and I had served as volunteer guides in the Frank Lloyd Wright designed Dana-Thomas House in Springfield, Illinois. The house was completed in 1904, and the infamous Springfield race riots, where two black men were lynched, occurred in 1908. I began to wonder if it would be possible to write a novel centering on the experiences of a young black maid employed at the Dana-Thomas House. The idea captured my imagination and I began researching the riots. Over the next two years, I became progressively more disabled but I could still struggle to the second floor of the Springfield Library to review microfilm copies of old newspapers and books. It didn't take long to before I was obsessed with telling my protagonist's story. I continued to work full-time, but I spent every evening and weekend at my computer, rewriting the book at least three times. By 2007, I had completed the book and sent it off with high hopes to almost fifty agents and publishers. No one bit though and by the end of the year I was ready to give up.

I got some encouragement at the right time. At the beginning of 2008, the local newspaper published a generous article about my book, with a tie-in to the commemoration of the race riots. What followed was a year of blessings that would not have occurred if I had not written and self published my novel, *Water and Fire*. I experienced things about which every would-be author dreams: a book signing at the Dana-Thomas House, a reading at Abraham Lincoln Presidential Library, presentations to book groups and retiree meetings and an appearance on the local TV station. I even discovered my book on the shelf of the local library.

But sweet as they were, these joys paled in comparison to friendships made and deepened, kind words from co-workers, honest feedback and recommendations from members of my church, and encouragement from the women in my book group. Relatives told me they read the book, boasting about having an author in the family. Total strangers wrote to me with heartfelt comments.

Although I would not recommend MS to anyone, I would not have written the book had I not received the devastating e-mail from my doctor that night in New York. A heartbreaking diagnosis can produce unexpected rewards—even great joy. I still have MS and there are uncharted roads ahead, but God will watch over me and the days will contain more happiness than pain.

~Melinda McDonald

Wake-Up Call

If you call a thing bad you do little, if you call a thing good you do much.
~Johann Wolfgang von Goethe

Opening the front door, I heard the piercing sound of an alarm in the darkness.

Hurrying toward the unfamiliar sound, I realized it was the newly installed carbon monoxide detector.

"What color is it blinking?" I asked Mike, my husband.

"Red," he answered. Even before I located the detector's instructions, I knew that couldn't be good.

Maybe that explained why we both hadn't felt well the past couple of days or why my heart suddenly was racing and I was struggling to breathe.

The pamphlet said: "If you hear the alarm horn and the red light is flashing, move everyone to a source of fresh air."

"Call 911," I yelled to Mike, as I opened the front door to let fresh air into the house despite outdoor temperatures in the teens.

Paramedics soon arrived and looked at the carbon monoxide detector and the furnace.

"Usually when we get a call like this the detector is malfunctioning," one of the paramedics said. Suddenly I felt foolish for summoning them on such a cold night. Although I purchased the detector months ago, we'd only had the detector hooked up for a day.

Soon the electric company representative arrived and turned on the furnace, testing the air coming out of several vents. I could hear the rapid beeping of his detector as he leaned over the bedroom vent.

"Sorry folks," he said. "I've got to tag the furnace and turn it off. Levels of carbon monoxide are four times the allowable limits."

We watched in shock as he turned off the pilot light and put a red "notice of improper condition" tag on the gas furnace, which had shown no sign of malfunctioning.

After everyone left, the enormity of the situation sunk in. Chances are, since it was a bitterly cold night, the furnace would have been running more than usual. There was a possibility we might not have made it through the night. If four times the allowable limits of carbon monoxide had seeped into the room in a matter of seconds, how much could have filled the bedroom during the night?

I shuddered to think what could have happened. Christmas was four days away and it was unsettling to think we might not have been alive to celebrate the holiday with my family. Just what, I wondered, had made me decide to install batteries a day ago?

No doubt someone was looking out for us.

Suddenly I had a newfound appreciation for life. I vowed never to take anything for granted again. Even spending a couple of nights in a bone-chillingly cold house until a new furnace was installed was a bearable inconvenience.

After a welcome weeklong vacation at my family's house over the holidays, I returned to work on January fourth, not even dreading the mountain of work awaiting me.

Soon after removing my coat, the newspaper editor summoned me. "Do you have a minute to come with me?" he asked.

As we walked toward the publisher's office, I said, "Uh oh, this isn't good."

"It isn't," he replied. "Layoffs."

We walked in silence, thoughts swirling through my mind. I'd worked at the newspaper for twenty-six years, as an editorial assistant, librarian and now a copy editor. I'd even met my husband here. But I can't say that I didn't think this day would come. I just wasn't expecting it so soon. I knew the newspaper industry was suffering and journalists nationwide were being laid off. I also knew this newspaper was struggling to reinvent itself to remain a community asset. But my role in that reinvention was no longer needed.

As I sat down in the publisher's office, she handed me a letter and a box of tissues. She explained that the company had eliminated my position due to financial difficulties. My mind tried to process what was happening in between focusing on snippets of conversation: "Joe (the editor) tried every which way to save your job"... "you've always been a good worker"... "have a lot of talent...."

After returning to my desk, I called my husband, gathered a few belongings and put on my coat. Co-workers came over to hug me as I numbly made my way to the door one last time. I stood outdoors in the blowing snow, waiting for my husband to pick me up. Once settled in the car, I began to cry again.

The rest of the day was a blur, mostly spent fielding phone calls from concerned former co-workers in between bouts of crying. "You're a smart girl, you'll find something else"... "don't worry, you'll be fine"... "you'll find something better" I heard over and over. But the assurance from my former boss that this was a "blessing in disguise" resonated with me. For some inexplicable reason, deep within my consciousness there was a gradual awakening to the notion that this might indeed be a blessing.

The next day, once the initial shock had subsided, I felt like a heavy weight had been lifted. It was an odd, unexpected feeling of liberation, of—dare I say it?—joy. Suddenly, I really, truly realized that the layoff was a blessing... no longer in disguise. Besides, what could possibly be accomplished bemoaning my fate? It was more important to focus on the future.

This, I felt, was a wake-up call: okay, you still have your life. What are you going to do with it? Life's far too brief to be miserable in your career. Although I had worked at the newspaper for more than two decades, it wasn't a job I particularly enjoyed anymore. I was merely going through the motions, pursuing a paycheck. Now was my opportunity to actually work at something I was enthusiastic about.

Years of frugal living had allowed me to accumulate a financial cushion to see me through some lean times. This safety net further bolstered my determination to take my time embarking on the right career path. Many years ago I realized I could be happy living on much less than most people. Materialism and the endless quest to "keep up with the Joneses," I firmly believed, was no way to live. Becoming mired in burgeoning debt and the endless pursuit of meaningless "things" wasn't living at all. As long as I had shelter, food and a few other basics, I was content.

Since I had always enjoyed the serenity and increased productivity of working from home when I freelanced years ago, it was apparent that that would be a natural choice. The comfort of working from home was something I often missed during my years in a chaotic, noisy, deadline-driven newsroom.

Furthermore, thanks to the Internet, freelance possibilities were endless. I could work for a client hundreds, or thousands, of miles away and instead of being beholden to an employer that often assigned me mind-numbingly dull, creativity-bereft tasks, I would be free to pursue whatever interested me.

Instead of slogging through a pile of work within a strict 9 to 5 schedule, I'd be free to work on my own terms at something more rewarding and fulfilling. As long as I had sufficient income to pay my bills, I didn't even need to return to full-time work. I could spend some of my time volunteering, relaxing or just "being." The choice was mine.

How many times had I heard "do what you love and the money will follow?" Whether it be writing, copyediting, indexing books or selling antiques, I would be doing something—for a change—that I wanted to do in the years remaining until retirement. No doubt it would take hard work and motivation to get established, but I was willing to do whatever was required.

Would I have ever had the courage to quit my job to follow my yearning to be self-employed? Not a chance. Being laid off was the prod I needed to finally follow my heart.

The carbon monoxide scare and a layoff a week later could easily have plunged me into despair. But I recognized it for what it was. Someone was simply trying to send me a message. All I had to do was listen.

~Debbie Dufresne

Italian Lessons

The only sure thing about luck is that it will change.

~Wilson Mizner

"Wallet stolen—contained passport and credit cards."
At the little police station hidden in a corner of the
Stazione Termini, the main train station in Rome, I
filled out the necessary forms while trying to hold back tears of anger,
frustration, and humiliation. Oh, yes, we'd been warned. First by
Rita, our Italian language instructor back in Indianapolis, and then
over and over since we had arrived in Italy ten days earlier. Watch
out for pickpockets! Guard your purse. And I had been careful. But
they found me, a seasoned traveler, anyway, waiting for a train to the
airport.

I felt so foolish. How could I have been so careless? The hotel
welcomed us back, but it took several hours to cancel credit cards,
notify our cat-sitter, and cover our two-day delay at our jobs. My
husband, Jimmy, tried to console me with a reminder that since we
were traveling standby with Delta Airlines Buddy Passes, we could
board any flight with empty seats, but I just felt stupid, stupid, stupid! Later, even one of those long, delicious Italian dinners didn't
alleviate my feelings of incompetency and humiliation.

The next morning we dressed in our traveling outfits and headed
for the American Embassy to get my temporary passport, intending
to make a mad dash for the airport if we finished in time.

"Tell me something about Indiana that is unique," the young

woman behind the counter said, looking up from my application. "I have to ask since you don't have a birth certificate with you."

Unique? My home state? "The Indianapolis 500?" I stammered.

She frowned. "Like a state park, anything like that? A famous mountain or beach?"

"I think the state bird is a cardinal. Or maybe not," I said, my mind a blank.

She must have decided an identity thief would have been better prepared, because ten minutes later we walked out with my new passport.

"Let's stay," Jimmy said as we waited to cross a busy street. "No one expects us home today."

"Really? Can we do that?" Suddenly I felt like a kid playing hooky. My depression began to lift.

It was a lovely day. We wandered all over the city, looking at sights we'd thought we would have to miss. Every so often, though, I had flashes of the embarrassment I was going to feel when I explained my carelessness to friends back home.

Our feet finally started hurting as we crossed a bridge near the block of ancient ruins where Julius Caesar was supposedly done in by Brutus. We headed toward a nearby bench. Several times during our stay we'd rushed past the ruins and even had remarked on the number of cats sunning themselves amid the broken columns fifteen feet or so below the level of the sidewalk. However, we'd never noticed the large hand-printed poster with a red arrow pointing down a flight of stairs near the end of the bridge. "Cat Sanctuary, Visitors Welcome." We couldn't resist.

At the bottom of the stairs was a small garden in front of an arched doorway that seemed to be built into the bridge abutment. Half a dozen cats were sunning themselves in the garden. It smelled like cat food. Okay, it smelled like cat urine, too, but not overwhelmingly. We obeyed the written invitation on the door and entered a large room lined with cages, all with open doors. From the information placards propped up on a long table, we learned the sanctuary serves over 600 cats, some feral, some abandoned. Once the cats are neutered and get shots and identification ear tags, they are free to roam, coming back to the room of cages for shelter and food. We bought a colorful picture book for our cat-sitter about a real-life, one-eyed cat that lived there. The woman who took our Euros told us to get Deborah to sign it and called over the writer, a slight woman with long, tousled hair and an energy force that was almost visible.

Deborah is American, intense, irreverent, and altogether delightful. She came to Rome for a visit sixteen years ago and never left. Helped start the sanctuary. She's passionate about taking care of the cats. The previous year they got 1,000 cats, adopted out 300.

The shelter survives on donations. It is occasionally threatened with closure by the city government because it doesn't have any legal right to be there. So far Deborah and her cohorts have won each skirmish by e-mailing to their list of donors around the world, which produces an enormous letter-writing campaign to the mayor and the threat of negative PR for the city.

Deborah spotted Jimmy's camera. "We're about to start a campaign," she said, "to show how we don't just help cats. There are many old people in Rome who spend way too much of their pensions on feeding homeless cats. Some give up food for themselves to do this. The sanctuary helps over fifty of them, giving them food or taking the cats in." She nodded at the camera. "We need photos for the posters."

An old woman, stooped over with osteoporosis, had entered the room. "Here's our model," Deborah said. "Carla has sixteen cats, lives in an apartment with no heat, and survives on her pension. She comes here for cat food and spends most cold days here helping with the animals and staying warm."

Deborah picked up two bowls of cat food and led us into the ruins. She set the bowls down and positioned Carla nearby as cats jostled each other for the food. The old woman leaned back to minimize her stoop and smiled into the camera. She was heart-wrenchingly beautiful. Jimmy and Deborah worked for over half an hour, snapping shots and then viewing them until they were satisfied.

As I watched, it occurred to me: this was why we needed to stay in Rome.

"Of course it is," Deborah said when I told her. "I've had my passport stolen three times and there's always a reason. Can you e-mail the pictures as soon as you get home?" We parted with hugs.

I smiled all the way back to our hotel, all through dinner, and was still smiling the next day as we boarded the plane. Several years later, I still smile when I think about Deborah and her cat sanctuary. She e-mailed to let us know her campaign was a success, bringing in enough to assure the sanctuary another year of compassionate care.

Sure, I know the campaign could have happened without us, but we were there at just the right moment, and for two cat lovers from the U.S., it was a blessing to be part of something so splendid and noble, so universal. Now when I'm asked to name the best thing that happened to me in Italy, I always say, "Well, it started with getting my pocket picked."

~Sheila Sowder

Around the Bend

In the depth of winter
I finally learned that there was in me an invincible summer.
~Albert Camus

The snow arrived earlier than predicted as I stuffed grocery bags into the Chevy's trunk and shut the hatch. Several feet of snow already covered our community, and this new storm was another cruel blast.

"It'll probably be the storm of the century," I grumbled, revving the engine and thinking about the past few difficult years. I'd worked through illness, financial loss, and the deaths of friends, but something else was distressing me—the hopelessness that results from unattained goals and broken dreams. And, now, the seeds of regret, something I'd never nurtured in the past, had sprouted.

"Another storm," I whispered aloud, usually relishing wintry evenings such as this. Tonight, though, my thoughts lay heavy as I edged toward our country home.

Usually a positive person of faith, I had always viewed life as a series of hurdles to overcome. In recent years, however, the hurdles seemed endless and more difficult to clear. Though I thought I'd handled the adversity well, I hadn't realized that the real me, the one whose passion for life had inspired others, had burned out.

In the past year, I had been faced with unexpected choices. And in my disillusioned state, I'd chosen wrongly, making critical mistakes.

Now I was afraid to trust my judgment, afraid to make decisions, and afraid of the future.

The headlights flashed along my home's white picket fence. I maneuvered the skidding car around a sharp curve, up the icy slope to our driveway, then parked and shut the engine off. Exiting the car, I lifted several bags of groceries, dropping a package of apples. The plastic bag burst—sending an apple rolling into the snow. Picking up the bruised fruit, I stuffed it into my coat pocket, thankful when my husband, Jeff, hurried out to help.

"I'm glad you're home," he said. "This storm hit sooner than expected, and that curve on our street freezes quickly. I prayed you'd remember to take that bend cautiously."

"And I did remember," I said, thinking of how well I knew the curves of our neighborhood roads. How I wish I knew what lingered around the bend for our future....

Jeff's hazel eyes studied me. "You've been crying?"

"It's melting snowflakes," I joked, attempting a smile.

"You don't have to be strong all the time," he pointed out later inside our home.

But I do, I reasoned. Too many people depend on me, and I can't afford to make more mistakes. Yet, I'm so tired and in need of a positive surprise.

After putting away the groceries, my children and I settled by the fireplace to play a board game. When nighttime arrived, I prayed with each of them by their bedsides and then returned downstairs. My husband had fallen asleep on the couch, and I covered him with a blanket before moving towards a window to peek outside. The white snow glowed against the dark backdrop of night.

I decided to take a walk in the crystallized world outside, and pulled on my coat and boots and gloves. Outside, my feet seemed to disappear in the endless white as I plodded along snowy fields toward the forest a quarter of a mile or so ahead.

The hushed quiet—a peace that only a freshly fallen snowfall provides—encouraged me to surrender my burdens. It was during heavy snowfalls like these, I'd told my children through the years, that time stood still.

Somewhere along my journey, I realized I'd been crying. Pausing to catch my breath, I felt a moment's panic. I'd somehow traveled off the recognizable path from my home. "Oh, no," I murmured, uncertain of my location. "Help me, Lord."

Through the windblown snow I searched for familiar landmarks and found none. It was symbolic of my life, making mistakes like going for a walk in a snowstorm, and wandering off course. I had fumbled in unfamiliar territory again, and I was suffering the consequences.

Tired and defeated, I slumped to the ground, resting my head on my drawn-up knees. Minutes passed, and then I felt a nudge against my arm. I slowly lifted my head and my breath caught.

A doe stood only a few inches away. She locked her gaze on mine, and then she snorted—sending swirling puffs of steam into the air. I studied her. She seemed thinner than most does I'd seen, and she was alone—an oddity since I'd always seen deer in groups.

My father, an experienced hunter, had told me that during harsh winters, hungry deer ventured closer to residential areas in search of food. Perhaps this was one of those times.

Mesmerized by her beauty, I waited. Her nervousness suggested she'd flee at any moment, so why had she approached me? The snowfall eased and peaceful silence seemed to encourage a mutual trust between this mysterious creature and me.

She stepped closer, my heart raced, and then she lowered her head and nudged the right side of my coat. I felt my pocket and realized I still had the apple I had retrieved from the driveway. I offered it to her.

A few moments passed as she sized up both the apple and me. I couldn't believe this was happening. I had walked off the beaten path, gotten lost, and was now experiencing a remarkable moment.

"You've given me what I'd hoped for," I said to my new friend. "Mistakes can bring positive outcomes, after all." As if she'd been waiting for me to say that, she took the apple in her mouth and sprinted away into the night.

"Thank you, God," I whispered, suddenly unafraid as I stood up. I was warmly dressed, not in imminent danger, and so I picked the most logical path to head home. If I made a new directional mistake, perhaps another astonishing wonder waited around the bend.

Just like in life, I told myself. Mistakes, regrets, and incorrect choices... they come with consequences, pain, and fear, but it's the wisdom and willingness to learn from the past and then press onward that can lead to a surprising and joyful future.

Excited by my new insight, I trudged ahead in powdery drifts of snow, growing tired but pressing onward, determined to be just as persistent in life... even if that life contained unfamiliar, unseen bends in the road... because maybe once-in-a-lifetime moments waited just around the corner.

~Karen Majoris-Garrison

If Only I Had Time

I've got dreams in hidden places and extra smiles for when I'm blue.
~Author Unknown

Sometimes, what at first seems like a negative event actually turns into an opportunity to try something you've always wanted to do. I had the perfect job. Well, the perfect job for me; it was part-time and flexible. My boss let me fit work around my kids' school schedule. It was great. I got out of the house, interacted with adults and as an added bonus, I made enough money to help with bills and give my family a little "fun" money.

Everything was great and then the economic downturn hit. Like every other company, my company started to feel the pinch. They specialized in large corporate meetings; once the economy went south, the first thing clients did was eliminate their large corporate meetings.

At first, the company insisted we would weather the downturn just fine. A few months later, a couple of employees were let go, but the company assured us remaining employees that they did not intend to let anyone else go.

No one believed them. I was especially worried, and it was only a matter of time before management decided that they no longer needed a part-time "office gal" in their satellite office. Each day, I went to work ready to hear the words "You're fired."

After a month of uncertainty, the day finally came. I walked into work to find my boss and the district boss huddled together. The minute they invited me into the conference room I knew this was it.

While they both were very nice and it wasn't a total surprise, I was shocked by my sense of loss. I'd worked in some type of job since I was sixteen years old. I went back to work after each child. It was part of my identity—what would I do now?

I cried on the way home, and I spent a few days moping. Then about a week later, I began to see the positives in the situation. Sure, I enjoyed working and goodness knows we could use the extra money, but this was an opportunity for me to relax a little bit.

Like most women, I spent the better part of my life juggling work and home. Now, I could finally enjoy myself a little bit. Who doesn't have a list of things to do "if I only had time"? I certainly did.

I could spend more time with my recently retired mom—we could do some cool day trips or just enjoy a long, laugh-filled lunch, something we hadn't done in a long time.

Speaking of the kids, this was a great opportunity to volunteer for more field trips and classroom activities. My kids were young enough to want me involved in school so why not take advantage of my suddenly clear schedule? I didn't have to juggle work and field trips. I could say "yes" on a moment's notice, which I was never able to do before.

Plus, there was something else, a little niggling question—what would happen if I actually dedicated myself to writing full-time?

For the past couple of months, I was doing a bit of writing on the side, squeezing it in between everything else. I wondered if given the opportunity, I could make writing into a full-time career?

I admit I was nervous. Who was I to think I could be a full-time writer? Sure, I published a few pieces in the local paper, but would this translate into a real job?

I continued to toy with the idea, filled with self-doubt, but then I remembered a piece of advice I read on a writers' forum.

"You have to fake it, until you make it."

On the surface, it is pretty strange advice. It sounds hokey, perhaps even a wee bit suspicious until you really think about it—you have to believe in yourself and present yourself as confident, capable and successful until you really are all of those things.

I wasn't going to become a full-time freelance writer by sitting there thinking about it. I had to go do it.

In order to succeed, I had to try and I had to fail. The trying is a piece of cake; it is the failing that is the hardest part. I had to view every rejection as an opportunity to improve myself. I won't lie to you—maintaining that attitude is easier said than done.

Receiving a rejection is hard. Writing is a very personal endeavor; you are presenting a piece of yourself to the reader. To a writer, hearing the words "Your piece isn't right for us" is akin to hearing, "We don't like you."

I try to maintain the attitude that a rejection means I tried. You only get what you put into it. I am officially a full-time writer; my work is published—not as often as I would like, but I have built up a client base and I do make money from my writing.

Some days I want to give up, but I don't. I keep trying. I am also a lot happier and I still find plenty of time to do the items on my "if I only had time" list.

~Jennifer Flaten

Think Positive

Moving Forward

*The only courage that matters
is the kind that gets you from one moment to the next.*

~Mignon McLaughlin

84

I Feel Like Crap Today

Just because you're miserable doesn't mean you can't enjoy your life.
~Annette Goodheart

Positive attitude? Yeah, right. You've got to be kidding, I thought, as my brother recounted his tale of this fabulous guy—who shall be referred to as Oliver Optimist from this point forward—who had multiple sclerosis and a sunny view of the world.

"You'd never even know he had it," my brother said. "He has the best attitude, exercises, works hard and is really doing great. MS can be manageable."

My jaw dropped, not literally, but in my mind. My brother must have been the one with the lesions on the brain, to suggest such craziness—this Oliver Optimist as a potential source of inspiration for me.

Just diagnosed with MS, fresh off the precipitous decline from exercising first thing every day, carrying two toddlers around at once, and part-time work at the University of Pittsburgh, to, in just two weeks, having to slide down the stairs with my kids in my lap so I wouldn't fall, with a body so numb I couldn't feel the keyboard to type or tell you if my hand was resting on my leg or the arm of the chair unless I looked. I was not thrilled with my brother's tales of disease contentment.

I was angry at what was happening to me. My sweet brother was only trying to help me see the bright side. He wasn't the only one.

As days went by I was introduced to other MS sufferers—everyone knew someone who had MS and every one of them had chipper stories of the way these people dealt with the disease as gracefully as saints, angels, or pixie fairies.

And when I'd hobble home after hearing one of these tales of ease in the face of man-eating myelin sheath, I was left wondering why I could not see lightness, joy or any of that upbeat gratification in my own life.

Frankly, it was nauseating.

Then there were the situations where I met and spent time with people worse off than me. You'd think based on my repulsion at the mere mention of Polly Positive or Oliver Optimism, that I might find a surge of happiness in the presence of people who had negative viewpoints or were severely incapacitated.

But those situations left me petrified beyond words and ashamed that the sight of these people did not evoke compassion in my heart, but instead, thoughts like "I'll never be able to live like that if I'm like her."

I wanted to live my life as I had for three decades, on my own terms. But I couldn't sleep due to the discomfort of my limbs, which alternated between prickly numbness and intense pain so bad that merely wearing socks felt like walking on needles. I had anxiety and two small children who never slept through the night and never managed to waken at the same time in the night. I think I went six years with only forty-eight hours of accumulated REM sleep.

"The best thing you can do for yourself is get a good deal of rest," my neurologist said. I think I cackled, looking unstable I'm sure.

"That's it? That's my treatment? Drugs that give me flu-like symptoms and rest? Please, my good doctor, let me explain to you exactly what my life looks like."

So, I went on, in excruciating detail, about how rest would not be a visitor in my home any time soon.

Then I waited. I waited for him to pull out a fat file, full of stories of others (Oliver Optimism and Polly Positive were patients of his) who were living grand lives with MS. I waited for him to delineate the ways I was lucky to have the degree of symptoms I did, that I should recognize how bad it could actually be.

But he yanked a box out of a drawer and plucked a Kleenex from it then another and handed them over to me. He leaned on his arms, toward me, as though he were a friend who asked me over for coffee. And, with the most sincere look on his face, he said, "This really stinks, doesn't it. It's the worst thing I can imagine. I can see how hard all this has been, that your life has been completely upended. I can't pretend to know how awful that is, but I can tell you there's so much that can be done. We'll try everything until you manage the life you want. But yes, for now, it just stinks."

It was the first time someone didn't try to talk me into either seeing how selfish I was for not appreciating that I could be much worse off. He was the first person who didn't tell me glorious stories of people who walk through life with MS as though they don't even have it.

I know how bad all that sounds, how awful of a person I was at that time, but the doctor's words released me from the argument I was having with myself and with others about how to live with this disease.

I realized that although I rolled my eyes at yarns spun à la Oliver Optimist, I was indeed an optimistic person. I may have moved slower than other people, my body changed for the worse, and some days all I could manage was to feed my children and lie on the floor and read with them. I couldn't show up for all the neighborhood mom activities because sometimes I couldn't manage anything except taking care of the kids. But every day I woke up and thought "today is the day I'm going to feel the way I used to; I'll do all the things I want to do," and every day that that didn't happen, I reshaped what I thought of as "everything I want to do."

I stopped hiding the fact I felt like hell. If someone asked me how I felt, I'd say, "I feel like crap." And they'd look away, that split second revealing their discomfort with my crappiness. And I'd add, "But I'm good. I'm getting used to feeling that way. We went to the grocery store and we played at home. That's it. And, that is a good day."

And even though in my mind I knew those were not raving accomplishments, I meant it. I began to understand Oliver Optimist and Polly Positive. Being a positive person isn't shaped by the words that come from a person's mouth, but how they approach their life. By admitting things stink, a person can then control his or her reaction. Being optimistic or hopeful, or happy in the face of something bad requires a deep immersion in the badness, it requires naming the stinkyness, to expose the awfulness of it, so that you can truly rise above it.

~Kathleen Shoop

85

Our Family Motto

Some days there won't be a song in your heart. Sing anyway.
~Emory Austin

One rainy Saturday morning I decided to tackle clearing out my e-mail inbox. Seventy-five e-mails later I came across the subject: THIS WILL BE OUR FAMILY MOTTO. The body contained a popular quotation from an unknown author: "Don't ponder life too much instead devote yourself to those moments that make each day worthwhile."

"Oh Amanda," I whispered, following with a silent prayer.

Abandoning the computer, I ran to my daughter's room, grabbed her sketchbook lying at the bottom of the bed and began flipping through the pages. There on page five was the motto again intricately inscribed against the backdrop of the family crest she had designed.

My only child, Amanda, spent two decades battling lupus. There were many bad days but mercifully, at times, not so bad days. When bedridden, she e-mailed and I remember the day she decided we needed a motto.

Our small, non-traditional family—mother, daughter, dog—meant everything to her.

Heroism and illness require sacrifice and she made many sacrifices over the years. She met every health challenge with grace and optimism.

"Do you ever wish you had a grandchild?" she asked one day out of the blue. This was the only indication I ever had of a crack in her optimism.

For me, envisioning a life different from what I always planned for my child was difficult. Incredibly, she found ways to make the transitions required by her declining health easy on me. She wouldn't permit the disease to diminish our life together in any way.

Her disease was systemic so we couldn't obtain health insurance at any cost. Unable to work, she discovered that continuing college provided access to student insurance. Adjustments were made to my work schedule and she selected classes based on the times I could drive her back and forth.

This inconvenience became an adventure, stopping at the fast food drive-thru before parking outside the classroom for an impromptu picnic. We ate while she reviewed her assignments. One afternoon she suddenly burst out singing. She set the title *Death of a Salesman* to Wagner's *Ride of the Valkyries*. "Death of a salesman," she sang over and over. Each verse growing louder. Before I knew it, I joined in. Her enthusiasm was contagious.

"Death of a salesman," we blared in harmony.

We sang. The car rocked. We sang louder.

At one point, I glanced over and saw her professor staring in the car window, laughing wholeheartedly. "Behind you," I mouthed with a nod toward the window. Turning, she waved to her professor without missing a beat. Still laughing, he headed into the building. Of course, Amanda finished her song before following.

At a time when most parents my age were becoming empty nesters, I was getting to know the talented young lady my daughter had become. During a short remission, she worked as a correspondent for a regional magazine covering the Central Florida entertainment scene. She photographed and interviewed recording and television personalities. Scheduled to interview Jerry Seinfeld, she insisted I accompany her. Arriving at the venue, there was only a photo pass at the will call.

She phoned Seinfeld's publicist. "What happened? Where are the tickets for the show?"

"The show's overbooked but your guest can wait backstage and join you for the meet-and-greet after Jerry's performance," the publicist assured her.

Backstage I found myself in the company of a local news anchor's mother and a dozen parking valets. We enjoyed the show over the PA system and eventually were escorted to the dressing room to rejoin our daughters while the valets scurried back to work.

Seinfeld was more than attentive. My daughter asked him to autograph the photo pass on her left shoulder but much to my dismay he scrawled his signature across the entire left side of her blouse. "Look what you've done," I yelled. "You ruined her blouse."

"Men have selective hearing," he quipped, grinning at me like a five-year-old who knows he's been naughty but likes it.

There was never a dull moment with Amanda.

Our relationship evolved as the disease invaded her kidneys. Becoming care partners, we learned to set up and administer dialysis at home. She spent ten hours a night connected to the machine.

"What are you working on so intently?" I asked her one night when she shoved a journal under the blankets as I entered her room.

"A surprise," was all she'd say.

On my birthday she presented me with an Advance Reading Copy of a novel she wrote, scheduled for publication that month.

"I took the stories you told me when you came back from walking the dog and turned them into a satirical murder mystery. Set in a deed-restricted neighborhood, I loosely based it on ours," she explained with a weary smile.

The Tampa Tribune ran a feature on the local author who wrote during dialysis. They arranged a photo shoot and asked her to do a reading of the first chapter for Tampa Bay Online.

Two weeks after a book signing at Barnes & Noble, Amanda was hospitalized. Greeting me with a dazed smile following surgery, she laughed "Do I get a balloon now?" Her body failed her but her spirit remained resilient.

I'd make excuses to leave her hospital room. Collapsing on the floor just outside her doorway, the agony of seeing my child suffer covered me in a cold sweat from head to toe. I didn't want her to discover my hope was replaced by fear.

Every morning we shared a quick breakfast. After work, I'd return bearing Happy Meals and magazines before connecting her for her nightly dialysis. On the drive home my screams filled every inch of the car.

I'd rush to exercise the dog before calling her. We'd talk until I'd drift off to sleep, the phone still at my ear. "Mom, wake up," she'd call into the receiver. "You need to hang up and get some rest." Those days she was in the hospital were the closest we'd ever been.

Illness has a way of reshaping life but Amanda managed to thrive in the face of adversity. I'll never know if she would have written the book had she been healthy. A quote by Stephan Hoeller sums up her remarkable accomplishment. "A pearl is a beautiful thing that is produced by an injured life. It is the tear (that results) from the injury of the oyster."

For me, Amanda's accomplishment remains a novel blessing. She greets me with a smile, her picture gracing the cover of her book when I walk among the stacks in the library. She welcomes my visits to Barnes & Noble where she resides in the company of my favorite authors. She gives me strength when I remember her tireless effort every time I hold the literary award bestowed posthumously. And when I listen to the recording of the first chapter of her novel, I hear her unspoken words encouraging me to follow our family motto and not ponder life too much but instead devote myself to those moments that make each day worthwhile.

~Toni L Martin

86

Savoring
the Sweetness of Life

Become a possibilitarian. No matter how dark things seem to be or actually are, raise your sights and see possibilities—always see them, for they're always there.
~Norman Vincent Peale

My ten-year-old brother elbowed me. "C'mon, I'll race you." I hated that. He ran faster, and being quicker than me, he always won. The race was to get the best water bucket, the one with the larger handle and fewer dents.

Back in 1964 in La Paz, Bolivia, every day at noon the electricity and water would be cut off. We expected and accepted the rationing as part of life. Right at twelve, lights and radio went off. And Abuela (grandmother) would sigh after listening to another dramatic episode of the "Count of Istanbul," her favorite radio soap opera. The only light bulb hanging from the ceiling went out, making our tiny kitchen even darker.

We followed our routine. Coming home from school, my brother and I took on the task, simple and mundane. With our metal buckets dangling from our hands, we dashed out the rusted gate of our home and skipped down the narrow, dirt hill. The buckets clanked as we placed each foot on the rocks we used as steps. It was steep, dotted with green weeds, uneven spots, rocks and debris. Once on the dusty field, we dodged stray dogs, all scrawny and with matted hair, sniffing for food. Then, we jumped over mud puddles and ran to the public faucet. Giggling with the friends we met, we sat our buckets in line behind other neighbors' containers.

The way back was tougher. The full buckets, now heavy, made our trip longer because we stopped often to rest. While the cold Andes Mountains wind cut at our faces, I'd sit on a rock and watch my brother throw dry sticks down the ravine.

At times, thirsty after playing outside, we ran into the kitchen and grabbed the large glass bottle where our family stored boiled water to drink. To our dismay, it was empty. We held it under the faucet, but only a few drops trickled out. Forgetting that noon had passed, we groaned and complained. But Abuela looked up from reading her Bible and smiled at us from her chair. She wore her wool black skirt, thick stockings to match and the brown sweater she had knitted herself. She gazed out the window to the mountain behind our home, called us over and pointed to the small mud huts among the sparse vegetation along the sides.

"We're so fortunate," she said. "See those folks who live there? They never have electricity, not even a faucet for running water." She took my hand. "C'mon, you're going to help me."

I sat beside her at the table in the small kitchen. She handed me a knife and three potatoes. "You need to learn this." She taught me to peel and chop them for the soup she prepared. Once she placed the contents in the pot, she added water from our cooking reserve. With frail and wrinkled hands, she placed it on a single burner over a flame fueled with kerosene.

An hour later, using a large wooden ladle, she stirred, tasted, and paused for a moment. "It's good." She turned to me. "Let's go."

I followed her to the old gate at the front of the house. By then, a few peasants had walked from their huts on the mountain and lined up. They sat on the dirt ground and, with dingy hands, held up their worn tin cans.

Abuela scooped ladlefuls of soup and filled their containers. "How are you?" Sometimes she knew their names and when she didn't, she still greeted them with genuine love. With sorrowful eyes in the middle of dark, cracked, wrinkled skin, they gave her their tacit gratitude.

Compassion filled me and I sensed new appreciation for the comfort we did have. Years later, after hard work, sacrifice and perseverance, Mami and Papi met the requirements imposed by the United States for us to enter her borders.

Our new home offered electricity all day long. Water, hot and cold, available all day—what a dream come true. Adjusting to the luxuries in America diminished the impact of other changes we experienced. Unable to speak English, my parents had to decipher newspaper want ads for jobs. Misunderstanding the picture on the can, we ate cat food, thinking it was tuna. Mami bought bloomers that I wore to gym class thinking they were gym shorts. We thought the name of a street was "One Way." Papi expressed effusive thanks to a police officer as he handed the officer his license. Later, we learned he'd received a speeding ticket.

Putting aside the effects of difficult moments, we grew aware of each blessing in our new American home. We committed to hard work. And determined to succeed, our family blossomed and prospered.

As the years passed, adversity touched our lives. Papi lost his sight to a hereditary retinal disease, and at thirty-one years of age, the gene I'd inherited from him caused me to also lose my sight completely.

Just as had occurred at noon everyday in Bolivia, the lights were turned off in the middle of my life, leaving me in physical and emotional darkness.

But God pointed to the mountains where there were those indeed more unfortunate. Those who never had sight. They never saw the beauty of a sunset, the radiant colors that paint a flower, or the smile on a child's face.

As I did at twelve, I grabbed my bucket of gratitude and filled it with encouragement, determination, drive and passion. Abuela's legacy lives on. Today, with my own recipe and through my work, I share with others ladlefuls of inspiration. I add large portions of the positive attitude that equips me to find joy each morning. I pour in lots of perseverance to quench uncertainty and insecurity. Often, I stir in a deeper sense of appreciation for things I had taken for granted. And fueled with passion, I sprinkle on top the philosophy that keeps me going: Rather than tasting the bitter flavor of a blind life, I savor each moment, relishing in the sweetness of life that my eyes do see.

~Janet Perez Eckles

87

Finding My Religion

Religion is not something separate and apart from ordinary life.
It is life—life of every kind viewed from the standpoint of meaning
and purpose: life lived in the fuller awareness of its human quality
and spiritual significance.
~A. Powell Davies

A few years ago, during a particularly stressful time, I sat down and wrote my own religion. Thumbing through a small, dog-eared dictionary, I came upon this definition: "religion: a specific system of belief built around a philosophy of life." According to that definition, my own personal beliefs and philosophies were, indeed, my religion. I jokingly called it "The Religion of Betsy-ism."

My "religion" ended up being ten pages long, and covered my views on everything from sin, heaven, hell, love, the Golden Rule, life purpose, God and even death. It isn't very reverent or solemn, but then again, my personal philosophy of life contains a lot of playfulness and humor. But to this day, if I start to feel off-track or un-centered, I can pull out my religion and re-read it and everything falls back into place for me.

To me, religion is a very personal thing, and is not something that is reserved for Sunday services. It is the rules and guidelines that we choose to live our life by. These philosophies are collected throughout our lives from places like our parents, our churches, books we read, friends. I even think there are some great philosophies in modern advertising or songs that can be incorporated into a personal religion. Some of those song lyrics or advertising mottoes that seem to tug at your heart are probably part of your own personal philosophy... the lines that, if you remembered to try to live by them, would help you to really "be all that you can be."

I think everyone has a personal philosophy of life. Some people have chosen to believe that life stinks, or life is unfair or it's a dog-eat-dog world. I feel sorry for those people, because I think if that's what they believe, then that's how life is going to treat them. My own personal philosophy is more along the lines of "If you are good to life, life is good back to you." I guess I just believe that if you lead a really good, kind, unselfish life, that life is going to be good, kind and unselfish in return. So far, this philosophy has worked out pretty well for me. When I am abiding by my "religion," life is pretty darn good. When life isn't going so well, it is easy for me to sit back and see where I have gotten off-track from my own personal beliefs.

I certainly don't claim to know all the answers for anyone else. After years of personal evaluation I do, however, know a lot of the things that work for me. And part of my personal religion is to always keep polishing my own philosophies as I go along in life and learn more about what things work and what things don't and which paths lead to good times and which lead to bad.

So anytime my life runs into another roadblock or obstacle that is trying to knock me down, I may stumble, but I rarely fall. I don't have to find the newest self-help book or run to a therapist and start back at the bottom for guidance. I know right where to turn. I turn to my religion. It's a wonderful reminder of all the progress I have already made in life, and all the wonderful things I have already learned.

~Betsy S. Franz

88

The Power of Mark

Courage is not the absence of fear,
but rather the judgment that something else is more important than fear.
~Ambrose Redmoon

No — I'm not talking about some supernatural phenomenon. I can't make a chair float across the room or anything like that. Rather, I'm talking about a special gift that I received from my son a few years after he died.

Perhaps I better explain a little about our family first. Mark was the younger of our two boys. Our kids meant everything thing to Cookie and me, and family always came first. Brian and Mark were less than two years apart in age and were always together when they were young. As they were nearing their teen years, they each developed different interests and identities.

Mark grew somewhat withdrawn and quiet.

During his teen years, we dealt with some "teenage issues" but we all seemed to get through them... or so we thought. He had grown from a skinny little kid into an amazing young man. At 5'9" and 175 pounds, Mark could dunk a basketball and bench press 400 pounds.

As Mark was nearing the end of his senior year in high school, life seemed good. Any problems he had had in the past were a distant memory. He was a week away from graduation — and then it happened. On Friday May 28, 2004, Mark never woke up. He died from taking a mix of prescription drugs that didn't belong to him. Life as we knew it ended that day!

For several years my life was consumed with heartache, emptiness, sadness, bitterness... and any other emotions that come from losing a child. I no longer laughed or smiled. Whatever friends I had once had were soon gone, and work didn't seem important anymore either. Except for my wife Cookie and our older son Brian, nothing much mattered to me.

Unfortunately, reality set in. With no job, no income, and no health insurance, I needed to find employment. The problem was that the work I had done previously—auditing hospitals and government agencies—was no longer important to me. The only thing that I felt was worthwhile was to teach people about the dangers of drugs—or helping people with substance abuse issues. The problem was that I had no formal training or background in that field.

Then it happened.... I realized one day that I had "the power of Mark." "What is that?" you're probably asking. It is something that has given me freedom from fears and phobias. It has allowed me to be honest with others... and with myself. It has, in fact, given me the courage to do things that I could never have done before.

Let me explain some of my previous traits and characteristics: Don't make waves... accept "no" for an answer... know your place... understand your limitations... fear failure... understand organizational "hierarchy"... respect people because of their status... etc. One of my biggest fears was talking in front of a group of people. I was so scared of making a mistake or looking foolish. If I knew that I had to talk to more than eight people at a time, I wasn't able to sleep the night before.

It came to me one day about three years after Mark's death. "How can anyone hurt me anymore?" I asked myself. My "baby boy" died—and there is nothing worse than that. "Why should I care what people think?" It gave me a feeling of relief... a feeling of power that I didn't have before.

About this same time, people and organizations began asking me to speak to groups and at conferences to share Mark's story—and to help people understand the dangers of abusing prescription drugs. Over the past few years, I have been a speaker at numerous national and statewide forums (in front of as many as 250 people), worked with TV and radio media, and have written several articles for print media.

In case you're wondering, I am also now employed by a non-profit organization in Pennsylvania—to help build a program to assist people in accessing drug and alcohol treatment. Ironically, it was the only job interview in my life where I didn't embellish facts, didn't try to hide my flaws, didn't lie, and didn't try to appear to be something I'm not. Why was I hired? It wasn't because of my education, work background, or experience—it was because of my passion and commitment for this cause.

It was, in fact, because I have "the power of Mark"... a true gift from my son.

~Phil Bauer

89

The New Apartment

He who fears something gives it power over him.
~Moorish Proverb

The realtor opened the door to the apartment. The floor-to-ceiling window in front of me revealed New York's Queensboro Bridge. Drawn to the view, I looked at the magnificent steel structure and then down seventeen stories to the bridge's snarled on and off ramps. All was quiet where I stood despite what I knew was a cacophony below. Yellow cabs, city buses, cars, livery trucks, and vans all jockeyed to be in front. As usual, the busy gears of the city were turning below, but the atmosphere within the apartment was calm. I turned from the window to find my mother's eyes. Hers were on mine already. I smiled, and she smiled back.

It was February and my mom and I were looking at rental apartments together. The previous July, I had been living in another apartment in Manhattan where a man walked through my unlocked door and raped me. The attack that took forty-five minutes left me bruised and sore on the outside, eviscerated inside. After the attack I fled the city to my mother's house in suburban Connecticut and landed, at age twenty-three, back in my childhood bedroom. The rape made the local news and the company where I worked generously offered me as much time off as I needed. In those first few weeks a team of family and friends, including my divorced parents and step-parents, scooped me up and did what needed doing on my behalf. Most important was starting my recovery. Together we interviewed psychologists, knowing that I would need long-term psychological support. Another day, we talked to rape counselors about how to deal with this type of crime. Despite good emergency room care in the ER after the attack, my parents set up an appointment for me to meet a doctor specializing in AIDS treatment since there was a fear I had contracted the disease. And, as much as was possible, we spent time together in places where I felt safe.

We also spent hours working with the police. Three separate policemen and two detectives interviewed me over the course of two days. I had some memories from the attack, but others were buried deep in shock. I flipped through books of mug shots and stared at hundreds of faces of convicted felons. Despite the hollowness of my soul and the shock that took away my emotion, I wanted the rapist caught, indicted, and imprisoned. Somehow I had the strength—either stored up within me or on loan from someone else.

On day two of working with the police I learned that the crime of rape is about power. The sex is secondary. A rapist's weapon is a body part rather than a gun or knife. When my attacker came from behind me, covered my nose and mouth, and did not let me breathe or move, he took control. I was powerless. I didn't fight back. I was crushed by fear. I have no way of knowing how the assault would have turned out if I had fought back. I learned later that he had been released from prison only twelve days before he attacked me. Had I fought back, would I be alive today? I don't know.

Using fingerprints found at the crime scene, two days after the attack the police raided the rapist's last known address—his mother's home. After his mother opened her front door, the police found him in bed with another woman. "What have you got me for?" he asked the arresting officer. After his capture I picked him out of a line-up and gave testimony at a grand jury. He was indicted and put in prison.

One of the books I read in the weeks following the assault told me that a crucial step in a victim's recovery is both the feeling of safety and regaining a sense of control and power. As the shock wore off and my emotions returned, I realized just how much this man had taken from me. He had rendered me a lifeless bag of skin and bones. Every so often my brain allowed a glimpse of the person I had once been not that long ago. I had been a young woman working hard in her first job out of college. One who easily rode a subway full of strangers to work, ate at the corner falafel stand with co-workers, and went to the Strand to buy used books. I was a woman who loved to travel by herself and play competitive sports, to hang out with friends, and laugh. Those memories made me yearn for "before"—despite finding myself deposited in a life-long "after." Many days I didn't think I would—or could—ever recover. Whoever that woman was before, she was gone.

After about a month I decided to go back to work for a few hours a day in an attempt to not only keep my job, but also to regain some of the cadence of the real world. After a few weeks, I could spend more than a few hours there. It was a relief to deal with clients who didn't see me as "the woman who was raped." Slowly things changed. One day when someone told a joke I laughed instead of not being able to feel humor. Another day when a friend called to check in on me, I picked up to phone not out of duty, but in a desire to connect. After weeks of feeling no desire for food, I heard my stomach's cries. These small victories came rarely amid the raging internal storm, but they were there. These tiny moments began to build day after day until without me even knowing it, a life was beginning again.

Slowly I realized that my recovery could only be engineered by me. My support system was still there, but only I could do the rebuilding. And it was hell. Moments of every day I was crippled with fear, depression, misery, and despair. Then, just as suddenly, I would see a flower and think that if I were dead, I would never see a flower like that again. My mind became an emotional battleground. A vivid, heart-stopping flashback would leave me in a fetal position on the floor, fighting feelings of helplessness and doom. But then I would remind myself what the books said: flashbacks were part of posttraumatic stress disorder. They would fade with time. Once my heartbeat became regular and I could breathe normally, I stood up and I found myself back on my feet.

Months passed, and with tri-weekly therapy sessions, love from family and friends, and the passage of time, I healed. I morphed from victim to survivor on the backs of others and an internal strength that I didn't know I had. The time came when I was ready to leave home again. For me, moving forward meant returning to the life I had chosen before the attack. Other options, like moving to another city or finding a roommate so that I didn't have to live alone, were actions based in fear. Fear was my attacker's legacy, and I decided that I would not live the rest of my life like that. I was going to do my best to pick up where I left off.

This apartment felt different. The last one was small and dark, and had the charm of a pre-war building. This one was modern. It had light wood floors, white walls, track lighting, and huge windows. I knew I could — and would — spend hours looking out at the beautiful bridge and the life buzzing around it. Still standing at the window, I saw yet another line of cars waiting at the stoplight. Suddenly the light turned green, and in seconds the cars were moving forward. Soon I knew I would be too.

~Jennifer Quasha

90

The Miracle

It's so hard when I have to, and so easy when I want to.
~Annie Gottlier

I was twenty-nine in 1974 when I rushed my seven-year-old to our family doctor. Doug, who was impulsive, had leaped from a swing in the park, somersaulted and landed on his head. The cut on his scalp wasn't serious although it bled profusely. "No worries," the doctor said calmly, needle in hand. Sure enough, three stitches and a Band-Aid later, the kid was fine. He left the office sucking a lollipop and bragging to his eleven-year-old brother Brad about his "operation."

I wasn't fine — more like a wreck — sitting anxiously on a stool in the antiseptic-smelling office with its paper-covered exam table, shelves piled with cotton swabs and bandages, its container of needles. My fists were clenched, my breathing shallow, and my stomach felt like I'd swallowed rocks. Tears stung my eyes as I turned to leave the office. The doctor noticed and put his freckled old hand on my shoulder. "You're upset, Dorothy," he said kindly. "What's going on?"

That bit of concern was all it took. Crying now, I sat down again and bored the nice doctor with the entire sad story of my recent split from my husband; how he'd taken off and now I had no husband, no job, and no child support.

Having bitten off more angst than he cared to chew, the doctor smiled and scribbled a prescription. "Here, dear," he said, handing me the piece of paper about to change my life. "This will calm you down."

"Couldn't I become addicted?" I asked, eyeing the prescription suspiciously.

"Follow the directions on the bottle," the doctor assured me. "And relax."

The prescription was for Valium; ten milligrams for anxiety, every four hours, or as needed. The bottle contained ninety small blue pills, each one providing hours of blissful, chemically induced calm, enabling me to present myself to the world as a functional person. I worked part-time as a substitute teacher, cared for my kids, even started dating. I sighed with relief; I could sleep again.

It took four years to disentangle myself from the drug.

My husband and I divorced in 1975. He and his girlfriend moved to Nevada. I loaded my sons and what possessions I could fit into Big Bertha, our battered station wagon, and moved across country to San Francisco's Haight-Ashbury district to start over.

Life was good. I made artwork and sold it to the public. I provided for my kids. I dated. I also consumed forty to fifty milligrams of Valium a day, but was so pleased with my new calm self, I didn't question my habit.

Truthfully, I didn't know I was an addict until I ran out of pills over a holiday weekend and had to wait three days for more. Within hours, my anxiety returned full force, erupting inside me like molten lava preparing to escape a volcano. Every muscle in my body ached. My solar plexus was as tight and hard as a trampoline; my head throbbed constantly—at my temples and between my eyes. I could barely perform routine tasks, like going to the supermarket, or having my car serviced. My moods swung wildly. I couldn't sleep.

I realized then I had a problem. My solution was to never run out of pills again. In the San Francisco of the 1970s, Valium was freely prescribed—easy to come by as alcohol or cigarettes. I had co-workers in the crafts community known as "the Valium for lunch bunch." They were always good for a few pills for a friend in need. I scored fifty once, no questions asked, by telling my doctor my bottle fell in the toilet. Another time I bought fifty from a disabled man who sold his prescription drugs for extra income, to addicts like me.

I wasn't the only rat in the Valium trap. In 1977 at the Balboa Theater, I saw the film *I'm Dancing as Fast as I Can* starring Jill Clayburgh, about a longtime Valium addict who finally quits cold turkey. She's overwhelmed by anxiety, becomes unable to sleep, feels like bugs are crawling under her skin, goes into convulsions, ends up in a straitjacket, and is carted off to a mental hospital. As a grand finale, she has a nervous breakdown.

"Don't attempt quitting without help," the doctor in the movie warns sternly. "This could happen to you."

Now I not only knew I was an addict, I feared insomnia, bugs under my skin, convulsions, and insanity if I tried quitting. I don't know what to do. I felt trapped. Getting off this drug would take a miracle.

The miracle happened in February 1978. Stuart, my best friend and lover, thirty-nine years old, was killed when his motorcycle was struck by a car that ran a red light. Devastated, I tried to stay strong for my sons' sake. Stuart was their friend and father figure. I saw the hurt and pain in their eyes.

At almost midnight, on the day of the funeral, my sons were asleep in their bedrooms. I sat, wide awake at my kitchen table, with a glass of water in one hand and three Valiums in the other. My intention was to ease my pain.

The thought of Stuart stopped me. He'd known his share of pain—from poverty, harsh parenting, drug use, and bitter divorce years ago, in which he lost custody of his only son. But I never saw him angry, or bitter, or blaming; he always saw the glass as half full. "Sometimes, life knocks you flat," he said, "but if you get right up again—and get up smiling—it can't ever beat you down."

I regarded the pills in my hand. Artificial courage, I thought. They cover the fear, but they can't make it go away. I decided I didn't want them any more and felt my mouth curve into a rare smile. I flushed the pills down the toilet and went to bed.

I can't account for why there were no withdrawal symptoms

the next morning, or the next, or after that. I can't account for how a miracle happened at my kitchen table that night, but thankfully, one did. My addiction to Valium was broken from that night, to now, thirty years later.

I wonder if what it really takes to break an addiction is realizing life has knocked you flat—and having the guts to get up smiling.

~Lynn Sunday

91

Lucky to Be Alive

We must embrace pain and burn it as fuel for our journey.
~Kenji Miyazawa

I attend college in a small Midwest town and live there year-round as I take classes and work several part-time jobs. The summer life is much different than during the regular school year. College students are more integrated with local young adults than they are during the regular school year. For the most part, everyone gets along pretty well. However, on June 19, 2009, I was brutally assaulted and almost killed by a local youth.

That day progressed like every day of the summer. I woke up, worked out at the university recreation center, came home to shower, did homework, then went to work. While I was working the evening shift at a local restaurant, I was invited to a work party. I wanted to get to know more people, since I was relatively new, so I accepted. When people started leaving the party, a co-worker offered my buddy and me a ride home since she was going to drive right past my house. I sat in front and Tyler, my friend, hopped in the backseat. We pulled into the back alley behind my house, and the car door opened. I thought it was Tyler opening my door as I was saying goodbye to my co-worker. But then I noticed that Tyler was still in the backseat and a second later I felt a terrible pain as my nose shattered, sending blood all over the driver and the car. I was immediately knocked unconscious.

As Tyler and my friend and neighbor Kyle recounted to me at the hospital, a local guy named Joshua dragged me out of the vehicle and began hitting me and kicking my head against the pavement. The assault lasted less than two minutes before neighbors who heard the screaming called 911 and pulled the attacker off me. Joshua fled the scene and I lay bloodied and broken until the police arrived. It turned out that Joshua was the ex-boyfriend of the girl who had given us a ride home. He admitted to the police when they arrived at his house that he had been stalking us from work to the party and then to my house, and had attacked me in a fit of jealous rage.

When I arrived at the hospital I was in shock and repeatedly asked Kyle where my mom was. The staff was horrified by the brutality of the assault and reported a severe concussion, broken orbital (eye socket), fractured jaw, broken cheekbone and shattered nose. The police checked on me and assured me that they had the offender in custody. In the months to follow, the case would go to trial where it was noted that this was not the first assault for this man and that this particular one had happened while he was on probation.

The past year has been filled with unimaginable physical and emotional pain. I have had three different surgeries to reconstruct my face. I have rarely missed classes even though I have to drive three hours to the hospital/surgeon in my hometown.

Through all this suffering, I felt myself shutting off from the world and keeping more to myself, full of fear and wondering how something like this could happen when I didn't do anything to deserve it. I sunk into a pit of depression every time the assault would come up, whether it was court, another surgery, or stories on the news about the incident. On the outside I acted as if nothing was wrong, but deep down I was lost, depressed, and broken. I couldn't cope with the fact that a human was capable of unleashing so much anger and hate on another human being, someone he had never seen before in his life.

I quickly learned that I was not the only one who was affected by this trauma. It hurt my family to see me so depressed and my mother broke down more than once when she saw my face. "That man took away my son's joy," was all she could say.

The words "lucky to be alive" were the first words the surgeon spoke when he saw my X-rays and scans. My nose looked like Corn Flakes inside and he remarked to me that three more kicks/hits would probably have killed me. Those four words remained in my head throughout the next year. One morning I woke up realizing that it was true—I was lucky to be alive and God truly had a plan for me. I realize that I am not the same person I was before the incident. I have used the pain to overcome the tragedy. I am now in the process of rebuilding my life and gaining back my spirit that was so abruptly stolen from me. The love of God and the support of my family and friends who never left my side turned this trauma from a devastating tragedy into a learning experience, one that would bring me closer to those I love. I never hesitate to say I love them and how much I care.

I am learning to let go of the anger I have felt towards Josh. I no longer hate the man who beat me. To this day I have not ever seen his face in the light of day. But through faith and prayer, I am moving on to my own future.

In the end, the attack in that dark alley deeply changed how I view myself and the world. Although I still think about it from time to time, I know that God is protecting me from any other strangers who lurk in the shadows.

~Thomas Schonhardt

92

Beauty in Breakdown

You have to leave the city of your comfort
and go into the wilderness of your intuition.
What you'll discover will be wonderful. What you'll discover is yourself.
~Alan Alda

'm sitting at my office desk trying desperately to hold back my tears. My body is numb and I feel excruciatingly heavy in my chair. There is something in the air today that I can't quite grasp, but I know today is unlike any previous workday.

My boss comes over and asks me to come with him to Human Resources. I have been with this company for four years, and never once have I been called to a meeting with HR and my boss. I'm not due for a raise or a promotion. The only rational reason I am being escorted is because they are going to fire me.

I become acutely aware of my surroundings. I feel as if I might pass out, so I remind myself to breathe and keep moving forward. I am asked to sit down. As I slowly breathe out, my boss begins to tell me that he is pleased with my positive attitude and that I am always a pleasure to work with, but that the roles of the agency have changed and the demands of my position are no longer being met.

As he talks, I find myself spacing out, watching his lips move, but in my mind hearing only static. I think to myself, "If you are going to give me the ax just do it — cut to the chase. The anticipation is killing me." Then I remind myself that this might be the most pivotal moment of my entire life. It's time to quiet the inner chaos and pay attention. I force myself to listen. At that point, my boss turns it over to the woman who signed my hiring paperwork, and she says, "This is always so hard to do, but we need to let you go."

The tears I have been holding in all day rise to the surface. As they look at me with sympathetic sadness, the water pours out. What they don't realize is that these tears do not come from a place of fear or pain. They are tears of relief, of unbounded excitement! It is in this moment that I realize all of my positive thinking and prayers have been answered! It is at this moment that I truly believe miracles do happen!

Let's travel back in time two years. I was walking home from work after working four fifteen-hour days back to back. This walk was the only thing I had done for myself in the past two weeks. I reminded myself that I had chosen this glamorous advertising job in the big city. As I scanned the Chicago streets, the faces became muddy. I picked up my pace in hopes of getting home quicker, but I couldn't hold the tears back anymore.

I made it home and burst through my front door. As I collapsed to the floor I was shaking and terrified. My face was now soaked with tears of grief and exhaustion. I looked around and realized I was not living the life I was supposed to be living. I felt like a foreigner in my own apartment. Everything should have been different. I was living my dream life, but it didn't feel like my life! It was as if I were renting someone else's existence.

From the outside it seemed I had it all. I had a man who wanted to marry me, and I had just received my second promotion in two years. I was travelling the world through my job, working at a big name advertising agency, and living in a gorgeous loft. I had hoped achieving these goals would make me happy and content. I should have felt alive and free. Isn't that what was supposed to happen when people got what they wanted? Instead I only felt trapped, alone and terrified that this was as good as it would ever get!

I prayed out loud. "Help me, please help me. I need you now." Instantly the air around me changed, and a calm presence filled the space. I sensed angels wrapping their soft arms around me. My tears dried up, and everything was calm. I heard a voice. It was my voice, but it was as if it were coming from above, as if the same angels who were hugging me were guiding me back into the light. The directive was simple: "Follow your heart."

When I woke up the next day, I took stock of my life. Listening to the voice, I knew I needed to overhaul my life from the inside out. I paid attention to my relationships with others and with me, my job, where I lived—everything. I asked myself how I could possibly make such large-scale changes. The gravity of the undertaking started to feel overwhelming, but I reminded myself that in life we always have a choice. Even if I couldn't see a way out now, the one thing I could control was my thoughts, and I had to choose positive ones. Those thoughts brought me back to safety, and that was how the journey to my true self began.

Like puzzle pieces, I broke apart every aspect of my life, determined to reconstruct it with positive energy and reinforcement. First I made a list of the things I wanted to do in my life, and I started to check them off. Focusing first on my health, I signed up for a triathlon. I lost fifteen pounds in pursuit of that dream and kept the positive affirmations coming. I volunteered at animal shelters. I started to travel, read and write more. I prayed and began to meditate daily. Slowly I was peeling off the Band-Aids I had used to cover my crying soul. I was connecting with my true self.

Everything around me began to change. My relationships became deeper, my self-confidence was stronger, and I even risked adopting an amazing dog, who became my favorite jogging and cuddle buddy. Even as the positive changes started having an impact, my job kept getting worse. Like a thief in the night, the fear and magnitude crept back in. I started to think that there was something really wrong with me, that I had a mental disorder, or something that was causing me to be so unhappy. I sought out therapy, even visited doctors; I was determined to fix me.

Despite my efforts, I knew I could no longer ignore the nagging in my heart. One day I stopped crying on the bathroom floor and said out loud, "What am I doing here?" I stood up, threw water on my face, looked at myself in the mirror and said, "This isn't you or your life, and this isn't who or what you want to be. So go get it." I grabbed my red lipstick and wrote my goals for the next four weeks on the bathroom mirror:

1. $10,000 (either a raise, or a new job with a pay increase).
2. I want to live near my family and loved ones in Oregon.

I didn't know how these goals would happen, but I knew in my heart that if I maintained a positive outlook it had to be better than my current state. Every day for the next two weeks I looked at that affirmation on my bathroom mirror. When I went for jogs on the lakefront, I visualized Mt. Hood and the bridges of Portland instead of Chicago's smoggy traffic. At work I put up pictures of Oregon, my future home, family members, and interior images of companies I wanted to work for. I thought of this as my mini dream board.

Now, in the place that was causing me the most pain, I had a visual escape. It was only two weeks after I'd written my midnight affirmation on the bathroom mirror that I was called into the human resources office to be let go. As part of my release they paid me just over $10,000 as a severance, and less than six weeks later I was in Oregon, living with my family.

I now feel more love than I ever imagined possible. I chose to turn my pain into a positive by focusing on the future. I manifested the life I truly wanted by holding positive thoughts and visualizing the life I needed. There can be beauty in a breakdown, but it is our job to be open to change and trust that miracles do happen. When we follow our heart it will never let us down, and having a positive outlook on life can turn our dreams into reality.

~Shannon Kaiser

Chapter
10

Think Positive

Gratitude

Gratitude is the best attitude.

~Author Unknown

93

The Gratitude Journal

If you want to turn your life around, try thankfulness.
It will change your life mightily.
~Gerald Good

Head down, I trudged around the walking path in the park. I did not want to be here. Actually, all I wanted was to climb back in bed and suffer. Depression can drain all of the zest for life out of you. The doctor had prescribed antidepressants and given me a number of suggestions to help me out of the doldrums. Exercise was one of them. My husband Ted had taken it to heart and practically pushed me out of the house toward the park.

Ted greeted me with a big grin as I plodded up the driveway. "How was it?"

I forced a smile. "Fine. I'm going to bed to rest."

"At least you can be thankful that you were able to take a walk in this beautiful weather," he called after me.

Yeah right, I thought. What have I got to be thankful for anyway? Beautiful weather? I hadn't even noticed. I sank into my bed, closed my eyes, and prayed for sleep, blessed relief. But it was not to be. Frustrated, I stared into space, trying not to think, when my eyes fell upon my long unused journal. On impulse, I picked it up and wrote at the top of the page: "What do I have to be thankful for?" Nothing came.

"Oh, for Pete's sake!" I muttered. Writing so forcefully that I almost tore the paper, I scribbled, "I am grateful that I have a roof over my head, food to eat, and clothes to wear!"

"There!" I slammed the journal shut.

Day after day, Ted encouraged me to walk. Mostly I did, just to please him or on some days, just to get him off my back. Sometimes, I'd take a shortcut through the woods. But I did walk. And surprisingly enough, I also wrote. It became my habit to pick up the journal when I came home from my walk. At first, I recorded the biggest, broadest things I could think of, much like my first reluctant try. I was grateful for my husband, my family, my friends. But as time went on, I became more particular. I was grateful for Ted rubbing my back and the call I received from Linda to check on me.

I amazed myself when I began to look for things to be thankful for, things to chronicle in my journal. I saw a tiny yellow flower trying to survive in the heat. It was so delicate. Into my journal went the yellow flower, along with a brief note to God about how good he was to sustain such a small bit of beauty. A crepe myrtle tree had two different color blooms. It was a lovely combination. So, pink and purple blooms became part of the journal. The more I walked, the more I wrote. The more I wrote, the more I found to be thankful for. The more thankful I became, the more my depression and self-immersion lifted.

I noticed that after a while my discovery of things to be thankful for extended beyond my walk. Like the man whose grocery cart was stacked to overflowing who let me in line ahead of him. Or, the woman who noticed my checkbook had fallen out of my purse and chased me down to return it. Grocery store heroes and heroines were recorded also. This made me more aware of things I could do to be helpful to others. Maybe I could be an item in a gratitude journal.

I began to mutter little "thank you's" through the day. Thanks, Lord, for letting me find that jar of pickles I need for my new recipe. The pickles went into the journal. Thank you, God, for letting me see that kid on his bicycle. What a tragedy it would have been if I had hit him. Of course, this one made the journal.

The words "thank you" came easily. I found myself thanking

people for things that I had previously taken for granted. There was the nurse that took extra care to straighten out my bedding when I was hospitalized and the dog walker who always waited while I crossed the bridge. Once I tried to write down all the things I had said "thank you" for during the day. I was overwhelmed that there were so many and I'm sure I didn't remember them all.

One morning, taking the short cut through the woods, I was brought to a hasty stop. There before me, standing in a pool of filtered, dusty sunshine was a fawn, no bigger than my Golden Retriever. Tiny white spots dotted her coat and ears that looked way too big for her perked high at my appearance. We observed each other for quite some time, and then she skipped off, searching for Mom, I'm sure. It was just too beautiful, mystical even. Tears came to my eyes and I sat down right there and gave thanks for this gift God had granted me. Needless to say, I went home and documented this marvelous event in my journal.

Thus, began my gratitude journals. I have a whole box full of them now. I literally count my blessings each day by writing them down. I look for them. I'm always watching out for the amazing surprises God has in store for me. If I ever doubt that I have anything to be grateful for, all I have to do is flip open a journal to see the countless blessings God has bestowed on me. My perspective has become optimistic and anticipatory, very unlike the droopy person that once couldn't think of anything for which to be thankful. Now, one of my frequent entries is "Thank you, Lord, for the gift of gratitude."

~Nancy Baker

94

Unexpected Gift

I learned there is a blessing sent from God in every burden of sorrow.
~Sherrie A. Hundley

Asperger syndrome. I had heard of it before, referred to as "mild autism." I had toyed with the thought of me having it, using it as an excuse to explain my social ineptitudes. But never seriously. So when some friends of mine started talking about it and one of them showed us a website where you could take a quiz for it, I took the quiz mostly out of curiosity, to learn more about it.

I laughed at some of the questions that I knew would score me high on the ASD (autism spectrum disorder) scale. But they were few.

So when I finished the quiz and got my score I was shocked. True, an online quiz is not an official diagnosis and they disclaim that all over the site... but my extremely high score was only the beginning of the revelations. "You are very likely an Aspie" was a bit surprising to me, but the amazement kept growing. My neurotypical score was less than seventeen percent. Then I saw the "general breakdown" which listed several areas and divided them into aspies and neurotypical. I was above average on every aspies category except one, and below average on every single neurotypical category. Could I seriously have Asperger's? Could I really have made it through nearly thirty years of life with Asperger's and not known it?

Then I began to read the detailed breakdown. It was fascinating, though disconcerting. Things I had assumed were "normal" were actually strong signs of Asperger's. No wonder I had so much trouble relating to people! We were working from different assumptions! So I began researching more and more about Asperger's. It was almost like reading my life story.

At first all I could feel was shock and surprise. When the shock began to wear off I was mildly relieved to finally understand the source of my social difficulties. But that relief was accompanied by a bit of despair. Yet another disorder to add to my list. Asperger syndrome. Me. I have Asperger syndrome.

The shock of this still hasn't worn off completely. Part of my despair is not having known it all my life. This is usually caught in childhood. Perhaps if mine had been caught in childhood as well, I would have been able to learn better how to deal with it, learn how my thinking differs from those around me, inform others so that both sides could understand each other better. Perhaps I wouldn't have lost so many friends if I'd know about it sooner. Perhaps there would have been a lot less hurt.

Part of me wants to curse the syndrome, as I think of all the pain it has caused me and those I love. Much of the damage that has been done is irreparable. All I can do is hope for the future. Making changes at the age of thirty is much harder... but knowledge is power, and now I'm armed with a better understanding of myself and of others. Perhaps it will help.

And yet... despite all the pain it has caused for me... within just a few days of this startling revelation I found myself crying with gratitude for the "gift" of Asperger's. How can this difficult syndrome be a gift?

I need only to think of a few very special, very close friends. The few whom I have always been able to understand much better than I could understand others. The few who understand me more than others do. The few most precious friends I would do anything to protect.

These are my friends with autism. And now when I think of them I cry with gratitude for my Asperger's. Whether it's true that it is "mild autism" or not, two things seem clear to me. It is related to autism enough that we understand each other. But it is also different enough that I have been able to communicate with "neurotypicals" much more easily than my autistic friends have been able to. So in myself, at least, I see my Asperger's as a sort of bridge. I had learned years ago that I had the ability to help someone with high functioning autism in a way few others could. I could talk about the way "others" think and act and expect us to, because I had had to study it very carefully myself my entire life. Yes, I still make many mistakes and it has hurt me, but for the everyday simple communications I had learned to cope. And I could pass on this learning, teaching my autistic friends, explaining in ways that made sense to them because they make sense to me. And then I could turn around and explain to others some degree of what my autistic friends are feeling and thinking. I could explain it because I have felt and thought so similarly, but also have the gift of words and communication.

Asperger's just might be a gift to help bridge the wider gap faced by those with autism. And when I see it that way, I weep with gratitude for this gift I was given.

~Susie Bee

Catching Ants

Turn your face to the sun and the shadows fall behind you.
~Maori Proverb

The North of Uganda has recently suffered from a long and brutal civil war. For the last few years, the area has been peaceful, but the lives of thousands of people are still far from easy. Packed together in "protected villages," or "internally displaced people's camps," the residents of this war-torn region are slowly trying to get themselves back on their feet. Agriculture, which had long been neglected due to the danger of being out in the fields, is slowly starting again. Schools are being rebuilt, and children who have known nothing but conflict are finally getting an education. But there is still a long way to go.

Recently, I was in one of these protected villages. Home to several thousand people, it is miles from the nearest shop, health centre or church. Families of eight people live in one small mud hut, eating one meal a day if they are lucky. A government army barracks sits next to the camp, in case of further violence. A team from the organisation that I work with went to this camp to help build a school and to provide health teaching in the community. In order to relate better to the villagers, we slept in mud huts, fetching our water from the borehole and cooking on a charcoal stove.

The people in the camp were very welcoming, and although we did not speak each other's languages, I soon became friends with several of the women. I began to learn something of the horrors that they had lived through during the war, and I was amazed at the joy and laughter that I saw in these victims. They must have been hungry, but they never complained or begged for food from us. I was truly humbled by their courage and resilience.

One morning in the camp, I woke up early to the sound of screaming. My heart stopped for a moment, and then started again, thudding hard in my chest. I lay silently, convinced that the rebel soldiers had come back. As I heard running feet outside my hut I froze, my blood running cold, but they passed by again. Still I remained where I was, desperately trying to work out what I should do. Was it safest to stay where I was? Or should I try to run to another hut? I did not know, and I was too scared to even think straight.

Then I realised with a start that people were laughing outside. I tried to clear my head, as I heard it again—the sound of children laughing with delight. My fear started to evaporate. The screams, I now realised, were the screams of people enjoying themselves. I jumped up and pushed open the rickety tin door of my hut, eager to see what was going on.

The sight that met my eyes made me laugh out loud. Thousands of flying ants, a delicacy in Uganda, had swarmed over the camp at dawn. Every child from the village, as well as most of the adults, were chasing them around, trying to swat them to the ground with tree branches, T-shirts, brooms, and anything else that they could find. Some were running around with containers, collecting the fallen ones. These ants have large white wings, which they shed as soon as they touch the ground, leaving the usually dull dusty place shimmering as the delicate wings caught the early rays of the sun.

I stood watching the mayhem, laughing and waving at the kids as they jumped high in the air, clapping when the ants came hurtling down. Everywhere I looked, people were giggling, guffawing, cackling, and laughing hysterically. Typically sullen men were joining in the fun, lifting their children into the air to better whack the insects to the ground. Tired-looking women forgot their burdens in the race to collect as many of these treats as possible. Soldiers from the adjoining barracks came over to the camp with guns by their sides, attracted by the noise, and soon left their weapons on the ground and jumped into the midst of the chaos.

Even as I stood laughing at the sights, tears rose in my throat. I was overwhelmed that people who had suffered so much pain and loss, and for whom life was a daily struggle for survival, could find such delight in catching bugs. I realised that nothing could truly suppress the sparkling life that was in the people of this region, and that I was privileged to have seen it uncovered for a short while.

That day, the smell of frying ants covered the village, and everywhere I went people called to me to come and eat. Overcoming my natural distaste of eating insects, I joined my new friends, and joyfully shared the feast with them.

~Rachel Spencer

96

Magic Stains

If you have lived, take thankfully the past.
~John Dryden

I am mortified by the myriad of stains on my carpet. It is so embarrassing when a new friend stops by for a visit. I find myself biting
my tongue to keep from shouting out, "I'm really not this gross!
Just don't look down! Ignore the nasty carpet!" I've even gone so far
as not inviting certain people over, knowing that they would never
leave wet Cheerios on their carpet long enough to stick there like
super glue. Now, I do have friends that are more like me — too crazy
busy to wipe up every spill. One morning, one of those wonderful
friends called.

For a while we both griped about the disgusting state of our
homes. And we agreed that the Health Department would surely toss
us in jail if they came over for an impromptu inspection.

"Maybe we should thank our floors," she said, out of nowhere.
Huh? Where did that come from? She told me about this group of
people who conducted a nifty experiment. After they'd use an item,
like a rake, they'd thank it for its kind service and gently put it away.
Eventually, this community of people discovered that they were quite
successful and highly productive. They attributed it to thanking, out
loud, their daily tools.

"Perhaps there's something to this thanking thing," my friend
said as she rang off to scrub her sticky kitchen floor.

Hmmm… maybe I should give it a try? I felt weird talking out loud to a bunch of inanimate objects, but I could certainly thank God for what I had.

So I went around my teeny home and thanked God that we had furniture and a roof to sleep under and comfy pillows and clean towels (some weeks, anyway).

Then I came to my living room and the horrifying carpet. I suppressed the four-letter word bouncing around my brain and prepared my tongue to whisper something nice about the beige floor covering. But then I noticed the big, orange stain beneath the dining room table next to my three-year-old's chair. I remembered that we got that stain from dying paper plates with food coloring as an art project. There was a greenish stain two inches from that one and I realized it was dried up play dough from the morning when we spent hours creating snakes and monsters.

I dropped to my hands and knees and inched around my living room and dining room trying to remember what event caused each stain. That one came from a carpet picnic on "family pizza night." That dark brown one by the couch happened when my coffee spilled because my boys tackled me and a huge wrestling match ensued. And the bluish one that speckled the carpet over by the rocking chair appeared after a fun evening of body painting and pretending we were wild animals.

As I glanced around my house I realized that all the stains represented something far lovelier than a clean carpet might reveal to me. They pointed to the fact that we were living our lives, together, with laughter and tears and messy projects and yummy dinners. We were alive! In our home we don't forbid laughter or the messes that often come with everyday life. Our home isn't sterile or oppressed. It is magical.

As I stood up with the first smile of that day, I whispered, "Thank you God for my stained carpet." And for that moment, I actually felt thankful for something I'd despised for so very long.

~Nikki Deckon

97

The Color of Gratitude

We often take for granted the very things that most deserve our gratitude.
~Cynthia Ozick

Hospitals are life-changing places, for better and for worse. Ten years ago in a New York City hospital a remarkable person gave me an unexpected gift that would forever change my life and perspective.

At the age of twenty-five, I found myself in one of those ruts we sometimes experience in life. The initial excitement of living in Manhattan had worn off and my life was dreary. Working in the public sector, I had started out with fresh idealism but had lost it somewhere along the way in the drudgery of trying to make a difference while seeing little immediate impact. Upon leaving the private sector, I had said goodbye to a cheery apartment and landed in a suffocating small and dank studio with only a sliding plywood panel covering the bathroom. My appendix had recently given out on me and I had never gotten back into exercise after recovering from surgery. My then-boyfriend (now husband) was attending graduate school out of state, so on weeknights I threw pity parties in my tiny apartment, wearing a groove in the bed while I watched hours of TV. At my low point I realized I had seen every last episode of *The Golden Girls* in syndication.

Around this time a friend invited me to participate in a service club. This opportunity didn't appeal to me much at first; in fact it didn't seem like an "opportunity" at all. I had sacrificed seventy-five percent of my pay to work in the non-profit sector and now I was supposed to use my free time to give back to others as well? Then I realized that perhaps all that "free time" was only worsening my funk. Using that time to help someone else could do me some good.

The service club offered various volunteer opportunities from which to choose. I listed activities helping children as my top preferences, as did apparently everyone else. When I received my placement information, my heart sank. My assignment seemed impossible — spend several hours every week visiting with bed-bound paralyzed adults in a hospital. I felt like I had gotten in over my head. What in the world would we talk about? Why would they want to spend time with me anyway?

Starting day arrived; I rode the subway to the hospital, second-guessing this decision all the way. At my orientation, the volunteer trainer told me that these patients were wards of the state, meaning they had no hope of leaving the hospital because they had no family or ability to live outside the hospital's walls. Volunteers weren't allowed to inquire as to how they became paralyzed. The trainer said that most had been victims of illness or tragic accidents. Volunteers couldn't ask any personal questions at all, but merely provide a (hopefully) positive point in the patient's week. The trainer informed me that my patient buddy, Charles, was paralyzed from the neck down and only able to talk and move his facial features.

With no small amount of trepidation, I headed to my assigned patient room. I remember wishing I had brought some talking points to get the ball rolling, as if this were some sort of staff meeting. Room 115 was upon me already — no time to strategize. I entered the room and introduced myself to Charles. He was lying on his back in bed with his head elevated on a pillow. He had a mop of unkempt hair and some stubble and appeared to be perhaps a few years older than me.

In one quick glance, I took in his constant environs, more claustrophobic than my studio to say the least. He had a tiny black and white television (but he had to rely on busy nurses to change channels or turn it off.) His room had a window, but it was covered with artwork: various papers painted with watercolor in a similar abstract style, all overlapped and taped to the glass. I wondered who had painted these for Charles but didn't ask since we couldn't get "too personal." He had a corkboard behind his bed displaying a few personal items, including one solitary birthday card. After the initial pleasantries, I stood there wondering what to do next.

"Are you ready to paint?" Charles asked me. My mind raced for a moment; what in the world could that mean? Maybe I was supposed to paint some pictures to hang by his bed, as someone had apparently done before me. I must have looked as clueless as I felt. Luckily, Charles saved me.

"In the cabinet—there's a brush and paints," he said. "You'll need to fill a cup with some water from the sink, too, for changing colors." Still not understanding his intentions, I opened the locker-style cabinet, the only other furniture in the room, and retrieved a large bucket of well-used watercolor paints and paintbrush. When I saw the paintbrush, it all became clear. On the handle end of the paintbrush, some sort of whistle-shaped adaptor had been attached with several rubber bands. Charles painted those pictures with his mouth, I suddenly realized. I busied myself with getting the water and paints ready, wondering how this was all going to work. Very simply, and very gracefully, as it turns out.

Charles explained how to arrange paint colors on a tray and set up a makeshift paper canvas about a foot away from his face. He entrusted me to daubing the paints with the brush, placing the paintbrush in his mouth, and rinsing the brush for color changes. He did the rest, and I watched, fascinated. Charles couldn't speak as he painted, so I chattered about his technique and whatever popped into my head that didn't require a response. Each time he wanted to change colors, he clamped the brush in his teeth and said, "New color, please."

We spent every Wednesday evening that fall and winter together, working on a fresh piece each week. Charles' passion for painting blew me away. I was amazed at how he didn't get bogged down by his social isolation or physical confinement to his bed in a dreary hospital room. He had found something that made him very happy: painting. He had that to look forward to, and that was enough. Instead of looking out his window at a world he would never again be a part of, he asked someone to tape his paintings up there because that made him happy and reminded him of something he loved.

That year, I began to appreciate my life with fresh eyes. Small things became bigger: the ability to hold my boyfriend's hand and feel his touch; the ability to run outside and fill my lungs with brisk winter air; even the ability to have a job at all. Charles had given me a wonderful gift: he had shown me the joy of gratitude, even for seemingly ordinary things.

Many years and miles separate Charles and me now. But whenever life frustrates or disappoints me, I think of him and tell myself, "New color, please." I have my family. I have my health. I have my freedom. There is so much to be thankful for.

~Barbara McKinney

98

Simple Joy

Be content with what you have, rejoice in the way things are. When you realize there is nothing lacking, the whole world belongs to you.
~Lao Tzu

There are times I have sat in my small, cozy home and wished for a larger living room, a tiled kitchen floor with a stainless steel glass-top stove, and a new couch with matching chair and ottoman. But I have come to realize through raising a child and having family and friend gatherings that what matters is not the furnishings of my house but whether love seeps into every corner.

Over the years the hair-shedding dog has slept on the couch in my absence, the latest kitten has repeatedly clawed the corners of the chair and cat pee and spit-ups have been cleaned up a thousand times from rugs, floors and down comforters. After raising our daughter, Aspen, and running a home daycare business, my house has that lived-in look. I admit I went through a period of railing against the universe each time I cleaned up the next mess: Why can't I have anything nice? All I want is simple elegance! Little did I know then that the lessons I needed to learn were just around the corner.

As the recession hit, we have felt lucky our small home is paid for. We have felt deep gratitude for our jobs and for our ability to save money for Aspen's college, although out-of-state tuition was killing us. Then Aspen recently decided to move back to Oregon to live with her partner who has been studying in Portland. Suddenly, our diligent saving made us feel rich.

After going through a clothing and shoe shopping spree, I began reading, meditating, walking, writing. With my daughter gone, our small empty nest loomed large, surrounding me with mothering memories. I had to reinvent myself. I felt overwhelmed by my wants and needs. Yes, let's hire a guy to tile the kitchen floor. Let's redecorate the bathroom. Let's dig up the side garden and put in a new lawn. The house projects became endless and my self-contentment diminished with each new décor I envisioned.

We made a visit to Portland to see Aspen's new living space. We parked across the street from the five-story red brick building. There was an old-fashioned broken buzzer by the locked front door, so we pulled out a cell phone to tell her we had arrived. She came downstairs and led us up to their studio on the second floor.

We entered their combined living room/bedroom, which had a bed and a shelf for the non-functional television and their modest DVD collection.

"Remember those large pillows in your bedroom that Grandma made? They might be great for your floor in front of the television."

Aspen's face lit up. "Yeah!"

On the left side of this one open space was a narrow kitchen in which only one person could cook at a time. They had a small, square card table, but no chairs. On the right side was a decadently large (in comparison to the other dimensions of their studio) walk-in closet with two tall dressers and one long wooden rod for hanging their clothes. One had to walk through the closet to get to the tiny bathroom, which had the usual wall sink, toilet and claw-foot tub with a removable shower device. Aspen absolutely praised this bathroom because she had lived in a college dorm where the only bathroom on her floor seemed miles down the hallway.

Jenny had spread out a simple lunch for us of cheese, crackers and fresh fruit, plus goblets of mineral water. We had wanted to take them out to lunch, but this thoughtfulness touched us. "We don't have chairs," they laughed as we sat on the bed or the floor to eat. The walls were covered with their own drawings; I recognized

Aspen's batik cloth print covering one window shade; the vase of flowers I brought now added color to a shelf by the stove.

I remembered when my husband and I were starting out in my small studio, even smaller than the one we now ate lunch in. We clicked glasses and made toasts. I swallowed their every loving glance; I drank in their contentment, their bubbling of gratitude for simply being together.

Since their apartment happened to be located in a lovely neighborhood, a walk seemed natural. Bustling, trendy Hawthorne Boulevard was to our right as we walked out the main entrance. We strolled the opposite way through Victorian houses towards a meridian circle rose garden. I was captivated by the lushness of this garden, which was one of four, one at each corner of the tic-tac-toe-like cross streets. The surrounding homes were a combination of well-worn two-story mansions and more modest one-story residences.

Across the garden was one such mauve-colored Craftsman. They were having a garage sale out front and there prominently displayed were a pair of chairs. My daughter and I simultaneously quickened our stride and were practically running to sit in those chairs. Each carved wood chair had a music staff design on the back and deep rose-colored tweed cushions. They were perfect; my daughter and her partner are musicians. "We want to buy them for your apartment," my husband and I said excitedly. The asking price was $35 for both chairs! What a bargain, we thought as we wrote the owner a check.

We proudly carried the chairs through the rose garden, down the neighborhood streets, through the halls and up the stairs to their studio. We placed the chairs by their table and Aspen and Jenny immediately sat down in them. "We can dine elegantly now," they teased. I have rarely felt happier than I did at that moment observing the glow on my daughter's face. It is all really so simple, I thought to myself.

When my husband of thirty years and I first met, we packed up all we owned in his van and my station wagon and drove north to Eugene, Oregon. When we rented our cozy one-bedroom duplex, we only had my childhood rocking chair and his childhood bureau drawers. We slept on a foam pad. I bought yarn and braided a rug. We found a used kitchen table, chairs and a loveseat. My husband made my desk by copying one I wanted at a furniture store. I don't think I have ever felt more fulfilled than I was during those early years. We filled our lives with friends. We filled our lives with family. We filled our lives with love. Sitting in my daughter's Portland studio, watching her radiating happiness, I gratefully remembered and reminded myself to treasure the simplicity in my own life.

~Victoria Koch

99

First Class Attitude

People are not disturbed by things, but by the view they take of them.

~Epictetus

A few years ago, looking to open an inspirational bookstore, a friend and I attended a booksellers' course in New York. After a busy few days filled with learning and sightseeing, we were ready to get home to our families. We left the convention center looking to hail a cab with what felt like plenty of time to make our flight.

No sooner than leaving the building it began to rain. "A little rain never hurt anyone," we thought. Besides we were about to embark on a business of inspiring people, so we couldn't let a little bad weather steal our joy. After a short while with no luck finding a vacant cab, it suddenly dawned on us, "It's five o'clock in New York City! This is rush hour traffic. We may never get a cab." My friend then remembered she had saved the card of the van company that had driven us in from the airport several days prior. As the rain began to pick up we scurried to a nearby awning and gave them a call. Over an hour later, our van finally arrived and shuttled us to the airport.

We arrived at the airline ticket counter with little time to spare, only to discover the airline could not locate my flight reservation. We looked at each other in disbelief yet somehow managed to maintain a smile as we worked with the attendant to find a solution. Fifteen minutes before take-off we were finally able to resolve the issue. Doubtful of making the flight, yet refusing to lose all hope, we headed through security and made a mad dash towards our flight gate.

A sigh of relief came upon us when we arrived at the gate to discover the flight had been delayed half an hour. Not only did we not miss the flight but now we had a few minutes to collect ourselves and grab a quick snack before boarding. About twenty minutes passed and we eagerly headed back toward the gate. Much to our dismay however, upon reaching the gate we discovered the delay had been extended another hour due to bad weather in another state. Although we were tired and ready to get home, we refused to end our trip on a sour note. Instead, we decided to make the most of our wait and grabbed a nearby seat on the floor to relax and chat about our trip.

We ended up sitting near a gentleman who at some point joined in on our conversation. After a bit of talking, the conversation turned to the gentleman sharing with us some struggles he was experiencing in his life. My friend and I, being women of strong faith, were then able to share some experience, strength, and hope with him that we believe influenced him in a positive way.

My friend and I talked afterward about how delays in life can be frustrating, but you never know why they may be happening. There could be some underlying purpose for them that you don't realize in the moment. Maybe it's to alter your life course for the better, maybe it's to afford you an opportunity you would not have had otherwise, maybe it's to share hope with someone in need, maybe it's to stop you from making a huge mistake, or maybe it's to protect you or someone else from harm's way.

We continued to sit and chat as announcement after announcement trickled in informing us each time that our delay had been extended. Being that we were sitting near the airline counter we also were able to hear passengers approach the airline employees and express their dissatisfaction and frustration. We were impressed with the empathy and style with which the airline handled each customer's concern. I admit, at this point, we were fighting ourselves to not let the frustration get to us, yet somehow we managed to keep smiling.

This furthered our conversation on how good it felt to make the most of the situation.

Well into the middle of the night, airline employees began bringing out refreshments to the passengers. My friend hopped up and offered to help. I jumped up after her, agreeing it sounded like a good idea. We then proceeded to pour cups of juice and water and offer them to weary passengers. We found ourselves sitting and sharing stories with some, while just offering smiles and encouragement to others.

Once all the passengers were served, we sat back down and continued our conversation. We talked about how great it felt to see frowns turn into smiles and how encouraging it was to us to sit and listen to others. We were truly realizing what it meant to look at the glass half full and what can happen when you chose to make the most of every opportunity. Life is going to throw you lemons sometimes. Will you make a sour face or add a little sweetener and drink up the lemonade? Sometimes we want so badly for our reality to change. Yet what we don't realize is that sometimes in order for our reality to change our perception must change. We may not be able to control the things around us, but we can control our attitude and sometimes that makes all the difference.

As my friend and I sat and chatted some more, an airline attendant walked over to us and bent down. He thanked us for our help and told us how much the attendants had appreciated our positive attitudes. He then asked for our boarding passes, telling us the airline wanted to upgrade us to First Class! Shortly after exchanging our tickets our plane was finally ready for take-off. We boarded the plane with a new enlightened perspective on how big an impact our attitude can truly make.

~Mandie Maass

Adopting
a Positive Outlook

As your faith is strengthened you will find that there is no longer the need to
have a sense of control, that things will flow as they will, and that you will
flow with them, to your great delight and benefit.
~Emmanuel Teney

I tried not to peek at the pregnancy test. This was the sixth month in a row that I was sure I was pregnant. The test was negative. I fell to the floor, distraught. "It's never going to happen, God," I sobbed, thankful my husband wasn't home to hear my pity party. "My dream is never going to come true. I don't know why I keep trusting in you! You aren't hearing me, God."

In the midst of my anger, I felt a weird similarity to Hannah in 1 Samuel. I remembered reading about how she cried out to God over the same issue of not being able to have children. "But God, how did she have the strength to give it over to you? How could she leave it at the altar and then choose to be happy?" None of this made sense to me, but I felt a strange pull to finally get rid of this awful burden that I had been carrying for so long.

"I don't think I can live without having children.... I mean, this has been my heart's desire since I was a little girl. God, I want to give this over to You. I want to finally have peace. I'm so tired of being disappointed over and over again."

As I prayed, I felt God speak a simple sentence to me that

impacted my life tremendously. "Will you still love me if I never give you children?" I thought about that challenge and wondered if I would have the strength to get through life without children.

"If You give me strength, God, I will. I will love You even if You never give me children. But God, I will be turning thirty on my next birthday. I know that will be a hard time for me, especially if I'm not a mother yet. Please help me through that." Stunned by my own words, I immediately felt a sense of relief as the burden lifted from me.

Over the next few weeks and months, I no longer counted out days on the calendar and took pregnancy tests. Instead, I left it in God's hands. But yet, part of me wondered what He was doing and if He would ever bless us with children.

A few months later, as my husband, Kirk, and I were talking, we suddenly started discussing the possibility of becoming foster parents. "Would you actually be open to doing that?" I was stunned that he even was entertaining the idea.

"Well, of course," Kirk said sympathetically. "Right now we have two extra bedrooms and no one to put in them. God hasn't blessed us with our own children yet, so we can use this time to help some kids who are in need."

I melted at his generosity and a new excitement filled my heart. Though I still had a yearning in my heart to have my own children, this open door was an opportunity I didn't want to pass up.

When the day for our foster class finally came, we walked into the building nervously, unsure of what to expect. We were in a class with about six other families, all of whom we had never met before. As the class started, the director came out to greet us.

"I know this class is about foster care," she started, "but I did want to let you know about something. If anyone in here is interested in adopting children, we have a sibling group of three children in our area who will be up for adoption in a few months."

Kirk and I immediately turned and looked at each other. I was totally excited but didn't expect Kirk to be open to the idea of three children at once. "We could do that," he whispered to me, surprising every ounce of my being. "We have the room. We should look into this."

Over the next few months, we completed our foster care and adoption classes and began preparing our home. We told the agency of our interest in the children, but we had no idea what would happen. Then we received a call that the three children needed a place to go for one weekend. We had them in our home, and had the time of our lives, but hated to see them leave our house. I didn't realize until after they left that my 30th birthday was just two days later! God had allowed me to be a mother, even if it was just for a weekend!

A couple of months later, they were in our home as a full-time foster care placement, but we still didn't know if we could adopt them. We had the adoption interview, but we knew that two other couples were being interviewed also. As we walked in, doubting our chances, we were stunned to find out that both couples had cancelled their interview. We were officially chosen as the adoptive parents and adopted our beautiful children the next year!

As I look back, I wonder what would have happened if God had answered my prayer and given us a baby years ago. Would we still have become foster parents? Would we have our three wonderful children? I am sure that we would not have applied to be foster parents if we had a baby of our own.

God knew our struggles, but more importantly, He knew the special plan He had for our lives! He made our children and set them aside for us, waiting for the perfect time. It amazes me to think that our son was born before I had even met my husband!

Even though this wasn't the exact plan I had for my life, God knew. He still answered my prayers… just in His own special way!

~Sandi Brown

Waiting with a Smile

The world always looks brighter from behind a smile.
~Author Unknown

I had no idea what the day would bring. I went to the dentist for my routine cleaning. The staff was friendly and happy as usual. After my cleaning, I visited the restroom as usual before embarking on my other errands for the day.

As I opened the restroom door heading out into the lobby, the thing I first became aware of was that it was extremely quiet and dark. At first, I thought there must have been some kind of power failure. I stepped forward and whispered a meek "hello," and then I uttered another "hello." No response. It was then that I realized that I was alone and that the staff had most likely gone to lunch. No problem, I told myself. I'll just let myself out, thank you.

The door wouldn't open. I tried a few times, but it was locked tight. I felt a mild panic but I reasoned I only had to occupy myself until they returned. After all, it wasn't a real emergency. I had what I needed: a whole cooler full of water, and the bathroom was nearby. What else could I need except for maybe a bottle of champagne while I was waiting?

I found a light switch, made myself comfortable on the waiting room couch and pulled out all those photo albums I never have time to browse through. They consisted of before and after photos of people who had their teeth transformed from crooked, uneven and discolored to straight, white and dazzling. As I turned the pages observing the changes in all the people, young and old, male and female, I began to wonder about the nature of a smile. I knew what people said about the eyes, that they were the windows to the soul. What about a smile?

I noticed that all the people who had undergone this transformation said that it improved their self-confidence drastically. I wondered how that happened. When you smiled at someone, you couldn't really see yourself smile… unless you saw your smile returned to you on someone else's face. So, I reasoned, a smile lightens the spirit of the receiver, if they are open to it. At least that's the way I felt when someone smiled at me. In returning to the sender, a smile is a message of warmth that most of us take for granted.

I began to think of all the unforgettable smiles in my life. I just closed my eyes and waited for the smiles that popped up in my mind.

The first was the unforgettable smile my son had on his face at nine months, the first day he started to walk. It was an amusing smile, as though it had been drawn on his face with a crayon. He was obviously very pleased (and surprised) at his newfound ability. I will never forget it.

The next smile that came to mind was my grandmother's as she stood at the threshold of her kitchen door, waiting for us to arrive after a few hours on the road, ready to fill our stomachs, growling with hunger for her homemade tortillas, beans and rice and delicious salsa that no restaurant could ever duplicate. She would have her apron tied around her with the blue rickrack trim and her flowery, button-front dress, her hair in loose curls peppered with grey that hugged her head and that we loved to touch.

The last smile that rose to the surface from my memory was my own faint smile reflected in the mirror in the middle of the night. I had undergone chemo for breast cancer and had been bald for more than six months. I had no eyelashes or eyebrows. Who could guess that such small things would mean so much in a time of crisis? Many times I would get up and look at my eyes and brows, examining them for any hint of hair. When there wasn't any, I would usually cry myself to sleep.

But one night, I had my magnifying glass in my hand as usual, when I saw the tiniest shoot of hair on my eyelid. It was so small, so fragile; it was white in its faint emergence. I drew back just a bit and I smiled at myself. I saw my smile in the mirror. It was one of relief. That night I cried myself to sleep, but this time, they were tears of joy.

When I emerged from my ruminations about smiles, I realized that nearly an hour and a half had passed. Knowing all the while that I could pick up the phone and call 911 at any time, the situation in which I had found myself appeared to be more interesting. I roamed around wondering if they had a refrigerator. I came to a small room and found a brownie. Not a bad meal for a surprise stay at the dentist's. (It would be a good excuse for going off my diet.) Thank God for little blessings! I was still thinking it might be nice to have some champagne when I heard the sound of car doors slamming.

I looked outside and saw my dentist and the entire staff emerging from two cars and heading for the office.

When the dentist opened the door, his ever-present smile disappeared as he saw me sitting in the waiting room calmly flipping through magazines as though I were waiting to be called in for my cleaning. It took him a second to realize what had happened.

The rest of the staff was on his heels, stopping abruptly at the door, and when it dawned on them that I had been in the office the entire time, they apologized again and again. It really was a good little reprieve, I told them. They all stood around, stunned and speechless, but I told them I had a chance to think about what a smile really means and that I just might write a story about it.

While the staff was still a bit disoriented, repeatedly offering apologies, I realized that I felt very, very good about just smiling. When I had them finally laughing about it, I headed for the door, going on to my other errands.

I was thinking that everyday inconveniences can transform themselves into unusual opportunities if we remain open to them.

Just then, I noticed a plaque on the wall that read: "A smile is over in a flash, but the memory of it lasts a lifetime." So, true, I thought to myself as I walked out the door... so true.

~Leah M. Cano

Meet Our Contributors

Debbie Acklin lives in Alabama with her husband, two children, and Duchess the cat. She enjoys outdoor activities, gardening and travel. Debbie is planning to collaborate with her daughter on a book of travel stories. E-mail her at d_acklin@hotmail.com.

Barbara Blossom Ashmun has written six garden books, most recently *Married to My Garden*, about her love affair with plants. She's been writing "Garden Muse," the garden column for the *Portland Tribune* since 2004, and has also contributed to many garden magazines, especially *Fine Gardening*.

Nancy Baker resides in College Station, TX with her husband and Golden Retriever. After retirement, she pursued her lifelong love of writing and has been published in numerous national magazines and anthologies. She has three children, eight grandchildren and nine great-grandchildren, all of whom are an inspiration to her.

Shinan Barclay is the editor of *Align with Global Harmony*, and the co-author of *The Sedona Vortex Experience* and *Moontime for Kory*. Her work has been translated into five languages and appears in numerous anthologies. A ceramic artist, she lives on the Oregon Coast. Contact her at www.facebook.com/shinanbarclay. www.shinanbarclay. author@blogspot.com.

Roy A. Barnes writes from southeastern Wyoming. His travel-related works have been published by *Transitions Abroad*, *Travel Thru History*, *In Flight USA*, *Northwest Prime Time*, *Live Life Travel*, *C/Oasis*, BootsnAll.com, and others. His works of poetry and prose have been published by *Poesia*, Skatefic.com, *Literary Liftoff*, *Conceit Magazine* and others.

Since the tragic death of his younger son, **Phil Bauer** speaks nationally on the issue of drug abuse prevention. He and his wife Cookie have been married for twenty-nine years. They enjoy spending time with their son Brian, daughter-in-law Lauren, and the grandkids. Please e-mail Phil at pbauer1@comcast.net.

Garrett Bauman has recently retired as a professor of English at Monroe Community College in Rochester, NY and is the author of a book on writing, *Ideas and Details*, 7th edition published by Cengage. He plays tennis, kayaks, gardens and writes about his students and family. He can be contacted via e-mail at mbauman@monroecc.edu.

Susie Bee loves writing many styles, including poetry. She also loves arts and sciences, and really loves animals. She understands animals so well that some have called her an animal whisperer. You can e-mail her at SusieSusieBee@gmail.com.

James Scott Bell has been called a "master of suspense" (*Library Journal*) and a writer of "heart-pounding" fiction (*Publishers Weekly*). He earned a law degree from the University of Southern California and practiced several years in Los Angeles before turning to writing full time. Visit his website at www.jamesscottbell.com.

Jennifer Berger currently resides in Queens, NY with her husband Aaron and her three-year-old son Josh. A former editor and freelance writer who loves to read and write, Jennifer is currently a stay-at-home wife, mother and full time advocate for her child.

Janet K. Brennan (aka JB Stillwater) is a poet, author, and book critic. She has released three books of poetry and two novels. She co-owns Casa de Snapdragon Publishing LLC, a traditional, independent book publisher. Her short stories and articles have been published in periodicals worldwide.

Sage de Beixedon Breslin, Ph.D. is a Licensed Psychologist and Intuitive Consultant, and an accomplished author. Her latest publications have been written to inspire and touch those who have struggled with life's challenges. Her books, stories and chapters are available on her website at www.HealingHeartCenter.org. She can be reached at Sage@HealingHeartCenter.org.

Elaine L. Bridge worked in the woods on the West Coast as a forester before becoming a stay-at-home mom to her three boys. Now living in Ohio she works part-time in a grocery store and is devoted to developing her relationship with God, caring for her family and writing inspirational material.

Sandi Brown is a pastor's wife and worship leader at Refuge Assembly of God in Bloomfield, IN. She enjoys freelance writing, as well as spending time with her family. Visit her blog at http://sandibrown. blogspot.com or e-mail her at safehouseministry@hotmail.com.

Lydia Calder's writing experience includes articles and personal essays published in a number of magazines. A former preschool teacher she now spends much of her time tending to a very active granddaughter. In the quiet times she writes.

Leah M. Cano received her BA in Spanish at University of California, Irvine and a Masters in Education at University of California, Santa Cruz. She teaches Spanish and French in Laguna Beach, CA, designs women's clothing and enjoys traveling, playing guitar and writing.

Brenda Dillon Carr lives in Enid, OK, with her husband Patrick, and children, Landry, Kelley, Carissa, and Aliceyn. Shane is now twenty-three years old and lives on his own in Enid. She is an avid football fan for the Nebraska Cornhuskers and enjoys sewing, writing, reading, and spending time with her pets.

Matt Chandler is a former chef who has always had a passion for writing. He is a reporter with *Business First* newspaper in Buffalo, NY and most importantly, he is a proud daddy to his daughter Zoey and son Oliver. Please e-mail him at matthewchandler@hotmail.com.

Emily Parke Chase survived her jungle training and now speaks at conferences and retreats across the country. She is the author of six books for teens about relationship issues, including *Why Say No When My Hormones Say Go?* Visit her at www.emilychase.com.

Jane McBride Choate has been writing her whole life. She is the author of more than twenty-five novels and hundreds of articles and short stories. She is also a loving mother and grandmother. Jane is thrilled to see her work appear in *Chicken Soup for the Soul.*

Shawn Decker educates at colleges in the United States about HIV/AIDS alongside his wife, Gwenn Barringer. The couple happily lives together in Charlottesville, VA. In 2006, Shawn's humorous memoir, *My Pet Virus*, was published. He's currently working on his second book. You can find Shawn at www.shawnandgwenn.com.

Nikki Deckon lives in the Northwest with her husband, two spunky sons and three spirited cats. Her writing desk is right in the middle of all the action—the kitchen. Some day she hopes to be more like Mother Teresa and a woman that her boys admire. You can e-mail her at reachnikkideckon@yahoo.com.

Gerald L. Dlubala has been a freelance writer in St. Louis, MO for over sixteen years. He looks at life's everyday occurrences through a unique perspective, and shares his thoughts with family, friends, two loyal dogs, and anyone else that will listen. You can contact Gerald via e-mail at gldlubala@swbell.net.

Debbie Dufresne earned a master's degree in library and information science from Syracuse University. After many years working for a newspaper, she is now a freelance copy editor/proofreader/writer. She is a New York Yankees fan and also enjoys reading and searching for antiques and collectibles at auctions, estate sales and flea markets. E-mail her at Debduf@localnet.com.

Although blind, **Janet Perez Eckles** thrives as a Spanish interpreter, international speaker, writer and author of *Trials of Today, Treasures for Tomorrow — Overcoming Adversities in Life.* From her home in Florida, she enjoys working on church ministries and taking Caribbean cruises with husband Gene. She imparts inspirations at: www.janetperezeckles.com.

Terri Elders, LCSW, lives near Colville, WA, with two inspirational dogs and three narcissistic cats. Over thirty of her stories have appeared in anthology series, including several *Chicken Soup for the Soul* books. She can be friended on Facebook and contacted via e-mail at telders@hotmail.com.

Shawnelle Eliasen and her husband Lonny raise their five boys in an old Victorian on the Mississippi River. Her work has been published in *Guideposts, Angels on Earth, Marriage Partnership, MomSense, Hearts at Home* magazine, Ourprayer.org, and several anthologies including *Chicken Soup for the Soul, Christmas Miracles,* and *Praying from the Heart.*

Jean Ferratier holds a degree in Psychology and a Masters in Early Childhood Education. Her passion is learning and sharing information through inspirational stories for children and adults. She enjoys teaching and spiritual mentoring. Dancing and participating in the arts are her special interests. Please contact her via e-mail at jferratier@gmail.com.

Inspired by her grandmother, **Kris Flaa** obtained an M.A. in Gerontology before she left corporate management to write, see the National Parks, and spend more time with her family and friends. She recently completed her first novel and lives near Minneapolis with her partner and their charming Westie. E-mail her at kmflaa@comcast.net.

Jennifer Flaten is a freelance writer living in Wisconsin with her husband and three children. In her spare time Jennifer enjoys gardening and jewelry making. Please e-mail her at flaten5@sbcglobal.net.

Betsy S. Franz is a freelance writer and photographer specializing in nature, wildlife, the environment, and both humorous and inspirational human interest topics. She lives in Melbourne, FL with her husband Tom. You may visit Betsy online at www.naturesdetails.net or by email at backyarder1@earthlink.net.

Erin Fuentes received her B.A. from Converse College and enjoys facilitating a support group for the caregivers of Alzheimer's patients. She lives with her husband, daughter, and multiple pets in Atlanta, GA. She has a collection of children's stories. Please contact her via e-mail at erinc.fuentes@gmail.com.

Mei Emerald Gaffey-Hernandez graduated from the University of Redlands in 2002 with a BA in Economics and double minors in Music and Religious Studies. She currently lives in San Luis Obispo, CA with her husband (Papi) and two sons (Chelo and John). Please e-mail her at meigaffey@yahoo.com.

Heather Gallegos is a married mother of three, wannabe runner, life saver and recreational writer. This is her first published work. Connect with her and find out how the story ends at http://elevenminutes.wordpress.com.

Grace Gonzalez is a young woman living with a terminal illness and wishes to share her story with others. She wants to make a difference in this world before her time comes.

Cindy Gore lives with her husband and family in El Cajon, CA. She enjoys writing, working at her church, and gardening. She enjoys a variety of writing styles, and is working on a young adult book called *Beatrice Fort aka Roxie — All Time Rootbeer Champ*. E-mail her at cjgore01@yahoo.com.

Carol A. Grund is a previous *Chicken Soup for the Soul* contributor. She has also published stories, articles, poems and plays for children. Her novel for ages 8-12, called *Anna Mei: Cartoon Girl*, was published in April 2010. Two sequels have been scheduled for 2011. Read more at www.CarolAGrund.com.

Lee Hammerschmidt is a graphic designer/writer/songwriter/troubadour who lives on the fringe of Portland, OR. His work has appeared in *Gumshoe Review*, *Page Forty-Seven*, Short-Story.Me, *Untied Shoelaces of the Mind*, *Chicken Soup for the Soul: Runners*, and more. Check out his hit parade on YouTube!

Melanie Adams Hardy received her BS with honors from Spring Hill College in 1984, and her JD from Concord University in 2007. She is an attorney and works for Cunningham Lindsey USA. Melanie enjoys cooking, Pilates, volunteering, and spending time with her husband and children. Please e-mail her at rhardy212@charter.net.

Julie A. Havener, PLMHP, is a counselor and curriculum developer at Friendship Home, a domestic violence shelter in Lincoln, NE. Julie enjoys helping empower individuals and groups through discovery and development of their unique strengths. If you wish to contact Julie, please e-mail her at jdhavener5@aol.com.

Ruth Heidrich is a six-time Ironman Triathlon finisher and has set age-group records in 100-meter dashes, ultramarathons, pentathlons, and triathlons. She holds a master's in psychology and a doctorate in health education. Author of *Senior Fitness* and *A Race for Life*, as well as cookbooks, she has an "Ask Dr. Ruth" column on her website, www.RuthHeidrich.com.

Miriam Hill is a frequent contributor to *Chicken Soup for the Soul* books and has been published in *Writer's Digest, The Christian Science Monitor, Grit, St. Petersburg Times, The Sacramento Bee* and Poynter Online. Miriam's manuscript received Honorable Mention for Inspirational Writing in a Writer's Digest Writing Competition.

Erika Hoffman has authored many inspirational non-fiction narratives for several anthologies and magazines. In addition, she has penned a novel: *Secrets, Lies, and Grace*, published by Comfort Publishing.

Jennie Ivey lives in Tennessee. She is a newspaper columnist and the author of three non-fiction books. She has published numerous fiction and non-fiction pieces, including stories in several *Chicken Soup for the Soul* books.

Shannon Kaiser received her BA in Journalism and Communication from the University of Oregon. She just moved back to Oregon, where she loves to write, hike, bike, run and reconnect with herself and family. She lives with her favorite jogging buddy, her dog Tucker. Contact her at Shannon.kaiser@mac.com.

Paul Karrer has been published in the *San Francisco Chronicle, The Christian Science Monitor* and many *Chicken Soup for the Soul* books. He was North Monterey County's LULAC Educator of the year for

2009. He is a fifth-grade teacher and union negotiator in Castroville, California. He frequently gives talks on education or writing matters.

Jean Kinsey resides in Brooks, KY, where she enjoys church, travel and grandchildren. Her creative non-fiction stories have been published in *Chicken Soup for the Soul* and *A Cup of Comfort* anthologies. Her award-winning fiction short stories are found in various periodicals. She is in the process of writing two Christian novels. E-mail her at kystorywriter@yahoo.com.

Victoria Koch received her Bachelor of Arts and Standard Secondary Teaching Credential from the University of California, Santa Barbara. Victoria has taught high school language arts and works with teen mothers and cancer students in their homes. She loves writing hopeful and true essays. Please e-mail her at victoria.a.koch@gmail.com.

Maggie Koller is a high school teacher in Charlotte, NC, a graduate of Eastern Michigan University, and was previously published in *Chicken Soup for the Soul*. She thanks her mom for telling her to write this story down, and her students who hear this story every year. Please e-mail her at scrappymags@yahoo.com.

Jeannie Lancaster, a freelance writer from Loveland, CO, celebrates blessings and delights in the beauty of simple things. She dedicates her story to her husband, who has danced with her through thirty-nine years of rain and sunshine, joy and sorrow. You can e-mail her at bjlancast@msn.com.

Linda L. Leary mother, grandmother, and former business owner is now a freelance writer including short stories, poetry, editing, ghost writing and magazine articles. She is actively involved in the international alternative justice movement called Restorative Justice and women's leadership groups. Please contact her via e-mail siouxlu@comcast.net.

Patricia Lorenz is the author of a dozen books including *The 5 Things We Need to Be Happy*. She also has stories in over fifty *Chicken Soup for the Soul* books. She's a professional speaker, willing to travel the country to deliver her inspirational messages. Visit her at www. PatriciaLorenz.com.

Mandie Maass is a certified life coach who has dedicated herself to motivating and encouraging others to become their very best person. She loves reading, writing, and most of all spending quality time with her husband and three boys. She is currently writing a book on experiencing fullness of life.

Karen Majoris-Garrison is an award-winning author, speaker, and editor, whose stories appear nationally in Barbour Publishing, *Woman's World*, *Chicken Soup for the Soul*, and other publications. Karen credits God and her family as her inspiration. For more information, please visit: www.soothingsouls.org.

Shawn Marie Mann spends her time researching the history of amusement parks, reading, and being with her husband and three children. Shawn loves traveling the state looking for new and unusual places to visit with her family on mystery trips. She plans to write as long as she has something to share. E-mail her at shawnmariemann@ yahoo.com.

Kids, critters, and country music give **Annie Mannix** plenty of raw material to inspire her tales about the sparks and giggles of everyday life. More of her stories can be found at www.anniesway.blogspot.com, and you can contact her via e-mail at eitman@mindspring.com.

Toni L. Martin, Wesley Chapel group leader for the Florida Writers Association, brings innovative workshops to the community through *American Idol*-style pitch contests critiqued by celebrity authors. Up next, she's arranged for a publishing house to judge a one-page synopsis contest with the winner receiving a full manuscript read.

Melinda McDonald earned a journalism degree from Iowa State University and was a reporter/photographer before starting a career in business communications. Until early 2010, she managed marketing communications for a manufacturer in Springfield, IL. Melinda lives near Springfield with her husband Ron and writes historical fiction. E-mail her at Melinda_mc_2000@yahoo.com.

Barbara McKinney graduated *cum laude* from Duke University with majors in economics and French. She received her Master of Business from Harvard University. Barb enjoys sunny days spent with family, creative expression through writing and art, and volunteer work. She may be reached at: barbaraboston@hotmail.com.

Donna Milligan Meadows is the mother of six adult children—including triplets. She worked for many years as an elementary school librarian and hopes to write a children's book someday. She loves reading, traveling, gardening and especially reading to her grandchildren. Please e-mail her at meadowsdonna@hotmail.com.

Beth Morrissey was diagnosed with, and underwent a thymectomy for, myasthenia gravis in 2009. She continues to run her own freelance writing, researching and tutoring business and can be visited on the web at www.bethmorrissey.com, or followed on Twitter where she is @HOHWWriter. Drop by and say hi!

Kathleen M. Muldoon is an instructor with the Institute of Children's Literature, as well as author of several children's books in the educational market. She recently adopted a shelter cat, Walter, and Kathleen's earnings go toward satisfying his tuna cravings. You can e-mail them at fxzwdx5805@sbcglobal.net.

Linda Newton is a counselor in California, and the author of two devotional books filled with stories, *Better Than Jewels*, *Sapphires from Psalms*, and her first book, *12 Ways to Turn Your Pain Into Praise*. A popular speaker at women's events, you can visit her online at www. LindaNewtonSpeaks.com.

Lindsay Nielsen is an author, psychotherapist, public speaker and athlete (2000 Paralympics) and was the first female amputee to complete an Ironman Triathlon. Lindsay is completing a memoir; *If You're Not Dead, It's Not Too Late! An amputee's triumphant run through love, loss and world records*. Please visit her website; www.lindsaynielsen.com.

Hailing from Copperas Cove, TX, **Jennifer Oliver** owes her inspiration to househubby, Stephen, and to their magnificent creative life forces: Cody, Ethan, Matthew, and Madison. Her stories have appeared in several *Chicken Soup for the Soul* books and other heartwarming publications.

Saralee Perel is an award-winning columnist/novelist and multiple contributor to *Chicken Soup for the Soul*. Her book, *The Dog Who Walked Me*, is about her dog who became her caregiver after Saralee's spinal cord injury, the initial devastation of her marriage, and her cat who kept her sane. Contact her at sperel@saraleeperel.com or www.saraleeperel.com.

Kay Conner Pliszka is a frequent contributor to *Chicken Soup for the Soul* books. She has been a guest speaker in Illinois, Wisconsin and Florida using her stories for motivational and inspirational material. Kay enjoys golf, bridge and music. To contact her please e-mail kmpliszka@comcast.net.

Jennifer Quasha is a freelance writer and editor who loves reading, and writing for, *Chicken Soup for the Soul* books. You can check out her website at www.jenniferquasha.com, and see some of what she's been doing since she went freelance in 1998.

Deb Roloson of Woodstock, Ontario has had a lifelong career working with people with special needs. She is the mother of four adult children and married to the wonderful Bob. She enjoys spending time with family and friends, playing volleyball and going on vacations. She is thrilled to have her first story published in *Chicken Soup for the Soul!*

Theresa Sanders is honored to be a frequent *Chicken Soup for the Soul* contributor. An award-winning technical writer, she managed a documentation and training department before turning to creative endeavors. She lives with her husband near St. Louis, where she is completing a novel. Theresa welcomes e-mails at TheresaLSanders@charter.net.

Jessie Miyeko Santala is a photographer who lives in Longmont, Colorado with her husband, Mike. She spends too much time at Starbucks because she just can't give up tall Americanos. Please e-mail her at J.Santala@yahoo.com.

Linda Saslow is a freelance writer and journalist. She has published three books and was a reporter for *The New York Times* for more than twenty years. She continues to write for several publications and non-profits, while also enjoying exercise, yoga, volunteerism and spending precious time with her two granddaughters.

Donna F. Savage teaches women how to meet life's challenges with faith and joy. A pastor's wife and popular speaker, she's published hundreds of articles in print and online. Donna and her husband, Hoyt, live in Las Vegas, NV. They have two young adult sons. Visit her at www.donnasavage.blogspot.com.

Kathi Lessner Schafer is a Chicago native and lives in North Carolina with her daughter, husband, and two ungrateful cats. In addition to homeschooling their daughter, she is actively involved with local wildlife conservation groups and natural habitat preservation.

Thomas Schonhardt recovered fully from the assault and is planning on graduating from Truman State University in May 2011. He owes much of his success to the support and love he received during the tough time from his friends and family. Feel free to contact him via e-mail at tms2618@truman.edu.

Tom Schumm is an inspirational speaker who received a BA from Alma College, and an MBA from the University of Michigan. He enjoys boating, travel, opera, and collecting antique fruit jars. He is currently writing a book about his journey with brain cancer. Please e-mail him at tomschumm.pma@gmail.com.

Jodi L. Severson earned a Bachelor's degree in Psychology from the University of Pittsburgh. She resides in Wisconsin with her husband and three children. Check out her other stories in these *Chicken Soup for the Soul* books: *Sister's Soul*, *Working Woman's Soul*, *Girlfriend's Soul*, and *Shopper's Soul*. Reach her at jodis@charter.net.

Kathleen Shoop earned her Ph.D. at the University of Pittsburgh — Go Panthers! She takes care of her children, writes, works with teachers and adores housekeeping. She is occasionally sweet to her husband! Please e-mail Kathie at jakenmax2002@aol.com.

Deborah Shouse is a speaker, writer and editor. Her writing has appeared in *Reader's Digest*, *Newsweek*, and *Spirituality & Health*. She is donating all proceeds from her book *Love in the Land of Dementia: Finding Hope in the Caregiver's Journey* to Alzheimer's programs and research. Visit her website at www.thecreativityconnection.com.

Alyssa Simon received her B.F.A in Theatre from Florida International University. She lives in New York with her wonderful fiancé Lynn Berg and their cat 180. She acts and writes theatre reviews for www.nytheatre.com.

Tulika Singh is a freelance writer and copy editor. She has earlier worked with leading Indian dailies including *Hindustan Times* and

The Times of India. She currently divides her time between the two loves of her life—writing and her four-year-old twins. Please e-mail her at tulika20@hotmail.com.

Sheila Sowder's stories and essays have appeared in anthologies and literary journals. She received an Indiana Arts Commission Individual Arts Grant and the Rose Voci Fellowship for Indiana women writers. Currently, she and her husband travel and occasionally work at resorts from New England to Death Valley. E-mail her at sksowder@aol.com.

Rachel Spencer is a qualified nurse who recently spent three years working in East Africa. She now works with mentally ill children in the UK. Rachel loves to write and is currently working on her first novel. She also enjoys reading, travelling, playing piano and singing. Please e-mail her at rachel.rnld@gmail.com.

Spring Stafford grew up in Hawaii where she received her college degrees. She is currently applying to work in Japan and has just finished her first novel.

Diane Stark is a wife, mother, teacher, and writer. Her work has been printed in dozens of publications. She writes about the important things in life: her family and her faith. She is the author of *Teachers' Devotions to Go* and she can be reached via e-mail at DianeStark19@yahoo.com.

Debbi Stumpf is an entrepreneur who has a passion for coaching people to success while building lasting relationships. Debbi has been blessed to work with amazing mentors, bestselling authors and people from all walks of life. She supports business owners and authors through social media volunteering within the community.

Joyce E. Sudbeck recently retired and is enjoying her free time by writing. She has been published in *Chicken Soup for the Soul* books,

Liguorian magazine, and has two more stories pending for fall 2010—*Good Old Days* magazine (Oct.) and *Thin Threads* (Nov). She won 2009 & 2010 poetry contests.

Lynn Sunday holds a BFA in fine art and a BA in education from Syracuse University. She is a professional artist turned writer. Her passions are animals and the natural world. She lives in Half Moon Bay, CA, with her husband and dog, Hootie.

Annmarie B. Tait lives in Conshohocken, PA with her husband Joe Beck and Sammy their Yorkie. Annmarie has contributed to several *Chicken Soup for the Soul* books, *Reminisce* magazine and the *Patchwork Path* anthology series. She also enjoys cooking and singing and recording American and Irish folk songs. E-mail her at irishbloom@ aol.com.

Writer, speech therapist, memoir teacher, wife and mother, **Tsgoyna Tanzman** credits writing as the supreme "therapy" for raising an adolescent daughter. Published in numerous *Chicken Soup for the Soul* books, her humorous essays and poems can be read on More.com, motheringmagazine.com, and in *The Orange County Register*. E-mail her at tnzmn@cox.net.

Jo Weinert lives in North Carolina. She enjoys hiking, traveling, water and snow skiing with her husband.

Lois Wilmoth-Bennett has a Ph.D. from Kent State University. After many years in special education administration and in private practice as a psychologist in Ohio, she moved to Central Florida. She is publisher/co-owner of Fireside Publications and has published two novels, and a non-fiction book, *Essays on Living with Alzheimer's Disease*. E-mail her at loisnett3@gmail.com.

Beth M. Wood lives in St. Louis with her three beautiful children and one three-legged Boxer. She is a marketing professional by trade, a writer by choice, a devout reader and semi-fanatic editor who will occasionally sneak a red Sharpie into restaurants to correct glaring, grammatical errors on the menu.

Dallas Woodburn is the author of two collections of short stories and a forthcoming novel. Her nonfiction has appeared in *Family Circle*, *Writer's Digest*, and the *Los Angeles Times*. She is the founder of Write On! For Literacy, an organization that encourages youth to discover confidence through reading and writing: www.writeonbooks.org.

Deborah Zigenis-Lowery positively delights in retelling folktales and writing young adult novels when not engaged in writing inspirational nonfiction. She loves reading, writing, teaching, and learning. Check out her blog at http://literatelives.wordpress.com where she strives to nurture a reading/writing lifestyle for you and your family.

Meet Our Authors

Jack Canfield is the co-creator of the *Chicken Soup for the Soul* series, which *Time* magazine has called "the publishing phenomenon of the decade." Jack is also the co-author of many other bestselling books.

Jack is the CEO of the Canfield Training Group in Santa Barbara, California, and founder of the Foundation for Self-Esteem in Culver City, California. He has conducted intensive personal and professional development seminars on the principles of success for more than a million people in twenty-three countries, has spoken to hundreds of thousands of people at more than 1,000 corporations, universities, professional conferences and conventions, and has been seen by millions more on national television shows.

Jack has received many awards and honors, including three honorary doctorates and a Guinness World Records Certificate for having seven books from the *Chicken Soup for the Soul* series appearing on the New York Times bestseller list on May 24, 1998.

You can reach Jack at www.jackcanfield.com.

Mark Victor Hansen is the co-founder of Chicken Soup for the Soul, along with Jack Canfield. He is a sought-after keynote speaker, bestselling author, and marketing maven. Mark's powerful messages of possibility, opportunity, and action have created powerful change in thousands of organizations and millions of individuals worldwide.

Mark is a prolific writer with many bestselling books in addition to the *Chicken Soup for the Soul* series. Mark has had a profound influence in the field of human potential through his library of audios, videos, and articles in the areas of big thinking, sales achievement, wealth building, publishing success, and personal and professional development. He is also the founder of the MEGA Seminar Series.

Mark has received numerous awards that honor his entrepreneurial spirit, philanthropic heart, and business acumen. He is a lifetime member of the Horatio Alger Association of Distinguished Americans.

You can reach Mark at www.markvictorhansen.com.

Amy Newmark is the publisher and editor-in-chief of *Chicken Soup for the Soul*, after a 30-year career as a writer, speaker, financial analyst, and business executive in the worlds of finance and telecommunications. Amy is a *magna cum laude* graduate of Harvard College, where she majored in Portuguese, minored in French, and traveled extensively. She and her husband have four grown children.

After a long career writing books on telecommunications, voluminous financial reports, business plans, and corporate press releases, Chicken Soup for the Soul is a breath of fresh air for Amy. She has fallen in love with Chicken Soup for the Soul and its life-changing books, and really enjoys putting these books together for Chicken Soup's wonderful readers. She has co-authored more than two dozen *Chicken Soup for the Soul* books and has edited another two dozen.

You can reach Amy through the webmaster@chickensoupforthesoul.com.

About Deborah Norville

Bestselling author **Deborah Norville** credits many of the successes in her life to a positive mental attitude. The anchor of *Inside Edition*, the nation's top-rated syndicated news magazine, the journalist is a two-time Emmy winner.

Deborah is also the author of a half-dozen books including the New York Times bestseller, *Thank You Power: Making the Science of Gratitude Work for You*. *Thank You Power* brought together for the first time the growing body of academic research proving the benefits of gratitude. Similarly, *The Power of Respect* presented research detailing the benefits of respectful behavior with real life stories.

A lifelong seamstress and crafter, Deborah recently introduced The Deborah Norville Collection, a line of fine hand yarns for knitting and crochet, available at craft stores nationwide.

Deborah Norville is a *summa cum laude* (4.0) graduate of the University of Georgia. She is married and the mother of three.

Deborah can be reached via her website www.DeborahNorville.com.

Thank You

We owe huge thanks to all of our contributors. We know that you pour your hearts and souls into the thousands of stories and poems that you share with us, and ultimately with each other. We appreciate your willingness to open up your lives to other Chicken Soup for the Soul readers.

We can only publish a small percentage of the stories that are submitted, but we read every single one and even the ones that do not appear in the book have an influence on us and on the final manuscript.

We want to thank Chicken Soup for the Soul editor Kristiana Glavin for reading every one of the thousands of stories that were submitted for this book, and narrowing down the candidates for final selection, as well as for her assistance with the final manuscript and proofreading. We also want to thank our assistant publisher, D'ette Corona, who works closely with all the contributors, and our editor and webmaster Barbara LoMonaco for their expert editorial, proofreading, and organizational assistance.

We owe a very special thanks to our creative director and book producer, Brian Taylor at Pneuma Books, for his brilliant vision for our covers and interiors. Finally, none of this would be possible without the business and creative leadership of our CEO, Bill Rouhana, and our president, Bob Jacobs.

Improving
Your Life Every Day

Real people sharing real stories—for 17 years. Now, Chicken Soup for the Soul has gone beyond the bookstore to become a world leader in life improvement. Through books, movies, DVDs, online resources and other partnerships, we bring hope, courage, inspiration and love to hundreds of millions of people around the world. Chicken Soup for the Soul's writers and readers belong to a one-of-a-kind global community, sharing advice, support, guidance, comfort, and knowledge.

Chicken Soup for the Soul stories have been translated into more than forty languages and can be found in more than one hundred countries. Every day, millions of people experience a Chicken Soup for the Soul story in a book, magazine, newspaper or online. As we share our life experiences through these stories, we offer hope, comfort and inspiration to one another. The stories travel from person to person, and from country to country, helping to improve lives everywhere.

Share with Us

We all have had Chicken Soup for the Soul moments in our lives. If you would like to share your story or poem with millions of people around the world, go to chickensoup.com and click on "Submit Your Story." You may be able to help another reader, and become a published author at the same time. Some of our past contributors have launched writing and speaking careers from the publication of their stories in our books!

Our submission volume has been increasing steadily—the quality and quantity of your submissions has been fabulous. We only accept story submissions via our website. They are no longer accepted via mail or fax.

To contact us regarding other matters, please send us an e-mail through webmaster@chickensoupforthesoul.com, or fax or write us at:

Chicken Soup for the Soul
P.O. Box 700
Cos Cob, CT 06807-0700
Fax: 203-861-7194

One more note from your friends at Chicken Soup for the Soul: Occasionally, we receive an unsolicited book manuscript from one of our readers, and we would like to respectfully inform you that we do not accept unsolicited manuscripts and we must discard the ones that appear.

This uplifting book reminds readers of the blessings in their lives, despite financial stress, natural disasters, health scares and illnesses, housing challenges and family worries. This feel-good book is a great gift for New Year's or Easter, for someone going through a difficult time, or for Christmas. These stories of optimism, faith, and strength remind us of the simple pleasures of family, home, health, and inexpensive good times.

978-1-935096-42-9

More Positive Thinking...

Chicken Soup for the Soul®

Tough Times, Tough People

TOUGH TIMES
WON'T LAST
BUT
TOUGH PEOPLE
WILL

101 Stories about Overcoming the Economic Crisis and Other Challenges

Jack Canfield,
Mark Victor Hansen
& Amy Newmark

Tough times won't last, but tough people will. Many people have lost money, jobs and/or homes, or made cutbacks. Others have faced life-changing natural disasters, or health and family difficulties. These encouraging and inspirational stories are all about overcoming adversity, pulling together, and finding joy in a simpler life. Stories address downsizing, resolving debt, managing chronic illness, having faith, finding new perspectives, and blessings in disguise.

978-1-935096-35-1

More Inspiration

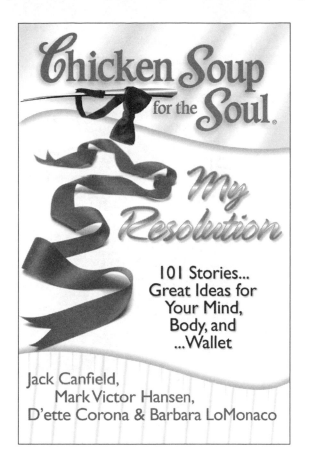

Chicken Soup for the Soul®

My Resolution

**101 Stories...
Great Ideas for
Your Mind,
Body, and
...Wallet**

Jack Canfield,
Mark Victor Hansen,
D'ette Corona & Barbara LoMonaco

Everyone makes resolutions—for New Year's, for big birthdays, for new school years. In fact, most of us are so good at resolutions that we make the same ones year after year. This collection of great true stories covers topics such as losing weight, getting organized, stopping bad habits, restoring relationships, dealing with substance abuse, changing jobs, going green, and even today's hot topic—dealing with the economic crisis.

978-1-935096-28-3

for You and Yours

Chicken Soup for the Soul

Shaping the New You

101 Encouraging Stories
about Dieting
and Fitness...
and Finding
What Works for You

Jack Canfield,
Mark Victor Hansen & Amy Newmark
Foreword by Richard Simmons

No one likes to diet, but this book will encourage and inspire readers with its positive, practical, and purposeful stories of dieting and fitness. Readers will find hope, help, and hints on getting fit and staying healthy in these 101 stories from those who have been there, done that, and maintained it. Stories about wake-up calls and realizations, moving more and eating better, self-esteem and support, make this a great book for anyone starting fresh or needing a boost.

978-1-935096-57-3

More Inspiration for Body

Chicken Soup for the Soul

for the Soul®

True Love

101 Heartwarming
and Humorous Stories
about Dating,
Romance, Love,
and Marriage

Jack Canfield,
Mark Victor Hansen & Amy Newmark
Foreword by Kristi Yamaguchi and Bret Hedican

Everyone loves a good love story. And we all love stories about how the love started and blossomed. This fun new book about dating, romance, love, and marriage will make readers laugh and cry. Stories of how couples met, when "they knew," good and bad dates, proposals, keeping romance alive, second chances, and all the other ups and downs of love will entertain, encourage, and warm the hearts of all readers.

978-1-935096-43-6

...and Heart

www.chickensoup.com